Social Science –
For What?

Hans-Henrik Holm and Erik Rudeng (eds.):

Social Science – For What?

FESTSCHRIFT FOR JOHAN GALTUNG

Universitetsforlaget

Oslo - Bergen - Tromsø

© Universitetsforlaget 1980
ISBN 82-00-05521-3
Cover design: Bjørn Roggenbihl

Distribution offices:
NORWAY
Universitetsforlaget
Postboks 2977 – Tøyen
Oslo 6

UNITED KINGDOM
Global Book Resources Ltd.
109 Great Russell Street
London WC IB 3NA

UNITED STATES and CANADA
Columbia University Press
136 South Broadway
Irvington-on-Hudson
New York 10533

Printed in Norway by
Tangen-Trykk, Drammen

Preface

According to the references in the *Social Sciences Citation Index,* no contemporary Norwegian social scientist is more referred to than Johan Galtung. As the new Galtung bibliography edited by Nils Petter Gleditsch *et al.* shows, his work is also prodigious in terms of sheer intellectual productivity. Being transdisciplinary from the very beginning of his career, he has proved a consistently difficult social scientist to evaluate in terms of quality and originality. Few people seem able to undertake a really comprehensive analysis of Galtung's work.

What friend and foe alike would acknowledge is his talent for linking research to social and political values. As a traveller in international social science, and as a public speaker, he is certainly one of the most sought after, accomplished, and provocative ones in the world today.

A *Festschrift* in Johan Galtung's spirit would have to focus on the uses of social science – *cui bono?* The editors invited contributors to present their own experience with social science research, the way they justify it and would like to develop it. Some of the contributors have gone off in a rather different direction, but we have included them as well, perhaps in order to illustrate the perplexing variety and surprises of Galtung's own contributions to social science.

Unfortunately, highly readable papers by George Asinero, Geneva, ('Technicians of Practical Knowledge') and Lim Teck Ghee, Penang, ('What Social Science – a Viewpoint') were received too late for inclusion in this volume.

Århus/Oslo, August 1980

Hans-Henrik Holm   Erik Rudeng

Contents

Dear Johan

When I first learned that plans were being made for a Festschrift in your honor, I must admit that my first reaction was 'What, so soon? At his early age? At the height of his activity?' It required only a minimum of reflection on my part to decide that on the basis of your contributions you are more deserving of this honor than the majority of those who have had to wait until the age of seventy or eighty for this symbol of respect for outstanding achievement.

We have known each other for a long time, my dear friend, ever since we met at Columbia University where you were a Visiting Assistant Professor, and where you did me the honor of occasionally visiting my seminar. Since then we have met in various parts of the world – Oslo, Paris, London, Rome, Geneva, Berlin, Partinico in Sicily – and always when we were together I was impressed by what you had to say, with your intelligence and originality, and the fertility and breadth of your ideas, and your willingness at the same time to listen to others. We did not always agree, of course, but when there was a difference of opinion between us – which did not happen too often – I could not escape the feeling that maybe, just this time, possibly for once I might be wrong!

One of my proudest experiences is to have spent a month with you in Oslo as a consultant when you were planning to organize the Peace Research Institute. The Institute represents only one of your successes, but it will always have a special significance for me because of your feeling that I could be of help in identifying some of its potential activities. I keep running into references to the papers you wrote for the Institute's Journal. Most recently, when I participated in a meeting on political violence, I was struck by the frequency with which your name and your theories were mentioned in the discussion. I had the inner satisfaction of thinking 'I knew him when . . . .'

A Festschrift frequently signifies the end of a career; I know that in your case it represents rather a mid-point, which will be followed by much more activity and many more contributions, plus a great deal of travel! You know that you have all my best wishes. It has been a joy to know you, to listen to you, and to read you over the years. My respect for what you have done and are doing is matched only by my warm affection for you as a friend. I wish you and your family many happy and successful years to come.

Yours affectionately,
Otto Klineberg

Some Thoughts on Methods of Analysing the Modern World*

SAMIR AMIN

I

A reader once observed that my works dealt with three sets of problems: (1) Concrete analyses of situations prevailing in Third World countries (Egypt, the Maghreb, West Africa, the Congo), (2) A theory of capitalist accumulation in its world dimension, and (3) An interpretation of historical materialism. This attentive reader is right. In fact, this classification also corresponds to the stages of evolution of my work. The concrete analysis of a situation is undoubtedly never neutral, in that it always implicitly presupposes an underlying theory. The concrete analyses which I first undertook (Nasser's Egypt, West Africa, the Congo and the Maghreb – all neo-colonial countries and so-called 'Socialist' attempts to break with imperialist domination) were certainly largely based on a theoretical interpretation of imperialism. This interpretation, formulated between 1954 and 1957 but only published in 1970 in *Accumulation on a World Scale,* was fraught with uncertainty, a result of the inadequacies of the type of Marxism still predominant in the 1950s, which was the period of my own political and intellectual formation.

That theory made it possible to criticise the bourgeois theoretical explanations of 'underdevelopment', but did not offer an alternative practical political formulation to the bourgeois nationalist policies of national liberation movements. My studies on the Arab and African countries mentioned above were produced between 1960 and 1967 and clearly bear the mark of these limitations. This dissatisfaction compelled me to re-appraise the theory of imperialism, which led me to rewrite the theory of accumulation (*Unequal Development*) and, I hope, to deepen it (*Unequal Exchange and the Law of Value*) between 1968 and 1973. This also coincided with the period of the open bankruptcy of revisionist Marxism and, with the Cultural Revolution, the search for a global alternative. These favourable circumstances thus necessarily led me to a reconsideration of the more fundamental as-

* L'oeuvre de notre ami Johan Galtung implique évidemment une méthode d'analyse qui lui est propre. Cette modeste contribution au recueil concernant cette oeuvre considerable précise, je l'espére, ce qui me parait constituer l'essentiel de ma méthode.

pects of historical materialism. *Imperialism and Unequal Development, The Arab Nation, The Law of Value and Historical Materialism, Class and Nation in History and in the Modern Crisis* (all written between 1973 and 1978) aim at clarifying my interpretation of historical materialism, but also, and at the same time in the light of these interpretations, to review the concrete situations with which I am concerned, viz. the Third World in general, Africa and the Arab world in particular.

If I were to 'sum up' in a few sentences what, in my view, are the essential points of these interpretations, I would mention the following:

1. There have been two conflicting interpretations of historical materialism from its inception. The first reduces the method in practice to a linear economic determinism. The development of the productive forces per se generates the necessary adjustments in production relations (through social revolutions where the actors act and in doing reveal the historical necessity), and the political and ideological superstructure in turn transforms itself to reflect the exigencies of the reproduction of production relations. The second interpretation emphasises the twofold dialectic between the productive forces and production relations, on the one hand, and between production relations and the superstructure, on the other.

2. The first interpretation draws an analogy between the laws governing the development of society and those governing the evolution of nature. From Engel's attempt at a *Dialectics of Nature* to the positivist interpretation of Kautskysm, even from Bolshevism itself (vide Bogdanov) to Soviet dialectical materialism (dia-mat), this interpretation follows in the trail of the philosophy of enlightenment and, ipso facto, constitutes the radical bourgeois interpretation of Marxism. The second interpretation uncompromisingly opposes the objective character of the laws of nature to the composite objective-subjective character of the laws of society.

3. The first interpretation either ignores *alienation* or extends it to the history of the whole of mankind without paying heed to the variable content of the history. Thus, alienation becomes a product of human nature transcending the history of social systems; it stems from anthropology; i.e. from the permanent relationship between Man and Nature. In these circumstances, man does not make his own history and never will do so, history being the product of 'force of circumstances'. The idea held by men – or classes – that they make history is naive. The determinism of 'technological progress' is so overwhelming as to render the margin of their apparent freedom very narrow. The second interpretation necessarily leads to a distinction between two different levels of alienation: that which stems from the permanent relationship between Man and Nature, transcends the

modes of society, defines human nature in its permanent dimension but which, for this very reason, does not directly interfere in the development of social history (we would call this anthropological alienation) and the second type of alienation which, on the contrary, constitutes the substance of the ideological superstructure of societies (we would call this social alienation).

4. In our attempt to define the successive contents of this social alienation, we came to the conclusion that all class pre-capitalist social systems undergo one and the same type of social alienation (which we would call alienation in nature), whose main features are the direct consequence of (a) the transparence of economic relations of exploitation and (b) the limited degree of control over nature at corresponding levels of the development of the productive forces. In these circumstances, social alienation necessarily assumes an absolute (religious) character, a result of the predominant role played by ideology in social reproduction. A contrario, the social alienation of capitalism is based on (a) the *opacification* of economic relations due to generalisation of commodity relations and (b) a qualitatively more advanced degree of control over nature. In commodity alienation, nature is replaced by economy (generalised commodity exchange) as the decisive external force in social development. The struggle to abolish exploitation and classes therefore implies the liberation of 'economic determinism'. In this sense, Communism must put an end to social alienation without for all that abolishing anthropological alienation.

5. This interpretation re-establishes the *unicity* of universal history. There is no reason to look for this unicity in an overdetailed succession of modes of production. In this context, the 'conventional' line (slavery – feudalism – capitalism) is not only specific but to a large extent mythical, for slavery was not a 'necessary' stage even in Europe, and feudalism is nothing but a specific form of a more general mode of production. The artificial and ideological distinction between a 'European' line as described and a so-called 'Asiatic' line (the pseudo-Asiatic mode of production) belongs to the family of Euro-centric, ideological and even racist philosophies. Unicity is restored by the necessary succession of three groups of modes of production: communal modes, tributary modes, and the capitalist mode of production (which is the first to present universal, homogenising features for the whole planet). The unicity of the group of tributary modes of production arises precisely from the universal feature of social alienation within nature in contradistinction to the commodity social alienation of capitalism. Hence the myth of 'Oriental despotism', the ideological creation of the philosphy of enlightenment, may be swept overboard.

6. The specificity of Western history in this context lies exclusively in the 'peripheral' nature (used here in the sense of incomplete) of its own

specific tributary mode of production, the feudal mode, which was the result of a combination with other communal modes of production.

The repetition in East Asia, in Japan to be precise, of this same combination of the feudal nature of pre-capitalist Japan compared to the advanced state of the tributary mode in China, is evidence that the theoretical conclusions drawn from the suggested conceptualisation are universal. *Unequal development* therefore appears as a universal law. The capitalist mode of production appeared earlier and evolved more rapidly in the backward areas of the tributary mode, just as today the possible transition to a classless society has begun to appear in the periphery of the world capitalist system.

II

The theses submitted above emerged gradually from a political and intellectual history, and I shall attempt to retrace here the main stages of each formulation concerning the concepts and definitions of (1) alienation (2) the tributary mode of production, (3) imperialism and (4) de-linking. Naturally, these four 'theories' emerged gradually with their natural complement to constitute the groundwork for an interpretation of historical materialism with which I personally agree.

1. The question of alienation, fundamental in the analysis of ideologies

The publication of the *1844 Manuscripts* was not only delayed (the French edition appeared in 1965) but it fell totally flat. At the time, all the currents of thought of Marxism and the left (Soviet, Trotskyist opposition, Social Democracy), with the exception, and that in parts only, of Anarchism (vide Castoriadis), had reduced Marxism to an evolutionism determined by the (autonomous) progress of the productive forces. The impact was even less considering that the way the *Manuscripts* were presented was, and still is, extremely faulty. Instead of offering a parallel reading of the chapters on wages, profits and rents, the editor has chosen an unfortunate format of successive chapters. This makes it more difficult to see what the *Manuscripts* reveal, namely the emergence of a critique of political economy (not in the sense of a critique of bad economics to be replaced by a better one but in the sense of a critique of the status of the economies in social life) and the discovery which makes possible this emergence, i.e. commodity alienation.

The publication made it possible at the time for the better reader of Marx to see how Marx had evolved from the position of an anthropological critique of a still general nature to that of the materialism of Feurbach and of the Hegelian left, to the fundamentals of a concrete critique of capitalist society. From a general concept of unqualified alienation he had come to the specific concepts of commodity alienation.

This was to be a definitive conclusion, and it is no mere coincidence that his *Capital,* subtitled 'A Critique of Political Economy', starts with commodity as fetishism. Yet, in spite of the definitive nature of his conclusion and the reminder provided by the publication of the *Manuscripts,* the predominant tendency of consistently ignoring its meaning survived for a very long time, even within those currents most ready to criticise *Revisionism.* Here, if at all necessary, is some evidence of this.

The subtitle, 'A Critique of Political Economy' seems to be generally misunderstood. Witness the fact that Marxist (or Marxian!!) political economies' are continually being produced. The dialogue of the deaf on 'value as a useless diversion' and 'the transformation of value into price as impossible' demonstrates that most Marxist economists in fact still reject the analysis of commodity alienation, which is the basis of the necessary value/price distinction. True to this logic, Althusser, in the early 1960s, went even further by openly rejecting the theory of alienation in order to reduce Marxism to a positive political economy.

However, even when the opposite line was adopted (up to the mid-sixties), i.e. recognition of the fundamental importance of commodity alienation in order to understand Marx's critique of capitalist society (as opposed simply to capitalist economy) and the organic link between this and the recognition of the value/price contradiction, there was a failure to draw all the conclusions.

Anyway, this was true in my own case. The dialectic productive forces/production relations was not yet fully understood. Techniques of production, for example, were still considered to be relatively 'neutral'. Nor was the dialectic infrastructure/superstructure fully understood. For none had realised the importance of the analysis of commodity alienation as a fundamental analysis of capitalist ideology in relation to the way in which the base of the mode of production functions. Thus, the interpretation of ideology as 'reflection' prevailed.

The theory of commodity alienation paved the way for a very different method of understanding the base/ideology relations. Commodity alienation defines the substance of the ideology governing the active social forces which determine the development of capitalist society. This ideology is not only the ideology of the ruling class but it is also the ruling ideology within society, despite the existence of social contradictions. Hence the necessary precondition according to this is that historical materialism must not be reduced to an 'economist' evolutionism. This observation is surely supported by fact, i.e. the working class movement is very largely fed on 'economist' ideology.

Hence Lenin's remark that 'Marxism is introduced from the outside' into the working class movement deserves some consideration. The rather too unilateral critique of this remark, even if well-founded, must be corrected by taking a new look (isn't it a return to Marx?) at the theory of ideology.

What stood in the way of all the necessary conclusions being drawn from this anlysis was the fact that it had been concretely erected as an analysis of capitalism. It had not been 'deduced' from a 'general theory' of the base/ideology relations within all social systems. It was only after a thorough investigation into these relations with pre-capitalist societies that this analysis assumed a more profound meaning to reach the level of historical materialism (vide Part II).

To come back to the problem of commodity alienation, a particular category of ideology viz. capitalist ideology, I put the question: As from when exactly were all the necessary conclusions drawn from this analysis? For myself, and many others, the answer is clear – as from 1966–67.

The trend towards deeper and more detailed analysis that led to these results was launched in 1957 and evolved over two periods: 1957 to 1966 and from 1966 onwards. I see a striking parallel between this world-wide trend, the waves of criticism of Revisionism and the movement of internal criticism in China.

Meanwhile, between 1957 and 1965, the criticism remained ambiguous and incomplete, the reason being that the nature and the scope of the problems underlying the 'Sino-Soviet' conflict were not understood in their full magnitude. The conflict still appeared to arise from China's refusal to be subjected to the dictates of the political strategy of the USSR aspiring, together with the United States, to 'dominate the world', as shown by the Joint Soviet American Declaration in 1957. Gradually, the critique of Revisionism became more precise. The two superpowers were not only two world political powers, they were also two class societies (it is irrelevant here whether one considers the USSR as a capitalist, 'state capitalist' or a new class society). The two ruling classes of these societies exploit their own people and oppress other peoples, yet each side tries to subject the strategies of the oppressed in the opponent's camp to suit its own goals; using their struggles to weaken the adversary. Thus, 'the USSR is no more the natural ally of the working classes in the West and of the national liberation movements than the Pope is the natural ally of the Polish people or the CIA that of the Czech workers'. To have a common enemy, which is the case in these two perfectly symmetrical situations, does not create a 'natural' alliance but only a circumstantial one. The aim of the oppressed peoples is to abolish classes and not to replace one type of class oppression by another, one type of domination by another. Oppressed

16

peoples cannot, therefore, have a class society as their 'natural ally'.

The 1963 Letter in 25 points established this relation between the superpower politics of the USSR and the class nature of its society. Yet another aspect has to be clarified, namely what was the nature of the Soviet mode of production and how had it come about on the basis of a socialist revolution?

The Cultural Revolution from 1966 helped to provide answers to these questions; it helped one to understand the origin of the inadequacies of Bolshevism. Its inadequate appraisal of the dialectic productive forces/production relations (based on an inadequate assessment of so-called 'neutral technology'); its inadequate evaluation of the base/superstructure relations (based on a theory of ideology as 'reflection'). Bolshevism had inherited these shortcomings from the positivist reduction of Kautskysm, who precisely neglected the importance of the analysis of commodity alienation.

The fact remains that this fruitful debate was restricted in scope to capitalism and socialist construction. The question of the nature of the twofold dialectic productive forces/production relations and base/superstructure in pre-capitalist societies remains outside the field of discussion. Yet, as we shall see, it was through delving deeper into this specific aspect of the question that it became possible, later on, to gain a better understanding of the nature of the Soviet system and of its ideology.

2. The concept of the tributary mode of production, a fundamental concept in the analysis of unequal development and the birth of capitalism

In my own personal thinking, this question largely took precedence over the previous one, and it was relatively late – by the end of the 1960s – that the conclusions I was reaching started to fit in and form a whole. In fact, as early as the 1950s the following issues were raised: 1) In the underdeveloped state of Egypt, the Arab World and the Third World, what was the interaction between the pre-capitalist inheritance and imperialist domination? 2) Were Egypt and the pre-capitalist Arab World 'feudal' in the same way as Europe? 3) Did Islam play the same role in Arab society as Christianity in medieval Europe? 4) Why did the 'feudal' Arab World fail to engender capitalism as had been the case of Europe? 5) What part did Islam play in the resistance to the ideas of Socialism and how can this part be explained? As a 'vestige'?

The debate here had developed in connection with vicissitudes of national liberation, and especially of Nasserism, even before the time when the question of the USSR was to trigger off a deeper analysis of socialism, and then even after 1960, without any understanding of the interconnection between the two series of problems. Obviously, there

17

2 – Social Science

had been a debate within Marxism on the question of non-European societies, in particular around the 'Asiatic mode of production' in the 1920s, and there was an academic tradition that survived the closure of this debate. However, all this was of little concern to us, since it was so obvious that the thesis of 'European exceptionality' smacked of pro-imperialist Western-centrism.

Thus, as far as we were concerned, there were only two possible theses: (1) The quasi-absolute identity between the pre-capitalist Arab World and medieval Europe or (2) if there was any difference, it was certainly not that embodied in the thesis of 'Oriental despotism'.

I think it would be wrong not to recognise that up to 1960 the essence of the analysis, albeit with certain shades of difference, arose from the first thesis. These shades of difference must be pointed out, however, for, as I have explained elsewhere, as early as 1957 I had established a distinction between the 'feudal mode of production in general' and the 'particular European feudal mode of production'.

These shades of difference basically expressed a certain degree of dissatisfaction. The thesis of identity left open the questions mentioned earlier. That is why when, from 1960, a sudden shift occurred towards the second thesis, it was possible to arrive at a precise formulation of that thesis within a very short time in a way that seems to us (still) to hold good.

The ground had been prepared. I should like to retrace its history, which, as far as I am concerned, is most curious. The work of Sayed Qotb (Al Adala al Ijitima Fil Islam), published in 1950, immediately aroused my curiosity. The author, who was an ideologue of the Muslim Brotherhood, drew a distinction between Christianity – which appeared in an organised world, the Roman Empire, and ipso facto was exclusively preoccupied with metaphysics and ethics ('Render unto Caesar the things which are Caesar's') – and Islam, placed in a position where it was forced to organise a State and therefore had to intervene in every area of social life.

That thesis had no great scientific value. Nonetheless, it constituted a powerful ideological expression which still basically permeates all the interstices of Islamic societies, where it represents an essential element of the predominant ideology. If this approach is obviously exploited by the most mediocre conservative forces, it is nevertheless true that even populist mass revolts remain within this ideology, vide the revolution in Iran.

This ideological thesis is interesting in that it reveals a certain truth, i.e. the totalitarian character of ideology in Islamic countries. Since this ideology claims to govern every aspect of social life, it therefore makes the separation between the State and the civil society a pointless exercise. The question was whether the situation had been identical in

18

Christian and feudal Europe. Undoubtedly the full development of civil society in Europe was due to capitalism, but that society has very deep roots and appeared in an embryonic form in the midst of feudal society (autonomy of guilds, private property . . .). Is it because the embryo of capitalist relations appeared at an early state in this society? Is it because it was tolerated or even encouraged by the ideology of this society? The first answer is tautological, because the question is precisely to discover the reason for the early appearance of elements of capitalist structure. The second question is idealistic (that of Qotb). A proper analysis should make it possible to uncover the real reason underlying both aspects, i.e. the early appearance of capitalist relations (infrastructure) and the 'incomplete', 'cracked' nature of the ideology. The reason is the *incomplete* state of the specific form of the tributary mode of production in Europe – the feudal mode. Even though our thesis only became clear in this 'definitive' form in the 1970s, its main constituent elements had already been drawn from the comparative analysis of the 'specificities' of Western and Eastern feudalism. For at the same time, the 'Oriental specificity' was attributed to the advanced stage of its mode of production, labelled 'tributary' (quite early on). It is a fact that this advanced stage was reflected at every level: (1) *the base* (tributary class and state centralisation of the tribute versus its feudal fragmentation and a weak state; the first condition corresponds to a *more,* and not less, advanced state of development of the productive forces, contrary to the claims of the 'Oriental despotism' and 'Asiatic mode' schools); (2) the *superstructure* ('better formulated' ideology, leaving fewer 'cracks' and hence more 'totalitarian' in its aspects); and (3) their *dialectic* (a higher degree of correspondence leaving less room for flexibility, thus less possibility of transcending the situation in a very short time . . .). The thesis that was gradually taking shape in the process of finding answers to the original questions also led me to an unexpected result. The features attributed to Islam by Qotb did, in fact, exist long before Islam, not, to be sure, in Arabia but in the Ancient Orient that was to undergo the process of Arabisation and Islamisation, in particular in Egypt, where the tributary mode of production had reached an advanced stage long before the advent of Arabisation and Islamisation.

The formulation of this thesis in connection with the Islamic world was made more complex because of the heterogeneous nature of that world (at the level of the development of the productive forces) and the important place occupied by internal and external commodity relations.

It is clear therefore that the thesis of the tributary mode in its general form as well as its advanced and non-advanced forms (peripheral) led straight to the question of unequal development. The European feudal non-advanced form, more backward (because based on primitive, alien societies), had a potential for more rapid development than the advanced form. In this relative contradiction flexibility/inflexibility, the degree of correspondence ideology/base played a decisive role. The fusion between the State and Islam, the pan-social nature of Islamic ideology and the advanced nature of the State were in complete contrast to the embryonic nature of the State in the West, the Church being only partially able to remedy the situation; hence the subsequent autonomous development of the State vis-à-vis the Church in contrast to the fragmentation, not only at the 'base' (fragmentation of surplus) but simultaneously at the top (a confused, 'incomplete' 'cracked' ideology, largely made up of juxtaposed segments of various origins . . .).

The thesis of unequal development, however, does not only explain the early appearance of the more advanced mode – capitalism – originating in Europe and its 'abortion' in the world of Islam. Within this explanation, it built up an analysis of the tributary ideology (and of its own alienation) and a method of analysis of the dialectical relations base/ideology. At that point, came the discovery of the analogy with Marx's method of analysis of capitalism and his analysis of commodity alienation.

The advanced stage of tributary ideology operated in fact within pre-capitalist class societies in the same way as commodity alienation in capitalism, i.e. as the ideology not only of the ruling class but as the ruling ideology within society (that is why it is almost as resilient as the 'economist' ideology in the modern world) in that it directs the development of the productive forces (technology is therefore no more neutral here then there). Obviously, the substance of the alienation which defines it is specific.

The question for us then was to analyse this specificity, and this led us to start thinking in a more systematic way about the main ideologies prevailing in pre-capitalist class societies – in addition to Islam and Christianity, we also considered Hinduism, Buddhism, Taoism and Confucianism, the ideologies of Ancient Egypt and the slave-owning societies of Antiquity. The conclusions we reached may appear simple today: the ideologies most representative of the 'correspondence' (base-superstructure) are those of the advanced tributary models, Egypt and China. The correspondence of the 'purest' of these ideologies, i.e. Confucianism, was moreover such as to be unbearable, to the point of constantly triggering off its opposite, Taoism. Hinduism, on the other hand, the most confused of these ideologies, continues to survive hand in hand with the 'permanent abortion' of the tributary mode in India . . . .

We came to the conclusion that the specificity of pre-capitalist alienation in contradistinction to commodity alienation was due to the transparence of economic relations in pre-capitalist societies compared with the opacity of these relations created by the market conditions. The decisive importance of the *1844 Manuscripts* lay precisely in this discovery of the basis of opacification (the market) and of its effects (the autonomy of 'economic laws' which impose themselves on society as the laws of nature). That being so, in both cases ideology (alienation) intervenes as an active factor in social reproduction and not as a passive reflection of the exigencies of the base. This active intervention explains why it is so difficult to transcend an advanced system. It explains the obstacles with which nascent capitalism had to grapple in advanced tributary societies as well as the obstacles in the way of socialist construction in our present day. Economic alienation, which constitutes this obstacle today (and provides an explanation for the deviations in the actual experiences of the USSR and China), operates in this respect like the tributary ideology did in the past (e.g. Confucianism) in order to delay the development of capitalist relations. In both cases, alienation deprives mankind of its freedom and subjects it to laws which appear external to itself, operating as laws of nature. However, the areas where these laws operate are specific to each of its two stages. In the tributary stage, it is the superstructure itself (the State, politics, ethics) and in the capitalist stage, it is the base (the economy).

This gradually evolving theory of ideology threw a new light on the question of Soviet society. In its ideology, this society carries, in its structure as well as in its functions, the seeds of reproduction which assimilates it to tributary ideology. The reason being the transparence of exploitation due to the centralisation of the ownership of capital, and that is why, in spite of its class character, Soviet society, to us, does not answer the criteria of a capitalist society.

3. The question of imperialism and the method of analysing class struggles on a world scale

This question has always been at the centre of our preoccupations. In this respect, we were among the very few who, from the beginning, saw capitalism as a 'world system from its inception'. This approach raised an important issue, i.e. what then is the specificity of the modern 'imperialist' stage?

In the 1950s, I was interested not only in trying to arrive at a critique of current theories of development and underdevelopment (a subject that was the basis of my academic thesis) but, even more important to me, in gaining a better understanding of the history of Egypt and of the

21

Arab world (see above) and in seeing the interaction between the struggle for national liberation and the struggle for socialism. In this context, the Leninist theory of imperalism seemed, and still seems, decisive. He argued, and this is now being confirmed by history, that the time had come for socialist revolution and that this revolution would start with the weak links of the world system, i.e. the dominated periphery.

The introduction of the centre/periphery concept as early as the 1950s expressed my concern for reconciling the vision of world capitalism from its inception, on the one hand, and the importance of the imperialist break, on the other. A number of critics, owing to the fact that they rule out the assumption of capitalism on a world scale, fail to understand the meaning of these concepts, which they misconstrue as imperialist centres and countries dominated by imperialism.

The importance of the imperialist break became clear in that until that break new centres could appear from peripheral situations, which has since become impossible, thus making socialism an objective necessity.

Meanwhile, the development of the thesis of world capitalism was no easy thing and the expositions of this thesis remained for a long time imperfect and even erroneous.

The pioneering work of A. G. Frank in the 1960s went much further in this direction than I had done. Taking America as a whole, he considered it as capitalist from the very beginning because of the way it was moulded into a periphery of the mercantilist system. The criticism levelled at him later on, that he did not pay enough attention to production relations, even if partially justified (but in general these critics have arrived at a wrong conclusion, namely that Frank's thesis was 'circulationist'), tends nevertheless to forget that the opposite thesis was, and still is, that Latin America is 'pre-capitalist' ('feudal'). Obviously, the question of the global qualification of mercantilist peripheries – which was to be decisive in the 'theory' of world capitalism – arose in the case of America but not for the Arab world, Asia and Africa more generally, at least not with the same urgency. However, once recognised, the hypothesis of world capitalism would make it easier to understand the mechanisms of the domination of capital over the peripheries of Africa and Asia. The rural, peasant, or 'feudal' societies of this continent provided innumerable and striking examples of the models of formal domination of capital. The analysis in these, and not in supposedly circulationist, terms constituted the second landmark in the evolution of this theory.

The origin of this second landmark dates back to the early sixties. The area under study was South Africa. The question was obviously not considered in 'academic' terms. It was a political question, i.e. how to define the social classes of the periphery upon which imperialist alliances were built and, consequently, how the national liberation alliance should be envisaged. The experience of Nasser's Egypt had led me from 1960–63 to challenge the 'traditional' theories on the so-called national bourgeoisie, as opposed to the compradores, and big landowners. The journal *Revolution* (1963) approached the South African question in terms which, at the time, were not acceptable. In effect, Apartheid was considered (by the South African CP and the ANC) as a politico-ideological obstacle in the way of capitalist development, reflecting the 'backwardness' of the Boers; and the 'liberal' argument against Apartheid seemed to support this point of view (this illusion is far from dead, even today). Our analysis, on the contrary, considered that the function of the 'reserves' in the reproduction of labour power was essential to the development of capitalism in South Africa. The work of G. Arrighi in Rhodesia came as a confirmation of this view, but we had to wait another ten years for these ideas to seep into the movement in South Africa.

I. Wallerstein was interested in the mercantilist period. As an American, he must have felt how much the Euro-centricity of the majority of historians (including Perry Anderson) had understimated the decisive role of the American periphery in this history, for it is this role that gave him the key to the explanation of the transfer from the centre of one region of Europe to another. It was ruling the seas that gave England its final, decisive victory, thus paving the way for the industrial revolution.

This work, exceptionally valuable because of its historical erudition and theoretical power, was carried out in an area very close to mine. I was not so much interested in the shifting of the centre of gravity within the central area of the system as in the forces which prevented other regions of the world (Asia and Africa) from reaching 'central' positions and condemned them irrevocably to gradual integration as peripheries of the world system. The assumptions that I was putting forward concerning unequal development were exclusively related to these questions. However, the simple juxtaposition of my findings on unequal development in the birth of capitalism in Europe, and not in Asia or the Arab world, with the conclusions which I could draw from my readings, of I. Wallerstein in particular, with regard to the shifting of centres in the European area, immediately suggested certain generalising hypotheses concerning the method of analysis of unequal development.

It was Arrighi who again raised the issue of the global nature of capitalism and its various stages and, in particular, the so-called imperialist stage. Written in 1972, the embryo of the *Geometry of Imperialism,* enchanced by two important related analyses – one on the

23

State/economy relations in the various stages of the development of capitalism and the other on the waves of class struggles in the West in the XXth century in the context of the 'reversals' of dominance in the State/economy relations – constituted a new starting point, which made it imperative to approach the question of 'a theory of world capitalism' at a higher and broader level, because of the important new areas to be integrated within the analysis.

Looking back, it is not possible to retrace the steps of this analysis of imperialism without recalling the tumultuous debates around 'unequal exchange'. There is no doubt in my mind today that the publication of Emmanuel's book in 1969 was timely, for it was going to lay bare the wound. The budding theory of capitalism had never been 'circulationist', i.e. solely preoccupied with commodity exchange and ignoring classes and production relations. At every stage, we feel that we had put the relevant question: How can different production relations and different sets of classes corresponding to them function in a system that has integrated them? The available analytical tools, however, in particular in the so-called field of the 'economy', were inadequate for any analysis in 'world' terms, for they had been invented for use in the exclusive context of an analysis of the 'international economy' (and a bad analysis at that!) The criticism that the first formulations of the theory smacked too much of the international economy is perfectly correct. The book *Unequal Exchange* reeked of it even more. Yet it was not rejected for this reason but its opposite, i.e. its potential ability to raise the issue in terms of world capitalism. With this in mind, I defined 'worldisation' in terms of the law of value operating on a world scale (globalisation of commodities, globalisation of capital, globalisation of the value of labour power); and this is where, once again, the analysis of imperialism cut across the study on alienation. (A summary of my theses on imperialism today and the globalisation of the law of value may be found in *Classe et Nation,* Chapter VIII, pp. 218–237.)

4. Integration within the world system or 'de-linking'?

According to the 'traditional' concepts of the working class and the socialist movement, socialism would be built on the basis of the advanced capitalist centres and the level of development of the productive forces reached by these centres. The 'worldisation' of production implied by this development forms the basis of the 'world (or at least European) revolution' thesis. This conception is shared by the 'evolutionists', i.e. the Social Democrats as well. It was replaced – by Lenin and Bukharin – by a theory based on the unequal development within an imperialist system divided between centres, where socialist transformation is delayed, and peripheries, where the combination of the national liberation movement, the peasant revolution and the workers' movement makes it possible to transcend the capitalist production relations at an earlier stage, even though the level of development of the productive forces may be rather backward.

The concept of 'rupture' appears to be indissolubly linked with the thesis of unequal development and socialist construction based on 'countries' opting out of the capitalist-imperialist system.

In fact, the concept of 'rupture' was already present in the thesis 'socialism in one country' which I supported and which still seems to me to be basically correct.

Nevertheless, the notion of rupture does not have the status of a scientific concept. It only refers to an empirical, complex reality (or objective) englobing various levels of the social object. For that reason, it is necessary to retrace the history of the development of this notion, which is far from being over, in order to unfold the constituent elements of its complexity.

Every revolution, is, by definition, a rupture of a kind. The Paris Commune, 1917, the Chinese Revolution are all examples of rupture.

The predominant ideas within Marxism were that this rupture: (1) was mainly concerned with the domain of production relations, transformed after the abolition of private ownership of the means of production, an abolition that was itself the result of a radical change in the nature of political power; (2) would operate in the already developed capitalist spaces. The question of the relations (economic, technical and cultural, political and military) between this space and the one governed by capitalism is not explicitly considered, because one assumes that the space concerned is sufficiently 'strong' not to be diverted in its transformation by the maintenance or cancellation of external relations.

Besides, the predominant ideas concerning the complex problems of productive forces/production relations, on the one hand, and base/ superstructure, on the other, obviously determine the content of the rupture in question.

There are two series of separate, though certainly interconnected, problems: (1) What 'changes' (what ruptures?) and (2) what relations (or absence of relations) with the rest of the world?

Perhaps the best way to consider these two sets of problems and the nature of their relationship is to consider in what way we interpret the historical ruptures nowadays and how they have been interpreted in the past, more particularly by the actors themselves.

The Paris Commune had brought about a decisive rupture at the level of political organisation from which Marx drew some conclusions, but it never had the time to be faced with the problem of organising the overhaul of production relations, and the external relations consisted only of armed confrontation and encirclement.

The Russian Revolution started with a similar rupture, also at the political level. Faced with the question of production relations, it initially produced a spontaneous radical revolution – not only was private ownership of the means of production abolished, but so were commodity relations during the period known as 'war communism'. At the same time, the situation created by the civil war and the war with foreign powers had reduced its external relations to military and ideological confrontation. The Bolsheviks believed at the time that the Russian revolution was only the spark that would set alight at least a European if not a world revolution and that, therefore, the transition to socialism would be rapid and that the problem of relations between the socialist and the capitalist worlds would be de facto settled in favour of the socialist world.

The expected spread of the revolution never materialised. Some people refused to draw the necessary lesson from this and to abandon the preconceived model of a 'world revolution'. It will never matter to them that their theories have reduced them to a state of total impotence; they can always resort to an academic Marxism or one restricted to a small clique and still be satisfied. Those who are concerned with the real transformation of the world have to learn from history: imperialism has made the social transformation of the centres of the system improbable, whereas it is certainly making this transformation a real possibility in the peripheries.

This fact clearly alters the reality in which the two series of questions referred to must be placed.

In Russia, after the 'war communism', the NEP re-established commodity relations and external economic relations. It would be wrong to draw the overhasty conclusion that the USSR was then 'reintegrating' within the world capitalist system. Foreign trade was limited in volume and very firmly controlled, while political power remained in the hands of the worker-peasant alliance. The subsequent negative development cannot be explained, either by some sort of 'fatal issue' of 'socialism in one country' or by the impact of foreign trade allegedly no less tragic. The explanation lies in the inadequacy of the Marxist vision of the time (shared equally by the opposition and the main current), i.e. the 'technicist' ideology of Bolshevism. The imported technologies in these circumstances helped to divert the strategy of transition, but only because the question of the development of another type of productive forces did not even arise.

In these circumstances, when from 1930 the worker-peasant alliance was broken and the country became engaged in a process of accelerated state industrialisation, a class society was gradually rebuilt on these foundations. But even here, external relations only played a secondary role in the rebuilding of this class society. Besides, the imported technology was disconnected from the world market through the administrative planning of prices, to be reconnected to a new mode of production – the statist mode. It was therefore not 'integrated' in any process of 're-establishment of capitalism'.

The Chinese experience made possible a new breakthrough in solving the problems related to 'rupture'. Undoubtedly, during the long period of civil war the 'de-linking' was to all intents and purposes complete. In this respect, Yenan has given a lesson in 'autarky' that is probably essential for any Third World country that would commit itself to the socialist path. Besides, the Vietnamese and Cambodian experiences reproduced this model and were compelled to go through the same stage. This is no mere coincidence. From 1949 onwards, Yenan's autarky spread to the whole of China, mostly owing to force of circumstances (the Western blockade). However, the importation of Soviet technology in the 1950s had the same effect as the importation of any similar European technology would have had; and yet it was not so much the negative effects of this technology on the development of production relations that lay at the roots of the Sino-Soviet rupture, as problems of international strategy. Subsequently, the development of the class struggle on the basis of a worker-peasant alliance made it possible to advance in the search for practical solutions to the issues raised. In fact, it was only after 1966 that it became possible to interpret Soviet history in the way that we have done above.

The Cultural Revolution certainly emphasised the first series of questions (what ruptures?) by subjecting to it the second series (what external relations?). The People's communes as a system of integrating agriculture-industri-education-administration-politics has pushed the transformation of society to the furthest limits ever known, by reducing China's external relations to a minimum.

The subsequent evolution of the country nevertheless raises the issue of the future of the social system (is China moving towards the establishment of a Soviet-type statist mode of production?) and, in this context, of the role of external relations (massive importation of technology reproduced locally according to the same model, nevertheless disconnected from the world capitalist system?) In our view, the crux of the matter is to be found at the level of political power and production relations and not at that of external relations, which is secondary.

In these very particular historical conditions, Vietnam and Cambodia were compelled to reduce their external relations practically to zero, not only during the war of liberation, but also after their victory.

27

If, as seems to be indicated by historical experience, what is essential is to be found at the level of class struggles and the transformation of production relations and if, by their importance and nature, external relations operate in such a way as to strengthen one way or the other the direction of development as determined by the production relations, why then talk about 'rupture', 'de-linking', 'self-reliant development' rather than simply talking about the 'socialist transformation of production relations'? Here, there are two conflicting theses attempting to answer this question.

The first considers that the only question at issue is that of the transformation of production relations. This would be very difficult on the basis of sufficiently advanced productive forces, developed by capitalism. The existing productive forces have been developed within the framework of an exchange system operating on a world scale. In these circumstances, the cancellation of external relations would constitute an additional handicap to the necessary development of the productive forces and would render the transformation of production relations even more difficult, probably impossible. This thesis is closely linked to the thesis of the neutrality of technology. If this thesis were correct, one would have to conclude that socialism is impossible in practice, precisely because, as a result of imperialism, it is not a practical proposition for developed countries. If socialism in one (backward) country is impossible, this means that socialism itself is also well nigh impossible.

According to the opposite thesis, the transformation of production relations can and must be carried out, even on the basis of less developed productive force. There is no alternative. Besides, if the productive forces have to be developed, they must be so on the basis of these new relations which, in turn, will channel development in different directions from those taken on the basis of capitalist relations (for technology is not neutral).

The first is whether this 'socialism in one country' is possible. Our answer is Yes. Whether it is certain? No. One alternative borne out by history, is the statist mode. Is not conventional capitalist development also a third possibility? Our answer is that this is probably impossible. This is where the concept of self-reliant development comes in, the definition of self-reliant development (S.A. 1960) being development whereby external relations are subjected to the requirements of internal accumulation, as opposed to externally oriented development, where (dependent) accumulation is the result of external relations and is moulded by them. Socialist revolution in the peripheries makes possible (and necessary) a self-reliant development. An inherited externally oriented economy and society are extremely vulnerable to the pressures of imperialism, from outside and from within, through the

28

medium of the classes moulded by imperialist domination. No doubt this concept of self-reliant development would be unnecessary if socialist revolution had taken place in developed countries, which are already self-reliant. But such is not the case. Thus, 'Normal' capitalist development within the world system does not require this transformation of the nature of the economy and society – from externally oriented to self-reliant. Furthermore, imperialist domination renders this impossible.

The second question is: on the assumption that society would evolve towards self-reliant development, which of the two strategies – cancellation or maintenance of external relations – would be the more favourable to the success of this transformation of the productive forces?

It is our submission that the reduction of external relations will, on the whole, be more favourable precisely because the technology that could be imported on the assumption of these relations being maintained is not neutral and is even unfavourable to social transformation. Stagnation of productive forces, however, is also unfavourable to social transformation. A certain degree of technological importation may therefore be useful or even necessary, which means that a certain balance must be maintained, which is a matter of practical politics.

Quite possibly, in certain cases a sudden and total rupture of external relations may have had rather negative effects. Is not this the reason for the current impasse of Vietnam after the liberation of the South, of Cambodia and perhaps even partly of the Cultural Revolution?

The (correct) (re) discovery of the fact that technology is not neutral may have caused the need for the development of the productive forces to be forgotten. It is therefore necessary to carry out a more balanced analysis of the problem of technology.

Two comments are called for concerning this analysis:

(1) Those countries of the periphery that never carried out a socialist revolution were never really committed to a policy of self-reliant development and have never really 'de-linked'. That is why these somewhat brittle experiences (Nasserism, Tanzania etc. . .) remain reversible, even if certain transformations (e.g. land reforms and nationalisation) appear to be irreversible. But are not these 'irreversible' transformations capable of being co-opted by the domination of monopoly capital in development conditions that continue to be outward-looking, whereas they would not be so in the context of self-reliant development?

(2) De-linking would probably be necessary even for a developed country committed to the transformation of its social relations. In fact,

to maintain external relations, i.e. imperialist relations of exploitation, means the establishment of a class structure hostile to change. Thus, if it is true that underdeveloped countries give the impression of having reached an 'impasse' and are facing a very real contradiction, this is even more true of the developed countries. Rudolf Bahro is perfectly aware of the nature of this problem, which makes him an exception. Neither in the developed capitalist countries nor in Eastern Europe do even the most advanced prevailing currents of thought appear to recognise this fact.

This analysis implies that the European workers' movement does not yield to the 'European' temptation. To yield to the requirements of the 'development of the productive forces' means to put off indefinitely social transition when it could be started on the basis of the rupture of the weak links of the European system.

One conclusion can be drawn from this analysis. If this is so and if the 'breaking up' of the world system is the only solution to the impasse of the modern world, the model of transition towards the abolition of class would appear just like that of 'transition from Antiquity to feudalism', i.e. as a model of 'decadence' rather than that of the transition to capitalism, which was a model of 'revolution'. (Vide the conclusion in *Classe et Nation*.)

Notes on the Making of a Third World Social Scientist in the Capitalist World

HERB ADDO

Certainly, it is too early for me to write the autobiography of the development of my scholarship. After all, it is still my intention to be a useful scholar in solving social problems I consider 'important'. It is not too early, however, to present some notes in this direction on the occasion of a *Festschrift* in honour of Johan Galtung, a teacher and a friend,[1] on the questions why I became a social scientist, what I consider to be the purpose of social science, and for whom my research is directed.

It all began in the mid-1950s when I was growing up in various Ghanaian towns and in the city of Kumasi, in particular, where I attended high school. In those years, the air in Ghana was filled with catchy political, economic and social terms. I can still remember some of them: elections, democracy, rallies, internal self-government, independence, opposition, the economy, balance of payments, racial discrimination and equality. The fact that I did not understand these terms did not stop me from finding them fascinating; and this fact encouraged me to sit, hidden from view, of course, but close enough to hear when the towns' sages, including my father, a teacher, explained, discussed and pronounced on them.

These words and terms haunted me all through the early months of my high school years, until later on I had developed enough appreciation of what they meant to be able to use them in school debates.

Two things helped most: the radio and the newspapers. They covered Kwame Nkrumah extensively; and he was my idol. They reported a lot of foreign news. My social vocabulary grew accordingly to include choice terms: the cold war, communism, atomic bombs, satellites, megaton, moral re-armament, Security Council, General Assembly, etc. This led to a situation where I preferred to read, and listen to, current affairs rather than work on the mathematics for which I was supposed to have some aptitude. So that when I emerged from my teenage crisis period, I had decided, against all advice, that I wanted to be a journalist, because I had come to sense that there was something unfair both in my country Ghana and in the world; and I could not think of a better way to tackle this unfairness I sensed than to write verbosely against it. I had come to ask myself whether there was a connection between the unfairness in Ghana, Nigeria, Kenya and elsewhere in Africa, and the wide world beyond. And I came to the unshakable conclusion that, as Kwame Nkrumah had said, colonialism and imperalism were to blame, and that all that Ghana and other African nations had to do was to seek the political kingdom after which other things, like economic kingdoms and African unity, would surely be added.

At twenty, three years after Ghana's independence in 1957, I abandoned unexciting journalistic dabblings and the silent pleasure of mathematical deductions. I decided to study in order to find out what exactly the rest of the world was doing to Africa which had led to the inexplicable situation whereby with the arrival of independence the 'other things' had come in the form of the bizzare reality in which nothing changed, except that Ghanaian and other African political leaders were doing precisely what I had not been led to expect. Naturally, I was called an idealist and a naive person whenever I voiced my disappointment and expressed my discontent with post-independence non-fulfilment of promised expectations. This frustrated me.

I ended up in a small English university to study politics and economics, as any true 'post-colonial colonial' would do, in search of answers to post-colonial social anomalies in Ghana and in the other African nations. Frustration mounted, however, when I discovered that one does not go to a university to explore what altogether interested one. One had to *do* and *pass* examinations on what one had not been consulted in putting together. It was even more frustrating to try in tutorials to ask to be made to veer in the direction one found interesting. Even worse, was to attempt, on the few occasions, to put asunder theoretically and analytically arguments that one had not put together. Strangely, I found that one was expected to study logic, which I liked, without posing logical queries at the dissertations on the many, and for the most part boring, theses in politics and economics to which one was subjected. No wonder then, that, to save my sanity, frustration thankfully turned into boredom half-way through my undergraduate years. What was a wonder was that I managed to pass my final examinations at all, and needless to say with the most inauspicious honours.

When the time came in 1967 for my graduating class to be counselled on what jobs they were interested in, or rather what jobs the graduands could find, I had the shining audacity to say I had not yet learnt the answer to my master problem of why Ghana and the other African nations had not lived up to the post-colonial hopes of the autonomy and the graceful unity which could make them develop as they had hoped, and that I would like to study further to pursue the answer to this question. My counsellor promptly reminded me that such thoughts occurred only to 'idle drifters who do not want to face up to their own intellectual limitations and are afraid to settle down to contribute to their societies. In your case, I refer to Ghana. The ICI has a job in Ghana for a representative of sorts. The pay is good and you will be back with your own people. And I must say you will be perfect for the job, if you abandon these unhealthy thoughts'. Being back home was a nice thought, I had to admit; but I said it could not be as nice as solving my problem.

With the words, 'don't be a drifter, think it over and accept to be interviewed', soundly ringing in my head, I set off to where I had to go only to be told that my Professor wanted to talk to me. We talked in his digs, sherry in hand, on the report from the counsellor. He was supportive of my intention and advised me to apply to some Canadian universities to do post-graduate work, but warned that my 'puzzle', as he called it, was beyond immediate solution as it appeared to him to call for a life-long dedication. I also talked to my lecturer in International Relations who offered to recommend me to do further 'worry' on my puzzle in any university of my choice in the U.S. and Canada.

So I turned up at another small university in Ontario, where my frustrations were relieved a little, in that directed reading led me to clarify the nature of the puzzle somewhat to myself. The year I spent there enabled me to accept that my English professor was right. I needed to devote my life to the unravelling of my puzzle. I had come to the conclusion that a social science researcher's job was to keep the accepted social conventional wisdoms foul or fair, under constant critical examination. I had come to accept that fact and value were not too far apart in conventional wisdoms. Importantly I had come to accept myself as an idealist, on the self-defence that any aspect of social reality, if contemplated for too long, soon appears too awesome to change; and that what a social scientist who is a critical researcher should do is to understand social problems just enough to understand their sources and the interest which they serve. Most importantly, I had come, through reading no more than snatches of radical liberal and marxist thoughts on societies, to sense that my puzzle was not new. It has a long intellectual tradition. The *world* appeared to have a lot to do with why Ghana and Africa, now blown into another term, 'Third World' to include Asia and Latin America, could not 'develop'. With my puzzle somewhat contained, I still had a problem, an old problem, which had matured. The question was for whom do I write? My peers, my professors or myself? I still needed to be told that my essays were 'good'. But whose criteria for good was I to accept. This bothered me as I moved on to do my doctorate in another Ontario university.

My stay in this latter university was long and sanguinary. It was long because I decided to relearn in order to approach my puzzle anew; and it was sanguinary because the grip of liberal ideology, and its conception of the idea of university education, did not make my long stay and my desire to relearn, in order to find a healthy approach to my puzzle, easy.

The puzzle remained, except that my long stay at this university, eased a lot through a close association with one of my professors, helped immensely to enable me to suspect, if not to convince me, after graduation about a few crucial things. The first was that the liberal ideology was incapable of providing fundamental solutions to the social problems from which the centre of its practitioners benefit. That is that liberal scholars approach solutions to social problems cosmetically and amelioratively. The second is that social problems have no panaceas in the orthodox and solemn readings of marxist texts. The third was that the solutions for social problems do not lie in the middle ground between the two – the domain of the 'end of ideology'. Most importantly, I came to accept that the problems relating to and deriving from my puzzle needed complete epistemological departures for their understanding in ways I considered satisfactory for the purposes of solutions. And not to be forgotten in this context was that I had come to resolve the dilemma of whom to write for in my own favour. I write to please my understandings of social problems and the most probable ways of solving them. But I do so constantly reminding myself that I owe it to students, who may have puzzles similar to mine, to so reason and write that they could use aspects of my research to approach our 'problems' in ways which will at least clarify the coherence between the separate 'problems' constituting the nature of the puzzles.

It is for these reasons that my professional research interests have veered in the direction of the epistemological re-examination of the underpinnings of my puzzle. The puzzle remains essentially the same as it was in the beginning, but in its less fuzzy and reasoned form is this: how can *colonialism* and *imperialism* be so understood as to suggest their *negation* in order to allow for the autonomy and the *development* of Third World nations, given that we live in an *unequal interdependent capitalist world* system, which has as its *historic motive* the accumulation of capital in the centre and away from the periphery, through the use of rising efficiency to exploit both human and non-human resources?

The italicised terms are those which, to my mind, call for new ontological referrents for the epistemological re-examination I mention above. The point is that all the other concepts should relate to the concept of *development* in such a way that the very exiology of the term development would imply by itself 'what is to be done to develop'. This would imply the recognition of the dialectical unity of the centre and the peripheral parts of the capitalist world. It would demand refinements in the meanings of such crucial concepts as imperialism and capitalism in the historico-processual sense, in order to remove their current meanings from the dead and oppressive hands of the Euro-centric interpretation of human history and human future. The argument is that we should try to understand key concepts and the relations between them within their world systemic context and not in the context of the 'European' peculiarity within this world context.

The suggestion is that, in order to unravel my puzzle, I should see it, at one and the same time, as 'problems within problems', 'processes within processes', 'contradictions within contradictions' and 'dialectics within dialectics'. I should then also resolve these problems, processes, contradictions and dialectics into a cardinal mode. I shall refer to this as the *imperialist problematique,* and I shall define it as the vexing, because of its persistence, exploitation nexus between internal-periphery and internal-centre problems, processes, contradictions, and dialectics, which combine to produce exploitation of the periphery.

This is precisely what Johan Galtung has described within the UNU-GPID methodology as 'a process with a centre and a periphery, both of them moving, the content of them moving, the exact processes within and between them changing, but the gradient of exploitation remains, enriching the centre, impoverishing the periphery in various ways'.[3]

This is the cardinal contradiction of things appearing to change and yet remaining the same. This is the cardinal contradiction, the imperialist problematique, the process leading to the enriching of the centre and the impoverishing of the periphery in various ways, expressing the historic constancy of the exploitation effects of capitalist imperialism.

This, clearly, is a huge research area. But faithful to my original puzzle of why 'things' appeared changed but the Third World remained exploitatively the same, my research efforts are now centred on showing that the dynamic source of negating the imperialist problematique resides in the internal-periphery end of it. Specifically, I am trying to argue that the politics of world-system transformation suggests that it is composed of a dialetical struggle between *valid transition potentials* and *arrested transition potentials,* and since the periphery nations should be the main carriers of the transformation process, their internal orders are of crucial transformational importance.[4]

Just in case the above is all unclear, and just in case it serves to confirm my undergraduate counsellor's view of me as a potential drifter, let me answer the following questions the following ways:

Q. What do you take to be the purpose of social science research?
A. They are two. One is to comment enough on a society's reality so that it would *reform* itself in the *short-run.* The other is to criticize it

fundamentally enough so that it will *transform* itself for the 'better' in
the *short-run*. In both cases the interests of classes and group should
not obscure those of the individuals who compose them. And at all
times the first law of political economy, production to meet the basic
needs of all, must be upheld.

Q. In what sort of specific research tasks are you now involved?

A. I am involved in the critical examination of the imperialist problematique to ensure that the world capitalist system transforms itself
enough to respect the first law of political economy.

Q. How is your own work related to social problems and issues which
you in some sense find 'important'?

A. The imperialist problematique, as explained above, sums up social
problems and issues and their relations to the all-important matter of
transforming the world-system enough to reduce exploitation to its
unimportant minimum.

Q. With what arguments, and for whom will you justify your work?

A. The justifying arguments are derived from the appealing sense which
the historic interpretation of the structural-relational development of
the capitalist world-system makes. I justify my research to the few who
have puzzles similar to mine and who want to know why in the midst of
all the apparent changes the imperialist problematique remains. My
research is not directed primarily to the politicians and bureaucrats
who tend to believe that the sources of imperialism always reside where
they themselves do live; and when they turn to confront them, they
appear, by their actions, to believe that the imperialist problematique
can be solved over a week-end, forgetting that it has taken nearly 500
years for capitalism to grow from its unsuspecting beginnings to its
present monstrous proportions. My research is addressed to those who
take a *respectable* view of the 'short-run' because they *respect* the
durable effects of world capitalism's arrested transition potential.

Q. Why are you engaged in social science at all?

A. I do not think I blundered, or drifted, into social science research. I
take the pursuit of my puzzle seriously enough to think now that it was
an involuntary decision. I cannot see myself, at the present time, doing
anything else. The overall and final resulting effect of my research on
transforming the world will most likely not be much, but this does not
disturb me. Granted that I live in a world where money unfortunately
counts most, the pressures are immense and the pay could be better,
but then, I must confess, the personal satisfaction I derive from research is enormous.

NOTES

1 It is difficult for me to write this piece conscious of the editorial caveat not to celebrate
Johan Galtung's research. I owe so much to him, as do many people from the Third

36

World, in the development of my research. But Galtung's research and scholarship are celebrations in themselves. My own research project, the 'Structural Interpretation of International Inequality Project' (SIIP) derives its inspiration from Galtung's earlier pieces on the structural approaches to imperialism, integration, violence, and conflict, all indicating the structural underpinnings of exploitation. My recent research products feed into, and feed from, the United Nations University's Goals, Processes and Indicators of Development project co-ordinated by Johan Galtung from Geneva.

2 Moral re-armament! How I still like the term! Except I understand and appreciate it differently now from what the Voice of America had in mind.

3 Johan Galtung, 'Towards Synergy in Networks of People with Networks of Problems: A Note on GPID Methodology', A report on 'The Theoretical Overview of the GPID Project (Synthesis/Integration)', p. 14, 1979.

4 Currently, I am working on the 'Dialectical Politics of Transformation'. In this piece I conceive transformation potential in any system as a dialectical struggle between valid and arrested aspects of its transition properties. This approach eliminates policies *per se* as tools for estimating transformation potentials, because each single policy is double-edged. It has *valid* and *arrested* contents. I apply this approach in 'Foreign Policy Strategies for Achieving the NIEO: A Third World Perspective', forthcoming in *Sage International Yearbook of Foreign Policy Studies*, VI, 1980.

Memoir of an Italian Sociologist

ANNA ANFOSSI

The reasons why we are engaged in something, now, seem more difficult to spell out than the motivations that first originated our engagement. This, at least, was my reaction, when confronted with this challenging question. An 'historical approach' therefore seemed appropriate in order to give a first, tentative answer.

To Italian sociologists who grew up in the Thirties and Forties like me, sociology was a late discovery, which certainly was not due to sheer hazard, although it did not involve a strict necessity either. The combined influence of Italian Idealism, on the one hand, and the Fascist régime, on the other, had wiped sociology off the academic map, condemned as a 'pseudo-science' by the former, and as an intrinsically subversive intellectual activity by the latter. Sociology made its formal appearance at Italian universities in the second half of the Fifties. It thus happened that most of us landed in sociology, in the Fifties, after journeying through either philosophy, or psychology, or both. Others reached sociology through jobs in industry, providing them with an opportunity to approach it, both as a mass of theories and a research practice. All of us, I think, eventually found out that, like Molière's *bourgeois gentilhomme,* who suddenly discovered he had been practising prose without realizing it, we had tried to practise a disguised sociology without knowing we were doing so.

My curriculum went step by step from philosophy to psychology, and social psychology, until sociology appeared as a promised land, a key – at least in my expectation – to a lot of unanswered questions, somewhat reminiscent of the big questions we keep brooding over in adolescence: Why inequality and social classes? How are individual drives related to the ways a society is set up? Why religions? How can contradictory beliefs be held together? Why violence and wars? Why Fascism? and so on. So, at last I thought I could find more precise contents for the up to then rather empty label that was sociology to me. This did not occur through books, in spite of the *Manuel de sociologie* I had got hold of in Paris, early in the Fifties, out of curiosity. It happened rather in the stimulating environment of Ipsoa, the first Italian Business School, set up in Turin by private initiative, and inspired by the model of the Harvard Business School. Its teachers came from the United States and were assisted by young Italians; students came from industries and banks, all over Italy. I joined Ipsoa in 1954, when it had been operating for a couple of years, and, because of my psychological background, I was assigned as an assistant professor to the course in Human Relations and Personnel Administration.

In the Summer of 1954, I attended the Salzburg Seminar in American Studies, where Talcott Parsons gave a course in sociology, the first in my life. There, one day at lunch time, a new student appeared, a unique combination, in a modern version, of a knight-errant and a *clericus vagans*. He had been riding his motor-cycle from Oslo to Salzburg, via Spain, France, and Northern Italy, and brought with him a typing-machine, a flute, a camera, and the draft of a book on Gandhi he was writing together with Arne Næss. This is how I first met Johan Galtung, and a close and permanent friendship started. He was to the Seminar what garlic is to Occidental cooking, if I may use this rather rustic, but appropriate, comparison. To me, he has been an unremitting source of inspiration, as well as of critical awareness, ever since.

Thus, it was by no hazard that in 1955, at Ipsoa, two colleagues of mine (one of whom had also attended the Salzburg Seminar in 1954) and myself set up, in a tentative way, an additional course, which was rather ambitiously called 'The business enterprise and the social system', and was meant to fill the existing gap between the American experience that the main courses were based upon, and the Italian situation, by discussing 'cases' and documents dealing with the latter. Gradually, in the next two years, our initiative resulted in a course in industrial sociology, concentrating on industrial relations in Italy; as far as I know, it was the first such course in this field that was given in Italy. To us, this was a unique experience: our interest in relevant, up-to-date problems in the Italian context could be combined with a theoretical approach: Weber and Parsons provided a specific sociological trend to the Marxian approach, which was current among young intellectuals, particularly in Northern Italy and in industrial areas. This rather peculiar combination, at the time, of references, and our tendency to deal with union problems were not, however, quite along the lines of the policy of an Italian business school in the Cold War period; some sponsors of the School raised strong objections. Our sociological course did not last long; in 1957, anyway, most of us Italian teachers left the School. Each of us went his or her own way. My way has henceforth been sociology; to me, too, it had been mediated by industry, although indirectly.

That same year 1957, I was involved in a field research project on development in Sicily; other field researches followed, on development in Southern Italy, on industrial and migration issues in the North. Now,

39

after teaching sociology in Sardinia for nine years, I have re-settled for some years in Turin, where I was born, and I teach sociology at the University where I had been a student in philosophy. Organizations, of which industrial organizations are but particular specimens, and 'development issues' have remained central in my interests; the meaning of development has, however, become more and more blurred.

At the present time, and since 1978, I am responsible for a research project on the ongoing reorganization process in mechanical industries of the Turin area. This project is sponsored by the Italian *Consiglio Nazionale delle Ricerche* (National Research Council), and is being carried on by an interdisciplinary team of sociologists and economists of various Faculties of Turin University. The project started through contacts between the local leaders of the Metalworker Federation and university researchers and teachers; its aim was to acquire better information and understanding of the ongoing organizational changes, and of their impact and implications, both on work conditions and work requirements inside factories, and on the labour market outside. In this contact, particular attention was devoted to the so-called 'production decentralization', namely the process by which big enterprises, like Fiat and Olivetti, in our case, allot the production of an increasingly large amount of components of their final items to other, and independent, enterprises, which, in turn, may spread the process, and thus involve a growing number of very small workshops. A sample of more than one hundred mechanical enterprises of the Turin area, each of them employing more than two hundred people, was selected, and the research began. A relatively new feature of the project was the fact that worker representatives, namely union leaders at the plant level, were asked to participate in the cognitive stage, thus acquiring and contributing information on the whole of the production process in their factories. Joint seminars with the workers were also organized, and held, by union leaders and researchers, to discuss the first outcomes of the investigation; papers on the work being done were also presented and discussed at seminars, organized by the *Consiglio Nazionale delle Ricerche,* and dealing with work organization in industry, at a national level.

The first stage of the research lasted a year and a half, yielding some interesting results, and raising a lot of useful critical questions concerning the approach to the issue at stake, and even the scope of the research itself. As to the former, although being confronted with these problems may have helped the workers grow aware of organizational facts and their implications, the limits of their acting as sources of information, regarding whole processes far beyond their reach, have become evident. Out of this realization, and because of the extra burden thus laid on worker representatives, the union withdrew from active participation in the project, though maintaining its external support to it. Concerning the scope of the research, some relevant aspects have come to the fore. First of all, the inadequacy of the traditional definition of the mechanical sector in industry on which official data and references are based: the network of enterprises involved in the production of 'mechanical' items almost always overlaps other sectors (electricity and electronics, the chemical sector, and so on); suggestions for different, and less abstract, groupings can already be drawn from the outcomes of the research. Secondly, it has become clear that no such network can be identified without encroaching upon other, and even distant, geographical areas, both national and international: at least some of the most significant connections must be identified, possibly as typical 'cases'. Thirdly, the original stress on the sociological aspects had to be integrated in a wider approach; the economic and technological aspects should get greater attention, as well as the international factors influencing them.

In this second stage of the research, its scope has thus been broadened, but, in order to make it feasible, the actual field of analysis has been restricted to three sub-sectors that had emerged in the first phase of the research as being particularly interesting: machine-tools, electronics (which is included within the national metalworker contract), and the automotive complex, or, at least, some relevant aspects of it. In all these sub-sectors, the main enterprises are examined in regard to their connections with the smaller ones: the distribution of work among them, their interdependent decision-making process, technological innovation, and new entrepreneurship are central items for investigation. Identifying their strategies, with their implications, should, if it is not too ambitious a goal, shed light on some of the possible outcomes in the Italian economy, owing to the major impact these sub-sectors have on it, and the relevance of the Turin area, which remains central in our analysis. If reliable results are obtained along these lines, our research project can make a specific contribution to a set of research projects and studies that are now being carried out to assess and interpret some relevant aspects of Italian society. These issues are: the 'submerged economy' ('double employment', i.e. moonlighting and 'black' or illegal labour); the thriving of small enterprises, particularly in the South; the evolution of the labour force and labour market; changes in work organization in industry; changes in union organization and policies, and so on. Characteristically enough, all these studies analyse economic issues in close connection with the sociological ones (and, as a matter of fact, many of them were initiated by sociologists).

A closer integration among social disciplines, including not only sociology, psychology, and economics, but also political science and history, has in fact been an emerging trait in Italy in the last decade. This certainly stems from the awareness of the inadequacy of each single discipline to cope with a multifarious reality, which is changing at an increasing speed, and often, apparently, in an unpredictable way. From this standpoint, the interdisciplinary approach is a response to a process of 'modernization' involving Italian society as a whole, but, at the same time, marked by deep unbalance. However, this fact also reflects the growing uneasiness all Western societies are undergoing, the deep crisis of which the economic aspect is simply the most consipicuous one. The belief in progress and its almost endless continuation, the confidence in being able to defeat poverty for good have been struck down. The combination of efforts on the part of social scientists is a response to this challenge as well.

Development has always been a relative concept, and a questionable one in its meaning. In Italy, development, with all its typically Western implications, has been a matter of concern, and of lively debates, with special reference to the Southern areas, ever since the early Fifties. Industrialization, and how to implement, it, was almost generally viewed as an unobjectional path to it, according to the established Western pattern. As a consequence of the economic crisis, and just as confidence in progress is dwindling, both the concept of development and its implementation have become more and more questionable, and are questioned indeed, overtly at least by some odd intellectuals. A feeling of helplessness in tackling a threatening reality is however widespread, and it affects not only intellectuals, but also a number of prominent actors in political and economic life. Many feel inclined to consider Italy as leading the way in underdevelopment, without ever having reached a generalized stage of 'development'. Here, too, looking for ways out of the impasse calls for joint efforts, involving intellectuals as well, and makes them inclined to explore alternative ways of life, and alternative societies, beyond the traditional Western models, be they capitalistic or Marxist.

My personal quest for alternatives has led me to approach Gandhian perspectives. A recent visit to India has enabled me to get a better grasp of Gandhi's views, by setting them in their social and cultural context, and to get first-hand information about some initiatives being carried on along his lines. The number of unanswered questions has increased, as was expected; possibly, it will take some time for me to unfold the riches of this experience. One point has however become clearer: the necessity of combining the inspirations drawn from other cultures with truly Gandhian self-reliance and a good deal of sociological imagination if we want to evoke future alternatives to a gloomy present. A bit of sociological imagination may first be applied to the fields one is more familiar with; in my case, to organizational thinking.

Now for some time, my interest has been centred on a particular aspect of the organizational theory, namely organizational interactions. This relatively new branch adds a crucial dimension to a mass of theories focussing on single organizations, or types of them, and thus dealing with them as partially closed systems. The dimension that is added by examining interorganizational relationships is a genuinely political one, as its kernel is power, and organizations are by themselves both a source and instrument of power. However democratic an organization – or society – is meant to be, its hierarchical structure is liable to defeat democracy, insofar as it concentrates control and information (our present research project deals with a typical case of this), and hence power, at the top. There, the organizational elites, in close, formal and informal, visible and invisible, interaction, can engage in the decision-making processes through which power is pursued and exerted over the environment, be it a local, or a national, or an international one. This power is exercised in a wide gamut of forms, ranging from open conflict and competition to various, and subtle, ways of bargaining and of alliances, or even more or less stable associations, insofar as the interacting elites are identified with their organizations, and can make them function as integrated units. Interactions, however, take place at all levels of organizations, characteristically enough at homologous levels, in ways that may be either functional or dysfunctional to the organizations involved – particularly from the standpoint of their tops. New organizations may even be originated through this process: unions and their federations are well-known examples, but this may take place in other social areas as well, for instance in the case of political parties. At the intermediate, and even at the lowest levels of hierarchical organizations, these interactions may always yield some power to those engaged in them, and, even indirectly, some control may be exerted on the formal power structures. At all levels, therefore, in spite of the extremely broad variety of forms that interactions take, some kind of personal power is also present, as a combined consequence of the inherent structural power and the interaction itself. The fine texture of visible and invisible networks thus involved closely connects the economic with the strictly political cultural subsystems of societies – Charles Wright Mills' analysis remains a classic one in this context. Sure enough, all this may make societies function, it may absorb the tensions inherent in any complex system, but it may also enhance these tensions, and prevent the system from working properly, at least from the perspective of the ruling elites.

Theoretical speculation about these issues may cover various aspects: models of interaction, at different levels, and their relationships with specific cultural traits (a *mafia* model, for instance, with its clientelistic variations, may be congenial with some cultural traits, whilst being incompatible with others); the verticality of organizations (and of societies), concentrating power at the top, is structurally non-democratic, but under what conditions, if any, can it be reconciled with egalitarian values and procedures, if we want to stick to these values? What alternative ways of societal functioning can be conceived for the future, with regard to organizational interactions, and particularly to the elitist interactions that are dominant today? Further empirical testing of some theoretical aspects can be envisaged, provided it is carried out on specific issues, restricted in their scope, although involving the joint contributions of different social disciplines.

This is where I now stand. I do not know whether I am still moving in the sociological domain, nor whose territory I am encroaching upon, but are labels so important?

Possibly, my present motivations in engaging in sociology are not so far away from the rather ambitious initial ones, but limits and contradictions in this engagement have come to the fore. Intellectual curiosity is still there, but the usefulness of its outcomes seems highly questionable. This attitude may well be what is usually called the critical awareness resulting from experience. I have been engaged in a number of research projects; some of them were centred on issues that were no doubt socially relevant, such as migration or development problems, organizational change, and so on. Some were even parts of action programmes meant to bring about, in particular communities, some desirable changes the communities themselves had agreed upon; the research projects were conceived of as instrumental, as a cognitive phase, to action-taking, and involved direct participation from below. I am afraid very few of them, if any, led to any substantial result. Their cognitive value may of course be questioned, but even if they had some, they never seemed to affect the solution of the problems they were supposed to deal with, almost always for external and political reasons. They often seemed at best, to be viewed by those responsible for action-taking as becoming rituals, sometimes even expensive ones, which at least suggests they were not regarded as properly backing the establishment.

So, we, too, feel that studying societies may be a necessary step, but it is not enough, and it is high time to start changing them. Indulging in the belief that we *are* bringing about some worth-while changes through our analyses would appease our consciences, were it not for the creeping suspicion that we are but flies on the wheel. Still, if we could achieve some flashes of insight and produce some good ideas, we should welcome them, and even rejoice at them. For ideas have a life of their own, and may be as important as structures – after all, structures are ideas at work, although often frozen ones. Ages ago, Leibnitz taught me that a sum of infinitesimal elements can eventually coalesce into a driving force, and we have watched a number of such cases in our lives, by now. Obviously, some infinitesimal fraction of a demiurge always dwells in social scientists, even though they, from time to time, feel inclined to envy artists, for art can be much more forceful in awakening awareness, creating brilliant visions of the future, and, sometimes, even bringing about action. Although there is no guarantee of the intrinsic goodness of forceful ideas, or of their outcomes, and the underlying values of good and evil remain open to question, this is a risk we took when we chose to live.

Anyway, despairing is out of question. We may no longer believe in progress; nevertheless we still are grand-children of the *Siècle des Lumières*, and may therefore indulge in the belief that we can, as human beings, somehow be masters of our destiny. With irony, of course.

And what if I happen to be engaged in sociology, or whatever it is, just because I am privileged enough to do something I like?

The Purpose of Social Science Research

MIHAILO MARKOVIC

I started social science research when I was already forty, writing a text on the meaning of self-management, which was presented at the second sessions of the Korchula Summer school and published in *Praxis* (No. 2–3, 1965, pp. 178–195). Both the moment when it started and the nature of my engagement in social science research, until this very day were determined by the nature of my previous activities and by the character of the social changes that took place in Yugoslavia.

Before I became a social scholar engaged in research on general social issues I was an active revolutionary and a philosopher. I was just seventeen when I decided that existing Yugoslav society (in 1940) was so unjust, inhuman, and corrupt beyond repair, that it deserved to be radically changed. Then the war came, followed by four years of Nazi occupation and the struggle in the underground youth movement and in the partisan army. When I eventually was able to start my studies in the University, it had to be philosophy. There was such a strong need to understand: What is the world as a whole? What is the meaning of human life and historical development? Where are the roots of human misery and incomprehensible destructive social forces? What is it in human nature that urges millions of human beings into a struggle for noble ideals, makes them able to take any risk, to make any conceivable effort and to prevail eventually? Whatever the subsequent disappointments, they were not able to erase that early basic experience: human beings cannot accept humiliation and misery indefinitely; eventually they rise and emancipate themselves.

This basic conviction was reinforced by the 1948 experience of Yugoslav resistance to the overwhelming authority and power of Stalin and the 'first socialist country'. No matter how much smaller and weaker you are, if you are ready to risk your life and mobilize all your rational and creative powers, the oppressor would have to pay such a high price that, on second thoughts, he might let you in peace. After surviving the first immediate danger Yugoslavia had to engage in a lasting ideological defensive war. My philosophical preoccupation throughout the Fifties, which explains my lasting interest in methodological issues of social research, was how to build up intellectual means that can be used for a rational critique of both an unjust, inhuman, reality and of a mystifying ideology. All my writings in the Fifties deal either with general philosophical issues of logic, epistemology, and scientific method, or with a critique of Soviet dogmatism and of Stalinist practices.

The early Sixties made a new step towards critical social science research inevitable. Together with a whole generation of humanist-socialism-oriented Yugoslav intellectuals I became deeply aware of the fact that our own society found itself on a crossroad. It could not go all the way back to Stalinism of the Soviet type. But the dilemma in 1963–1965 was: whether to continue a process of democratization, of gradual replacement of bureaucratic structures with new truly self-governing organs which would take care of all indispensable social coordination, or whether to substitute a mere economic liberalization for political democratization: to preserve a strong authoritarian bureaucratic state, decentralized along national lines, and offer a considerable degree of *laissez-faire* market economy. It became increasingly obvious that professional political cadres preferred the latter; with the 'Economic reform' of 1965 it became official policy. To me and my colleagues from *Praxis* there was no doubt what it meant: prevalence of a selfish particular bureaucratic interest over a general, emancipatory one, renunciation of initial revolutionary commitment, choice of a road that would indefinitely keep a self-appointed vanguard in power but at the same time would generate all kinds of new social inequalities, produce a hopeless confusion, and eventually destroy enormous existing moral and intellectual forces that thus far supported a genuine self-governing socialism.

In order to resist this trend we had to pass from our purely philosophical studies towards a more concrete social research, from a general criticism of Stalinism and Bourgeois liberalism towards a specific critique of our own Yugoslav bureaucracy and of the capitalist tendencies in our own economy. In order to make our ideas an objective social force we created *Praxis* and the *Korchula* Summer school.

What is the basic purpose of social science research is implicit in this story. One can state it briefly and explicitly by saying: the purpose is building a critical self-consciousness that helps a society in a given situation to become aware of its optimal historical possibilities and to take practical steps for their realization. Such a formulation of the basic purpose of research in social sciences is integrative and obviously value-laden. It embraces all existing forms and directions of actual social research and finds a meaningful place for them within a larger framework. On the other hand, it rejects any ideology that tends to reduce social science research to only one dimension: mere description, explanation, understanding, model building, utopian projection, critique in the name of abstract ideals, pragmatic preoccupation with strategies.

Anything that deserves the name of social science must be concerned with a most serious study of *what there is*. If I study Yugoslav self-management I must establish what the facts are about worker's councils, basic and complex organizations of associated labour, local communities, communes, networks of communities for education, culture, scientific research, health service and others. I must find out not only what is written in the Yugoslav Constitution and the laws, but, much more important, how organs of self-management actually function, how much decision-making power they really have, how they are related to the State, the ruling Party, trade unions, the managerial elite.

The next question is *why?* Whatever there is must be both *explained* in terms of certain regularities of overt behavior and structural set-up, and *understood* in terms of subjective and inter-subjective aspirations, intentions, beliefs and frustrations. In order to give an account of the actual state of Yugoslav self-management, one has to develop a considerable theoretical background and to become well acquainted with relevant historical information. Without a sound knowledge about the nature of the modern state and political parties, especially about one-party systems, about the history of self-management and the history of the Yugoslav socialist revolution, one would not be able even to begin to explain why Yugoslav self-management functions the way it does, why there is so much ambiguity in the Yugoslav political leadership's attitude toward self-management: giving to it the highest priority among all social goals, making out of it the very backbone of the official ideology, but also constraining its further development in all kinds of ways. It would also be impossible to explain why Yugoslav workers pay so much importance to it and invariably express a readiness to defend it against bureaucratic and technocratic encroachments, but at the same time, in practice, do not use nearly all the rights that existing forms of self-management offer, and exhibit a striking passivity in all but distribution issues. On the other hand, the question *why* cannot be fully answered only on the basis of well-known methods of *explanation* in terms of objective, institutional, and behavioural patterns. One has to penetrate rather deeply into the mental set-up of different groups of Yugoslav people – which can be done only by living and communicating with them – in order to *understand* why are they so optimistic, so hopeful about the future, and at the same time so critical and sometimes revolted about their present condition.

The next question is what *could be*, what is the potential for the future, what are the most probable possibilities. How likely is it that Yugoslav self-management would continue to develop in the Eighties, increasing the autonomy of the workers councils, generating higher level self-managing bodies, embracing the political sphere in addition to the economic one? What are and how likely are other possibilities?

Answers to the questions *what is, why* is it the way it is, and *what could be* in the future provide *positive knowledge,* the moment of *consciousness* about a given social reality. If one stops research at this point one surely provides useful information, but the question remains *to whom* would it be useful. Clearly a positive information could be used for both emancipatory and repressive, creative and destructive purposes. Taking into account that a great deal of scientific research is being financed, directed, and controlled by the state, the army, and other institutions committed to the preservation of the *status quo,* it is obvious that a considerable amount of mere positive knowledge will be misused and abused. That is why it is essential in my opinion to make a step from positive science to critical science, from consciousness towards critical self-consciousness.

That means, first, to ask the question: *What is inadequate, what are the basic limitations* in the examined social reality? Second, to ask such a question not only about another society but about the society to which one belongs and *for which one is responsible*. Besides, it is comfortable to criticize other societies; sometimes this criticism is itself part of an official ideology. On the other hand, critique of one's own society is much more risky and leads to conflicts that may be extremely painful but are indispensable for any development. Yugoslavs produced a vast descriptive literature on self-management but not enough critical analysis. Once one begins to study its basic weaknesses: too many constraints imposed on self-governing bodies by the state legislature, heteronomy in decision-making that results from the predominant power of the league of Communists, enormous pressure exerted by the 'informal groups' manipulated by the technostructure, inadequate efforts to educate workers for a more active role in self-managing organs – one touches the most vulnerable areas of the system and must count on its growing hostility.

This happens even more if one asks the question *what is the optimal possibility* of future development? Is it compatible with the prevailing officially supported trend? Thus, the optimal possibility of further Yugoslav development would be: transformation of all organs of the state into organs of self-government, decentralization of decision-making power on all those issues which are not of common interest, making the ruling Party (the League of Communists) a truly educational organization (as in the period 1958–1968), socialization of mass media, a radical shift in education from preparation for a narrow specialized role in the professional division of labour to preparation for a meaningful and creative communal life. This is *not* the envisaged direction of development in present-day Yugoslavia. By advocating an alternative

4 – Social Science

course of development a social scholar would almost certainly be classified as an 'enemy of self-management'. But one must take such a risk – if his research and his basic value-orientation lead him in that direction. Everything else would be conformism and self-betrayal. Naturally there are all kinds of ways to avoid this kind of self-destruction and to develop 'false consciousness', a will to believe that things are better than they are, or a philosophy that justifies conformism and apology.

The idea that critical self-consciousness is a basic purpose of social science research involves a rational and critical reflection of one's own philosophical position. Some ontological, epistemological and value assumptions are always implicit in any social research. One need not be aware of them. To pretend that they do not exist, that one is a pure, 'anti-metaphysical', 'value-free' scientist, is a well known case of self-deception. Since they are always there, it is an obvious advantage to know them, to control their interaction with concrete knowledge, and to be able to solve problems that arise in connection with them, such as: Are my philosophical assumptions consistent? What are the priorities in the case of a conflict between them? Do I mean what I say when I try to express them: do I accept all their implications? Am I ready to live my philosophy and to act according to its practical consequences? What follows from this is that one cannot be irresponsible about one's philosophy: unless one *means it* and is able to *live it* either one must avoid any rational dialogue or else one proves to be a split human being whose words, thoughts and deeds entirely fall apart. For example one loses all integrity if one claims to be a champion of self-government and at the same time seeks to preserve an existing monopoly of dominating power. The only philosophy compatible with self-government is a philosophy of universal human emancipation. And the only way to live that philosophy is by constant struggle against all monopolies of political, economic and cultural power.

Since practice cannot be separated from theory, critical social science research does not end with the projection of optimal historical possibility and indication of basic limitations of examined social reality that ought to be overcome. The question is *how* to do it, what practical steps are to be taken, what are the phases of the process leading from the present situation towards the realization of specific emancipatory goals. This is the question of *strategy,* or better, of *alternative* strategies, among which one should choose the optimal one. To be sure the optimal one is not just the most efficient one, although other conditions being equal, more efficient means are preferable. One must beware of strategies that eventually let the goals alone justify the means. When means are chosen merely on the ground of being efficient and not because they satisfy the *same* rational and moral criteria as the goals, they may profoundly and irreversibly corrupt the agents and bring to life an entirely different social reality from that to whose realization they were supposed to be instrumental. For example, if full development of self-government is a social goal, it cannot really be achieved by using a dominant political party as a means; a strong political authority tends to establish itself as a lasting power rather than to 'wither away'. Thus, a means turns into an end in itself; the former goal becomes a means of its legitimation. Similar inversion takes place when market competition and group egoism are construed as the means of self-management (as opposed to state control). The very basic purpose of self-management – increase of freedom, human dignity and solidarity – gets lost in endless conflicts over the issues of profits distribution.

The specific research in which I am now involved is closely related to self-government, the crucial issue of Yugoslav society. I am especially interested in two problems: one is the development of new forms of political democracy in self-governing socialism, the other is the abolition of alienated labor, the humanization of socially necessary work. The first is of essential importance, since there is such a tremendous gap between the socialist ideal of an emancipated self-determining community and the oppressive reality of those societies that claim to be really socialist.

Yugoslav experience, especially from the late Fifties and early Sixties indicates the direction in which new solutions may be found for some basic problems of democracy in socialism. On the basis of that experience it is possible to conceive of a synthesis of centralism and decentralization, a process of deprofessionalization of politics, a transformation of parties into primarily educational political organizations, a participatory democracy in which people have much greater control over the decision-making process. Research of this kind differs from mere abstract model building; one must take into account historical tendencies and actual cultural and psychological constraints. Factual information, especially data from the period (1953–1968), confirm the *possibility* of new alternative social forms.

The other problem on which I am now working: *humanization of labour* is a major issue of worker's emancipation but has not attracted much attention from sociologues in 'socialist' countries so far. At a time when some Scandinavian, Western European and American enterprises begin to be seriously concerned about the worst aspects of alienated labour and begin to experiment with alternative technologies and 'job enrichment', state socialism still uses capitalist forms of the organization of labour and manifests an almost total indifference towards what happens to the workers as human beings in the process of modern industrial production. The whole issue of the *quality* of life

51

seems to be reduced to the *quantity* of material goods to be enjoyed in the free time. On the other hand, attempts to improve the quality of working life within a capitalist economy have so far been constrained by the profitability demands. Entirely new perspectives of the resolution of this problem open up when emancipation from alienated labour becomes one of the primary social goals in which it is worth investing social funds. This implies a search for alternative technologies and alternative ways of organizing production which would increasingly liberate human work from its present monotony, mechanical repetitiveness, and heteronomy.

This kind of engagement in critical social science seems to me indispensable for the understanding and clear sense of direction of any rational and emancipatory social praxis.

The Lawyer as a Social Scientist

BERT V. A. RÖLING

'The occasion makes the thief', so the saying goes. And in many cases this is true. But the occasion also makes the judge, and even the peace researcher. The occasion often explains the behaviour, the choices in life, the intentions and aims of activity.

I chose the law because I considered the world, the social order, the existing 'system', unjust. From the very start I wanted to know more about it, to discover the causes of injustice and the means to bring about changes. The treatment of criminals I especially considered disgusting, the penalties undeserved, and without any connection with the protection of society. Protest against a social institution such as criminal punishment is for a good part based on misgivings about the social system as a whole. Punishment is seen as the instrument to maintain this reprehensible order. As a matter of fact, socialist anti-militarism was in the same way based on the perception that national military power was the principal means of maintaining a detested social order.

I started, as a student, with the intention of finding decisive arguments against punishment as such, and of discovering other, more decent, means of dealing with criminals. I must confess that further research made it clear to me that punishment neither aimed at changing the criminal nor at giving him his due, but at restoring the mental order of society. This order, being undermined and disturbed by the crime, has to be restored. It was not the criminal who needed the punishment; it was the society concerned that could not do without it. Thus I learned the significance of cognitive dissonance at an early stage. For everyone who approaches society with specific idealistic ideas, social science research constitutes a fount of unwelcome information.

My main interest as a law student was criminal law. I realized that one should know more about the individual and social causes of crime, should know more about the social effects of crime, and about the ways and means to restrict the punishment. For that purpose the first criminological institute in Holland was established at the University of Utrecht in 1934, where I was a junior teacher of criminology. It was to serve as a place where all the relevant disciplines could cooperate in an endeavour to know more about the causes and effects of crime, and to arrive, on the basis of this better understanding, at a more reasonable policy with respect to the prevention and treatment of criminal behaviour. Criminology is a problem-oriented social science. It concentrates on one social phenomenon: crime, and tries to combine the concerted insight of several scientific disciplines on this issue.

If one looks at the history of the social science called criminology, starting with Lombroso's theory of the 'born criminal', then moving to the theories of the French school: 'les sociétés ont les criminels qu'elles méritent', the socialist theories that regard capitalist society as the main culprit, the psychological theories and so many other one-sided explanations, one is struck by the fact that apparently scientific theory is inclined to follow the moods of the day. The main theories of criminology, with which are connected the names of great and famous criminologists, give one-sided explanations, emphasize one aspect of the social evil. What they teach is not incorrect. The aspect they describe may be an important aspect. But it is not all. It is only one side of the story. It disregards other aspects, and in this respect the given theory is wrong. The famous names in criminology, Lombroso, Lacassagne, Manouvrier, Tarde, Bonger and so many others, represent inadequate theories, errors in judgment. But these errors had an impact on society. For that reason they might be called vital errors. Their effect was two-sided. First of all they destroyed the former traditional opinion that crime was the result of pure individual wickedness which should accordingly be punished. They demonstrated that other factors played a role, hereditary factors, social factors, for which the criminal could not be blamed. Secondly, they stressed the evil influence of the one factor, that, in their opinion, played the decisive role in the cause of crime and criminality. They drew the attention of the government to this special factor, and something could be done, and was done, in the struggle against crime. The vital error had, in its simplicity, a great appeal to the public, a convincing power. It was effective, it led to something. The slogan 'open a school and close a prison' was incorrect in its simplicity, but had an impact on politics.

When criminology approached a kind of maturity, it became more relativistic. The many aspects, the innate predisposition, the effects of education and environment, the impact of situation and occasion – they could all be combined in nice formulas which gave weight to everything. But the strength of every factor in relation to the others, the interaction between the different factors, remained unknown. The formula is, scientifically, correct. But it is a sterile truth, which cannot have much impact on governments or other decision-makers.

Perhaps every problem-oriented social science is bound to develop in the same way, from vital errors, generalizing specific features, to sterile truths, in which the interplay of many factors is recognized. But it is still impossible in that phase of scholarly research to have a clear insight into the strength and impact of the different elements of the process. That insight may come later, but I do not know of any problem-oriented social science in which this problem has been solved.

After the war I was invited to participate as the Netherlands' judge in the International Military Tribunal for the Far East, established to try the major Japanese war criminals. The Tokyo Trial – the Asian pendant of Nuremberg – was the largest trial in recorded history. It had before it 27 leaders of Japan accused of playing a decisive role in bringing about the Pacific War, starting with the attack on Pearl Harbour. Many of them were also held responsible for the misconduct of the military during the war. The question whether the leaders of Japan were responsible for crimes against peace and for conventional war crimes was the main issue.[1]

The Tokyo trial, which lasted 2 ½ years, changed my interest from criminal law to international law, from crime to war, or it might be said: from bad to worse. The foreign policy of Japan from 1928 to 1945 was analyzed and discussed at the trial. It could not be correctly understood, without consideration of what had happened in former centuries. It meant going deeply into colonial history and into Japan's response to the European intrusion into the Asian world. First a response of withdrawal out of fear. Fear of ideological aggression in the form of Christianity followed by military conquest and political domination in a colonial relation. Later, after Perry's demand that Japanese ports be opened for trade, the response was one of re-entering the world, but at the same time of taking revolutionary measures to build up sufficient strength with the aim of maintaining national independence. Japan, at that time, was well aware of the nature of international relations in which power was the predominant feature and war the *ultima ratio*. Japanese statesmen were prepared to adapt themselves to the rules of the international game. As Haushofer wrote: 'So wurde Japan von einem harmlosen Tier in seinem Paradies zum Tiger unter Tigern'. Its succesful wars against China and Russia demonstrated its capacity to handle modern weaponry. As a consequence, Japan was admitted to the charmed circle of 'civilized nations'.[2]

Japan's position within the 'civilized nations' was a delicate one. White supremacy still prevailed. In vain, Japan demanded the recognition of racial equality in the Covenant of the League of Nations. It was insulted by American behaviour (the restaurants on the West Coast with the signs 'Forbidden for dogs and Japs') and felt betrayed by the Washington Treaty. From its underdog-position it developed the idea of its historical mission: to expel the European powers from Asia.

The trial of government leaders for questions concerning international policy rests on the assumption that individual activity, individual wickedness, contributes fundamentally to the occurrence of events, in casu the Pacific War, of which they were accused. Their specific role, however, remains an open question. What will have had the greater impact, the social forces, in our case the changing relations between the white and the non-white races, or the individual opinions and actions of specific Japanese leaders?

The role of the individual in international affairs is sometimes quite clear. Hitler, Mussolini, Tito, Stalin, all determined the fate of their countries. But in many cases the persons whose names are attached to specific periods are nothing more than the *étiquettes de l'histoire,* as Tolstoi called them. And it may be surprising that he considered Napoleon as falling under this category *étiquettes de l'historie* or *marionettes de l'histoire,*[3] those who play the role that history confers on them.

Were the accused in the dock the causes of the Pacific War? One of them, Hirota Koki, prime-minister and minister of foreign affairs in the thirties, was found guilty of the crime against peace and of conventional war crimes (the Rape of Nanking) and was condemned to death. It is true that Hirota formulated when premier the Konoye-Hirota policy, which determined the future fate of Japan. Its principal aim was the elimination of the European powers from Asia. 'Asia for the Asians' was the slogan underlying the policy. But Hirota realized that this could not be accomplished by military means. The U.S., the U.K. and France were simply too powerful. He therefore chose other, indirect, means: economic penetration and ideologically subversive activities, stimulating liberation movements and awakening nationalist Asian thought. Should a colony, or an island declare itself independent, Japan would immediately recognize this independence. A treaty of mutual assistance would confront the colonial power with the prospect of war with Japan should it decide upon military action to reconquer its lost possession. Should, so ran the argument, Japan have real military strength, the colonial power would not dare to take that military action. Consequently, the aim of expelling the European powers would be achieved without war. The build-up of Japan's military strength was, in Hirota's policy thus not aimed at war. Consequently, he was prepared to conclude treaties of non-aggression with European states, as he did, for example, with Holland.

Hirota's policy failed because the military took over after it had been made really powerful. But as a policy it did not at all amount to preparation for an aggressive war. It did not constitute the crime against peace. Only a misunderstanding of its contents can explain the majority judgment of the IMTFE.[4]

56

It should be added here that the Hirota-policy was later to receive both recognition and a name. General Beaufre introduced in his writings the concept of the *stratégie totale* or *stratégie d'ensemble*. He, too, realized that military power could not be used as a means of achieving political ends. War, in the sense of Von Clausewitz, does not have a reasonable place in the atomic era. Political ends must be achieved, according to Beaufre, by a *stratégie indirecte;* that is by economic, ideological, and political means. But a strong military power is still needed to prevent an adversary from retaking by military means that which he has lost in indirect ways.[5]

The Hirota-policy has in our time practical significance. Franz Joseph Strauss, perhaps a future Bundeskanzler, has taken up Beaufre's strategy with the aim of applying it to the liberation of the 'satellite countries'. They should be liberated, according to Strauss, because they belong to the democratic West. But military action is precluded. It would lead to the destruction of Europe. These countries should be seduced to come over to the West on their own initiative, attracted by the wealth and freedom of Western Europe. The danger is that if they do come over to the West, the Russians will react as they did with respect to Czechoslovakia in 1968. To prevent this reaction, through deterrence, Europe needs a strong nuclear force. It must have established itself as a *Grossmacht* which commands the same respect as the United States of America.[6] Strauss aims at 'die Kraft eines integrierten Grossraumes' (p. 213), so powerful that the Soviet Union simply would not dare to take any military action. Strauss' policy is in essence nothing more than the policy of Hirota, applied in Asia a quarter of a century before it was endowed with a name in the writings of Beaufre, and an application in Europe by Strauss.

There is still one other relation between the policy of Hirota and our present world. Part of his policy was the struggle against colonization, the stirring up of liberation movements, the awakening of Asian nationalism. After the war the world recognized the universal validity of the concept of human rights. It meant the outlawing of colonialism. In the Decolonisation Declaration of December 4, 1960, the colonial relation was declared illegal. Later, the colonial relation was branded as criminal, a crime against humanity (Resolution of the General Assembly, December 20, 1965). The General Assembly recognized the right of a people to struggle for its independence, even 'with all necessary means' (G. A. Res. of December 4, 1970). In short: legal developments after the Second World War were such that the UN propagated – a quarter of a century after Hirota adopted the standpoint – that Asia should be for the Asians.[7]

Hirota was condemned to death and hanged. That sentence was wrong. It was based on ignorance and misunderstanding of the real contents of his policy. The judgment was correct in its analysis: 'This policy of far-reaching effect was eventually to lead to the war between Japan and the Western Powers in 1941' (*The Tokyo Judgment,* Vol. I, p. 447). But Hirota, apparently, did not foresee this inevitable consequence at the time. Ignorance about the effects of a policy played a role in shaping a policy that could only lead to disaster. As ignorance about the same policy led to the judgment of death by hanging.

After the Tokyo Trial the Netherlands' government invited me to become a member of the Dutch delegation to the General Assembly of the United Nations. The UN was going to implement the principles of international law recognized in the Charters and judgments of Nuremberg and Tokyo. Agenda items were the International Criminal Code, the International Criminal Court, and the definition of aggression. I participated in the work of the Sixth Committee and was a member of the Special Committee on defining aggression and on establishing an International Criminal Court. I saw the UN in action in its endeavour to contribute to the progressive development of international law.

Here again I realized that one should know a lot more about the forces at work in society before setting out to furnish it with a better legal order. Law results from conflicts of interest, from power-positions and value-judgments. The lawyer should have a clear picture of these different elements. Only then will he be able to determine what kind of progressive development has a chance of being realized.

The lawyer's task is easy if he concentrates his attention on existing positive law and restricts his activity to making the law more consistent, more systematic, more in accord with logic. Law does not develop in a logical way. It develops haphazardly, adopting in one area legal principles that play no role in other fields. The lawyer may try to instil some order into the prevailing legal system, staying within that system. His work is then restricted to an evaluation and adaptation of positive law according to its own intrinsic values.

But this method is demonstrably insufficient when factual circumstances fundamentally change, as was the case with the introduction of atomic weapons or with the political emancipation of colonial peoples. In such circumstances, the prevailing principles in existing positive law may no longer be adequate to cope with the new realities. The lawyer may then turn to 'natural law' for a yardstick, for rules which, according to reason, are needed to reach the goals of the legal community. He may, for instance, in this way formulate 'the natural law of the atomic era': the complex of rules which would guarantee the existence and well-being of mankind in a period in which atomic power has fallen into the hands of men. Eméric de Vattel, who wrote in the middle of the 18th century, called these kind of norms of natural law *jus necessarium:* the law needed for achieving community goals. But a society in most cases will not be prepared to adopt these rules. Vested interests and traditional values or opinions will oppose the norms. It is not reason which determines what shall be the contents of the law, it is the will and desire of the parties. De Vattel called the positive law established as a result of the *Kampf ums Recht, jus voluntarium.*

This distinction between *jus necessarium* and *jus voluntarium* still has significance in our world. William Fullbright has emphasized the difference between 'our needs' and 'our capacities'. Our needs respond to the concept of natural law, our capacities determine the contents of positive, valid law.

With the yardstick of natural law as his ultimate goal, the lawyer needs the social sciences – sociology, social psychology, political science, economics – to learn the 'capacities' of a legal society. He needs that knowledge because he needs to know the legal developments which a society is willing and able to accept. He needs, next to his knowledge of the existing law, the other social sciences to grasp what is – at that moment and for that legal society – possible and feasible in the progressive development of the law.

The implementation of the principles of Nuremberg and Tokyo failed. The Cold War made it impossible to apply to the whole world the legal principles which in the judgments were applied to the vanquished. In later years at least the issue of aggression was again taken up, leading to a G. A. Resolution 3314 (XXIX) of December 14, 1974. This resolution purports to constitute a definition of aggression. Strictly speaking it is not a definition, although it remains important. It strengthens the prohibition of the use of force, as formulated in art. 4 sub 2 of the UN Charter.

It emphasizes that the state may never use military force except in case of an armed attack by another state (art. 51). And it explicitly states in the first paragraph of article 5: 'No consideration of whatever nature, whether political, economic, military or otherwise, may serve as a justification for aggression'. This consensus of the world community is important, especially at the present time, now that the United States is establishing 'rapid deployment forces' in connection with economic problems concerning oil.[8] Strong and unequivocal reaffirmation of the prohibition of force in international relations is urgently needed in view of this new trend, a trend that sees the need to guarantee 'economic security' as a military responsibility.

The lawyers' method differs from the method of other social sciences. This may be demonstrated with respect to the other factual change in the international community: decolonization, the political emancipation of the colonial peoples. It was the logical consequence of the universal recognition of human rights. It meant the democratization of international society. A European elite had ruled over the remainder of mankind. That elite at first consisted of the 'Christian Nations'. Later following the admittance of Turkey 'to participate in the public law and concert of Europe', it called itself 'Civilized Nations'. The third phase, beginning with the Charter of the United Nations, brought the process of democratization to a close. The nations participating in the world organization call themselves 'Peace-loving Nations' (art. 4 UN Charter). Every independent nation that is willing to accept the obligations imposed by the Charter has the right to become a member of the UN.

Decolonization meant an essential change in the composition of the world community. Previously, 'the world' had consisted of a small group of developed, rich, self-sufficient states. Decolonization meant that the majority was formed by poor, weak, vulnerable, destitute states. It was quite clear that this fundamental change would have far-reaching consequences for the contents of international law. In a little book, *International Law in an Expanded World* (Amsterdam 1960), I tried to outline the possible and probable consequences. For that purpose I compared the international situation in the twentieth century with the national situation in the Netherlands in the nineteenth. The national process of democratization ended in the recognition of universal suffrage (1919 for men, 1922 for women). But here it was possible to analyze the desires of the newcomers, their opinions and value-judgments, their power, position, and the means at their disposal for ameliorating that position.

Traditional Dutch domestic law, made by the elite in the interest of the elite, had been a law of freedom. The man of property, the *homo economicus,* forming the governing elite, could take care of his own interests. He demanded freedom to pursue his interests. In his view the principal task of the law must be to square the freedom of the one with the liberty of the other. What we call 'liberal law' – that is liberal law for the happy few – was the result. The have-nots, who gradually developed a voice in the law-making process, demanded several changes. First of all, they demanded the abolition of all discriminating provisions, and thus the right to vote and the right to form coalitions (trade unions). They wanted equality. Next to that, they claimed the right to make use of the means of power they had at their disposal, such as the right to strike. But apart from liberty and equality, they demanded protection against the might of the economically powerful; labour law provided that protection, regulating labour-conditions, working hours, wages. They also needed protection and assistance with respect to adverse circumstances: illness, invalidity, unemployment, old age. The laws concerning social security answered this demand.

60

The emergence of the labour-class as fully fledged citizens also brought about a change in the tasks of the State. The elite had preferred a state in which the principal task was internal and external security, the *Nachtwachtstaat*. The new majority demanded from the state that it play an active role in promoting the well-being of all its subjects. They required an active 'welfare state', one which accepted a certain responsibility for the well-being of the individual citizen: state policy in favour of full employment, but also special measures in the field of education, housing, medical care, and aimed at raising the status of the poor and destitute. In short, they demanded action for development in addition to a new legal order in which the principles of liberty and equality were supplemented by the principles of protection, assistance (by provisions of positive discrimination), correction of the market-mechanisms, when too favourable to the powerful, and general arrangements for the common good.

The same principles would be applicable – *mutatis mutandis* – in the world. Liberty, universally applied, equality, protection of the vulnerable and weak against the powerful, assistance to the indigent and destitute, the correction of the liberal order founded on the market-mechanism in favour of the have-nots and powerless (positive discrimination); changes in the structure for the sake of the advancement of the poor. In short: change in the legal structure and legal rules guaranteeing factual assistance.

The needs and desires of peoples and states in a process of democratization are more or less the same as the needs and desires of individuals in a comparable social situation. They, too, have identical means of building-up the power-position needed in the *Kampf ums Recht:* just as the labourers found positions of strength in their trade-unions, so the developing countries have sought to enhance their power position through 'the group of 77', and through 'producers-associations'.

There is still another connection between domestic and global development. In domestic law the concept of the welfare state can be considered as a general principle of law recognized in the community of nations. As such the legal principles deriving from that concept have a claim to be applied in world relations. Moreover, art. 28 of the Universal Declaration maintains that everyone has the right to a social and international order in which his human rights can be realized.

As in the domestic field, a *Kampf ums Recht* is foreseeable. We are witnessing it already in the conferences on the Law of the Sea, and in the struggle for a New International Economic Order. The lawyer has a specific function in this struggle. He has the task of elucidating the factual and legal situation, of indicating the road of gradual change. He should also indicate the possible consequences of a refusal by the rich world, sticking to its vested interests, to cooperate in elaborating the new legal order. Resistance to peaceful change in this field might have disastrous consequences. As a matter of fact, the lawyer-peace researcher could contribute to the debate by focusing attention on the conflicts that will inevitably result if the pattern of North-South relations is not fundamentally altered.

In this connection attention should be drawn to the concept of 'structural violence', to which Johan Galtung has given such a prominent place in peace research. It indicates the restrictions placed by laws and customs and social structures on the possibilities of individual or group development. Structural violence may have the same or an even more devastating effect than personal, physical violence in war. The old question of Mark Twain 'What is the horror of swift death by the axe compared with lifelong death from hunger, cold, insult, cruelty and heart break?' is still valid. Naming these situations 'violent' is a kind of metaphor, suggesting that structural violence and the violence of war should be put on one and the same footing and, consequently, should both be the object of peace research.

The concept of structural violence is more or less identical to what jurists are used to call 'social injustice'. The name is new, and with the name, the focus on its evils. One is left wondering, however, whether peace research should focus on both forms of 'violence', aiming thereby not only at the maintenance of peace in its negative meaning (no war or threat of war), but also at the establishment of a global situation of justice, of 'positive peace' (a generally acceptable social and legal order based on human dignity). Kenneth Boulding protested against this extension of the concept of peace research and proposed a separate area of investigation, which he called 'justice research'. I am inclined to agree with him. Peace research, as a problem-oriented branch of scholarly endeavour, should have the evil of war as its main focus, and aim at contributing to the maintenance of 'negative peace'. That does not mean that structural violence would be excluded from the field of peace research. Social injustice, especially in our time, is the cause of social unrest and conflicts, leading to internal civil strife with clear external implications. Structural violence may be at the root of civil and international war. As such, it is of very great importance to the peace researcher.

There is another link between 'structural violence' and the physical violence of war. It is the old link between the value of justice and the value of peace. Neither of the values are absolutes. Justice may be preferable to peace, as the UN expressed in its recognition of the legitimacy of the struggle 'with all necessary means' against 'apartheid'. Peace may be preferable to justice in cases where the violence needed to restore justice might destroy all participants. That was the situation with respect to Czechoslovakia in 1968. Justice and peace are relative values. Both deserve research. But Boulding's proposal disregards the fact that research on justice has long been the traditional field of the lawyer. 'Justice research' has been done as long as jurists have existed.

Peace researchers and lawyers may help each other in their respective tasks of contributing to the realization of the maintenance of peace and of justice. In his struggle for a better legal situation – I may mention as an example the struggle of the lawyer for a New International Economic Order – the lawyer may profit from the peace researcher's arguments concerning why the maintenance of the old order will inevitably lead to conflict and violence. The peace researcher may profit from the lawyer's contribution in cases where legal arguments, based on the human sense of justice, can be added to polemological argumentation. Legal arguments have a power of their own. Though that power is not always very strong, it plays its own role in promoting or preventing specific policies.

At the end of the fifties preparations begun for the establishment of a peace research institute at the University of Groningen. It took some years to convince the authorities that the problem of war and peace deserved to be studied in an interdisciplinary way. As a professor of international law (I had exchanged my chair of criminal law and criminology for one of international law), I convinced the faculty of law that fundamental changes were required in international law as a consequence of the introduction of nuclear energy (and in view of other technological developments) and the emancipation of the colonial peoples. I argued that more insight into world affairs, greater awareness of existing interests, opinions and power relations, was needed if the lawyer was to contribute to the progressive development of international law. Hence the Polemological Institute (P. O. Box 121, Haren, Groningen), established at the beginning of the sixties, in which scholars from several relevant disciplines could collaborate in research on conflict and violence.

We did not call the new brand of scholarship 'peace research': in those days the Cold War dominated much thinking and the peace propaganda of the Soviets had made the concept of peace suspect in the West. Hence another name, an imitation of Gaston Bouthoul's 'Institut de polémologie', Polemology. This name (from the Greek word *Polemos,* conflict) does not imply a choice with respect to the different schools of peace research. It indicates the same branch of scholarship as 'peace research', *Friedenswissenschaft.* The aim of the researcher in this field is to contribute to the maintenance of peace by clarifying relations, by showing how specific events will probably carry specific consequences. The peace researcher is quite aware of the fact that greater insights do not in themselves result in a change of policy. But action groups can use them to spread knowledge, to awaken the public conscience. Not only the military establishment but also politicians are supposed to make use of the results of peace research. Contacts with political and military decision-makers are established in the Netherlands through state advisory committees, in which peace researchers are represented. Links with action groups are more informal, but Dutch peace action relies heavily upon the data and insights derived from peace research.

The polemological institute, with a permanent staff of about 12 people and some 10 part-time collaborators, has to restrict its work to specific topics. They range from empirical research on peace education to the inner dynamics of armament processes. This is not the place to elaborate on this. Rather, I should like to indicate the field in which I was most engaged, as a lawyer and a peace researcher (from 1972 I occupied the chair of international law and polemology).

As an overall generalization one could contend that the lawyer deals with the question of how far international law can play a role in the maintenance of peace. That is, its role in preventing conflicts, in solving conflicts, in preventing the violent solution of conflicts, in mitigating violence in cases where a violent solution cannot be prevented. An outline of these different fields I gave in *International Law and the Maintenance of Peace*.[9]

The progressive development of international law is obviously a very wide field and the individual lawyer has to make choices. My participation in the Tokyo trial led to a profound interest in the prohibition of war and the individual responsibility for violation of this prohibition. One wonders whether such a prohibition still makes sense now that a war in the sense of von Clausewitz, between the nuclear weapon states, has become absurd. Another type of war has assumed a far more threatening significance: the accidental war, resulting from a misperception or miscalculation, or due to the fact that a crisis could not be kept under control.[10]

The contents of the prohibition of war are again under discussion. Is self-defence only permissible against an armed attack? Or is humanitarian intervention legitimate?[11] Here the conflict between the maintenance of justice and the maintenance of peace is very clear. But the main clash between these principal values is related to the universal applicability of human rights: the most important legal event after World War II. It is self-evident that the recognition of human rights, including the right to a decent economic existence, contributes to civil unrest. The former 'static poverty' is replaced by a 'dynamic poverty' which leads to protests against situations seen not only as hard to endure but as an unbearable injustice. Conflict-opinion and conflict-attitude are awakened by the conviction that the situation can be altered and should be altered, as a right of the group and the individual. The same applies to other violations of human rights.[12] The conclusion is that the realization of human rights is more or less a condition of peace. It is thus entirely understandable that the Security Council should consider the continuation of 'apartheid' in Southern Rhodesia a 'threat to the peace'.

But here we touch upon another aspect. Realization of human rights demands the social and economic development of the Third World. Economic development for more than two-thirds of the world population, however, means more consumption and thus more demands for scarce raw materials. According to Gunnar Myrdal, 20 to 30 per cent of the world's population, the rich part, at present consumes 80 per cent of scarce raw materials. If development in the Third World really takes place, a serious clash about raw materials, for instance oil, might ensue.[13] How intense will be this clash? Will the rich world adapt itself to the new circumstances, or will it react with military measures to assure adequate supplies of needed goods? Schlezinger told military officers that it was 'a military responsibility' to assure regular inflows of oil, and Carter's 'rapid deployment forces' enable such a 'responsibility' to become a reality.

At Groningen University interdisciplinary research is under way to tackle this problem. The first part of this research effort consists of research around the concept of 'security' (military security, economic security, etc.) and its impact on the military function. The second part consists of extensive economic research on the consequences of rising living standards and levels of economic activity, both here and in the Third World, on the claim on scarce goods, and the clashes of interests ensuing therefrom. The last part of this research will be devoted to research on the impact of scarcity-problems on wealthy societies. Lowering of the economic standard of living, and even 'limits to growth', needs adaptation. The question is what form of democratic government would best be suited to cope with a long list of very unwelcome government decisions. Here the research will focus on the capital problem of governance.

There is one other field of law that is emerging and which demands the full attention of international lawyers: the law of arms control and disarmament. At present this law is developing only at the periphery: restrictions on nations with respect to specific weapons (such as biological weapons or anti-ballistic missiles), restrictions of quantities of certain weapons (SALT I), restrictions on the liberty to place weapons at specific places (space, antarctic, seabed). The question is

5 – Social Science

whether the problem should not be approached from the centre of the issue: the weapon function.

With the emergence of weapons of mass-destruction, the function of weapons, reasonably speaking, should be restricted to 'military security'. Defence in the case of nuclear missile powers has become impossible if one party wants to destroy the other. The risks for society, and for humanity in general, have become so high that, reasonably, weapons should be considered unusable. Their only function would be to keep the weapons of the other party similarly unusable. That can be done by deterrence. Deterrence, however, knows of all kinds of variations, ranging from maximum to minimum deterrence. A specific variant of the latter is interesting: the concept of defensive deterrence, in which the military posture deters by the prospect of unacceptable resistance, but where the composition and choice of arms render it impossible to use the arms for purposes of attack and external domination. In short: research is done on the function of weapons, based on the presupposition that the progressive development of international law may lead to a denial of the legitimacy of possessing military capabilities which go beyond the recognized legitimate function of national military power. The General Assembly of the UN should start by elaborating principles and norms restricting the national freedom in that respect.[14]

The law of arms control and disarmament is a new chapter of international law. It should be supported by the progressive development of the humanitarian law of warfare. Technology introduces every year more diverse and more horrible weapons. There exists a long-standing (1868) obligation to evaluate the military usefulness and the humanitarian aspects 'to conciliate the necessities of war with the laws of humanity'. With respect to specific new weapons, this was done at the diplomatic Red Cross Conferences.[15] The laws of war are not only important because they may diminish the suffering caused by war. Prohibition of the use of weapons may further the prohibition of the possession of these weapons. Moreover, they may provide, in the long-term, strong arguments for the general prohibition of the use of atomic weapons.[16]

As noted earlier, there are many fields of international law which are directly related to questions of peace and war. The impact of technology is not only felt with respect to arms.[17] The emancipation of the colonial peoples should not only lead to fundamental change in the law of nations, but may also have a considerable impact on the structure of international society. The organization of world society which started in 1945 as a peace-organization is bound to develop into a welfare organization; that development will have a considerable impact on the function and structure of the United Nations.[18]

Peace, in the sense of the absence of war and of the threat of war, will be impossible to maintain without establishing in the world a minimum order of justice. International lawyers from all parts of the world should cooperate in research to elaborate feasible developments. They should form a group which considers international law an instrument of world order, rather than a means of protecting national interests. Such a group might work more effectively when it establishes strong links with peace researchers from other disciplines. To their combined constructive, imaginative research – a type of research that Johan Galtung so successfully stimulated – the lawyer will contribute the image of rational justice with which he is thoroughly familiar.

NOTES

1. The judgment and the dissenting opinions have been published in BVA Röling and F. C. Rüter, *The Tokyo Judgment*, 3 volumes, Amsterdam University Press, 1978. About the trial see Richard H. Mincar, *Visitors' Justice. The Tokyo War Crimes Trial*, Princeton, 1971.

2 For a more detailed elaboration of the three phases of international relations and international law, of the 'Christian Nations', the 'Civilized Nations' and, since 1945, the 'Peace-loving Nations', see my *International Law in an Expanded World*, Amsterdam, 1960. An intelligent Japanese diplomat stated at the time: 'As soon as we showed ourselves your equals in scientific butchery, at once we were admitted to your council tables as civilized men'.

3 I refer here to his very interesting abstract chapters in *War and Peace*, the classic novel about Napoleon's war in Russia.

4 In my 'dissenting opinion' *(The Tokyo Judgment*, Vol. II, pp. 1041–1148) I gave the arguments for my conclusion that Hirota should be acquitted of all the charges brought against him (pp. 1121–1127). The relevant documents in which the Konoye-Hirota policy was outlined are given in full (pp. 1092–1102).

5 See André Beaufre, *Introduction à la Stratégie*, Paris, 1963; *Dissuasion et Stratégie*, Paris, 1964; *Stratégie de l'Action*, Paris, 1966; with the final conclusion: 'La stratégie totale sur le mode indirect est vraisemblablement la stratégie de l'avenir' *(Stratégie de l'Action*, p. 128).

6 F. J. Strauss, *Herausforderung und Antwort*, Stuttgart, 1968, p. 125. This book deserves more attention. The theories developed therein are as dangerous as the theories developed in *Mein Kampf*.

7 For a further elaboration of this development see my *Some Aspects of the Trials of Nuremberg and Tokyo*, Haarlem, 1978 (in Dutch).

8 Further about the definition see my 'Die Definition der Aggression', in *Recht im Dienst des Friedens*, Festschrift für Eberhard Menzel, Berlin, 1975, pp. 387–403.

9 *Netherlands Yearbook of International Law*, 1973, pp. 1–102. See also my 'Völkerrecht und Friedenswissenschaft', *DGKF Hefte*, No. 4, Bonn, June 1974; 'Friedenssicherung durch Völkerrecht – Möglichkeiten und Grenzen', in W. Schaumann (ed.), *Völkerrechtliches Gewaltverbot und Friedenssicherung*, Baden-Baden, 1972, pp. 89–118; 'The Function of Law in Conflict Resolution', in De Reuck and Knight (eds.), *Conflict in Society*, London, 1966, pp. 328–350.

10 Further elaboration of this aspect in my 'The Limited Significance of the Prohibition of War', in Lepawsky, Buehrig and Lasswell, *The Search for World Order, Studies by Students and Colleagues of Quincy Wright*, New York, 1971, pp. 228–237.

11 On these problems, see my contribution: 'Aspects of the Ban on Force', in *Essays on International Law and Relations in Honour of A. J. P. Tammes*, Special Issue of the Netherlands International Law Review, 1977, pp. 242–259.

12 Further elaboration in my 'Human Rights and War', *Netherlands International Law Review*, 1968, pp. 346–361.

13 Further elaboration of this theme in my 'Disarmament and Development: the Perspective of Security', in Dick A. Leurdijk and Elisabeth Mann Borgese, *Disarmament and Development*, Foundation Reshaping the International Order, Rotterdam, 1979, pp. 65–101.

14 Further elaboration in my 'The Function of Military Power', in Carlton and Schaerf, *Arms Control and Technological Innovation*, London, 1977, pp. 288–302; and 'Feasibility of Inoffensive Deterrence', *Bulletin of Peace Proposals*, 1978, pp. 339–347.

15 See for a further elaboration of the principles of the law of warfare the SIPRI publication *The Law of War and Dubious Weapons* (Stockholm 1976), which I wrote in collaboration with Olga Suković.

16 See further my 'The Significance of the Laws of War', in A. Cassese (ed.), *Current Problems of International Law*, Milano, 1975, pp. 133–155; and my 'Aspects of the Criminal Responsibility for Violation of the Laws of War', in A. Cassese (ed.), *The New Humanitarian Law of Armed Conflict*, Naples, 1979, pp. 199–231.

17 Further elaboration in my 'International Responses to Technological Innovations', in Christopher Freeman, Bert V.A. Röling, Alvin M. Weinberg and Herbert York, *Technological Innovation: A Socio-Political Problem*, Boerderijcahier 7710, Enschedé, 1977, pp. 83–122.

18 For further elaboration see my 'The United Nations – a General Evaluation', in A. Cassese (ed.), *UN Fundamental Rights*, Alphen aan den Rijn, 1979, pp. 23–38; and 'Peace Research and Peace-Keeping', in A. Cassese (ed.), *United Nations Peace-Keeping. Legal Essays*, Alphen aan den Rijn, 1978, pp. 245–255.

Parabole du dragon sec et de la grande pyramide et biographie politique d'enfance

ALAIN JOXE

J'ai voulu être historien du Bas-Empire Romain et ce fut ma première orientation sous la direction du Professeur MARROU, avec qui j'étudiai la relation – inexistante – entre le christianisme et les révoltes paysannes en Gaule entre le III° et le V° siècle après J.-C. Ceci me préparait sans doute à devenir historien du Bas Empire Américain, lorsque, après deux années de service militaire à la mauvaise époque de la guerre d'Algérie, je me lançai dans les études stratégiques qu'animait le Général Beaufre à l'Institut Français des Etudes Stratégiques et Jacques Vernant au Centre d'Etudes de Politique Etrangère. Mais si j'ai constamment préféré la Paix à la Guerre, et qu'il me parait toujours nécessaire de spécifier que je suis plutot 'Peace Researcher' que 'Strategy Student', même si la matière est la même, c'est pour des raisons qui remontent à l'enfance, et probablement à l'enfance du monde.

Les sciences sociales n'ont pas d'autre but propre que de satisfaire les curiosités de l'enfance. Cependant elles peuvent être utilisées soit pour lutter contre l'oppression soit pour perfectionner l'oppression. Plutot qu'un papier savant, je veux dédier à Johan Galtung 1°) Une parabole sur le commencement des temps de guerre 2°) Une biographie d'enfance politique devant éclairer les motivations d'un chercheur français, espèce connue pour son rationnalisme apparent.

1° Parabole du dragon sec et de la grande pyramide

a) Le dragon curieux

Le dragon qui sort du fleuve, souvenir de notre ancêtre batracien, cesse de jouer pour vivre et rencontre le feu du ciel pour la première fois et meurt. Cesse de jouer pour vivre, cesse de vivre pour jouer s'il rentre dans l'eau ce retour qui n'est pas la mort, dans l'univers liquide des $n+1$ dimensions du noeud, menace la vie et la recrée. Après 10.000 dragons morts de curiosité quelques uns sont restés serrés les uns contre les autres dans une grande promiscuité. Passons sur les reptiles, les oiseaux et le mammifères. Nous sommes pleins de mélancolie et de jeux oubliés. Le feu du ciel nous tue encore, la piscine, la mer, les caves où l'on danse pour y échapper c'est peu. Pour échapper au feu du ciel il a fallu se serrer. L''amour' est né de la malédiction céleste. Dans le paradis des jeux aquatiques, il n'est nul besoin de se toucher pour être avec, mais bien plus plaisant d'entrelacer des itinéraires frolants. La plus grande Hérésie fut de nommer amour la malédiction qui obligeait les êtres à se serrer et à se pénétrer pour se féconder, à coquiller les oeufs et même à les couver finalement à l'intérieur de soi dans une réserve d'eau autonome jusqu'à l'éclosion, bref à nommer amour ce qui dérivait simplement du manque d'eau, du manque de milieu universel non hiérarchique, au lieu de nommer amour honnêtement comme les poissons ou même bien des animaux retournés depuis dans l'eau ou certainement les oiseaux qui tentent de nager dans l'air, le jeu infini des approches. Cette grande malédiction comporte cependant de nouveaux plaisirs, pour la première fois *aliénables*. Le culte du soleil et du ciel, feu et air déssèchant, compensé par celui de la lune, eau et air humide, commence certainement avec l'un de ces dragons curieux qui choisit d'être sec. Le soleil devient alors pour ceux qui rampent au ras du sol le symbole de l'amour égal entre tous parcequ'il touche tous les individus à la fois, ce qu'aucun homme ou bête ne peut faire avec toute l'espèce, sauf en rêve. En somme parceque seul le feu du ciel avec ses rayons fait ce que faisait autrefois la Grande Mer avec tout son corps unifiant. Et du soleil, *sommet unique,* reliant tous les pauvres dragons déssèchés qui ont oubliés les jeux latéraux nait la grande pyramide qui se prétend l'image de l'amour alors qu'elle n'est qu'arbre de viol et menace de mort.

b) *La Grande Pyramide*

L'empilement des grades repose sur *rien*. Plus personne au dessous du simple soldat, sauf quelques femmes, chevaux de parade, dauphins à l'étude pour détections de sous-marins, et virus pour la guerre bactériologique. Puis des machines qui sont plutot, face aux structures majestueuses et complexes de la Grande Pyramide, à refouler au rang d'outile. La vraie Machine, c'est la pyramide des grades et dignités. La Hiér-archie, commandement sacré, posé sur ce désert comme celle de Guizeh, symbole de mort parceque forme de l'inerte, du tas de sable, de la fin de toute possible cata-strophe (en grec: passage cul par dessus tête) ou éboulement faille mutation soudaine du tout sous l'effet d'un petit incident local. Un tas de sable cuirassé contre les vents. Du haut en bas de la pyramide dégouline du carburant pour hommes: intendance, cantine, du lubrifiant: permissions; le système de refroidissement: punitions; s'emboîtent les carosseries, les carters, casernes, guérites, uniformes, godillots. Dégoulinent aussi des vibrations, secousses et explosions ordres, contre-ordres, manoeuvres guerres, parfois aboiements. La pyramide *remue,* mais ne bouge pas. Du bas en haut, ça recrute et ça dégage des cadres. La pyramide mange de l'homme et en excrète. C'est aussi une pyramide des âges, un peu déhanchée pour plaire: il y a de vieux capitaines et de jeunes lieutenants, mais aussi de jeunes colonels et de vieux commandants. Mais *en soi* la pyramide n'a pas d'âge, elle n'a que de l'ancienneté, comme les momies, et le déhanchement des âges et des grades n'est qu'une vue des vivants. La pyramide ne peut pas vraiment vivre le temps des vivants car elle doit visiblement être leur mort. Quand la pyramide bouge, elle tue mettant en oeuvre ses outils, mais c'est devenu accessoire. Il y a la concurrence des accidents de voiture et des désespoirs passionnels, des famines et des épidémies, de la sous-alimentation et statistiquement sont travail *outillé* est seulement honorable. Son oeuvre de mort la plus grave est l'étalement. La Grande Pyramide en effet s'étale lentement, elle grandit.

2°. Biographie politique d'enfance

Né en 1931, j'ai le souvenir des slogans et des foules du Front Populaire, des photos de la guerre d'Espagne, des discours hystériques de Hitler à la radio, d'un sentiment de soulagement intense lors de la déclaration de guerre en 1939: depuis le temps qu'on l'attendait.

a) De la Guerre

J'ai fait l'exode dans une voiture d'occasion conduite par ma mère, enceinte, et qui n'est tombée qu'en panne d'essence. J'ai vu déferler les troupes hitlériennes sur la France et je peux même préciser que les fameuses colonnes de tanks de Guderian étaient doublées en parallèle, sur les routes secondaires, par des partis de cavaliers qui passaient au galop dans les villages et s'arrêtaient seulement pour se jeter nus dans les fontaines en s'aspergeant et en riant avant de reprendre leur train d'enfer. Je les ai vu passer dans un bourg de Vendée. Peu après chevrotait le discours du traître Pétain, au grand enthousiasme d'un sénateur royaliste qui tenait table ouverte aux réfugiés. Ma famille est bretonne républicaine. Mon père, enfant, chantait le chant du départ le jour de la mort de Louis XVI pour agacer une tante royaliste qui voulait faire manger un gâteau fleurdelisé, appelé chez les Chouans 'le non-autorisé'. Le Maréchal était-il un roi? Tout cela ne présageait rien de bon. Quand nos alliés héréditaires, les Anglais, nation de mon arrière grand mère maternelle, peuple aimé de mon oncle l'historien socialiste Elie Halévy, eurent coulé la flotte française à Mers El Kebir, je l'appris en lisant un journal qui trainait dans une escalier d'une maison sordide à Clermont-Férrand, où l'exode nous avait fait échouer. Je fus désespéré par la trahison de nos alliés, si bien décrite dans le journal. Assis sur une marche, je pensais que, avec les Allemands sur le dos et les Anglais qui nous tombaient dessus, la France était vraiment foutue. Je pris à témoins une voisine qui passait, des extrêmités desastreuses où paraissaient réduites les affaires de la Patrie Républicaine. Nous n'avions connaissance, ni l'un ni l'autre, de l'appel du 18 juin lancé par de Gaulle. Mais elle me rassura en me disant textuellement: 'ne t'en fais pas, petit, avant deux ans, les Russes feront la guerre aux Allemands et finalement ils les battront. Elle en était sûre parcequ'elle était communiste et que, 'entre les communistes et les nazis il ne pouvait pas y avoir d'entente durable'. Cette brève prophétie en 1940 m'a toujours laissé un certain respect pour les militants du PC, quels qu'aient été par ailleurs les insuffisances et les vices qu'ils ont hérité du stalinisme. Plus tard, réfugié en Afrique du Nord, j'ai suivi la campagne de Russie sur la carte en attendant l'ouverture du 'second front' et en appréciant en historien le concept de 'défense élastique'.

b) Des alliés et des amis

Après le débarquement des Anglais et des Américains à Alger, évènement à la préparation duquel mon père joué un role important aux cotés de René Capitant, dans le réseau Combat, j'ai assisté à la succession de Darlan, Giraud, puis à l'arrivée de de Gaulle, en connaissance des jeux 'florentins' et des enjeux mondiaux. Lorsque Giraud ent pris le pouvoir et ouvert la chasse aux gaullistes, je me souviens d'avoir vu arriver un soir Capitant chez nous, entre chien et loup, accompagné d'un immense officier britannique portant un immense pistolet d'ordonnance et ces shorts ridiculement longs imaginés par les services d'habillement de sa Majesté Britannique. Capitant, poursuivi par Giraud (protégé des Américains), etait sous la protection de l'armée Anglaise. C'était transparent. La France avait donc retrouvé des alliés. Mers el Kebir était effacé. La personnalité pragmatique, désagréable et incompréhensible de nos alliés anglais prenait peu à peu consistance. Il était clair qu'avec les Anglais, on ne s'entendait pas mais on pouvait quelquefois se mettre d'accord, c'était des alliés. Aves les américains, au contraire, on s'entendait parfaitement mais on ne se mettait absolument pas d'accord. C'était seulement des amis.

c) De la décolonisation

Et puis la France était assez compliquée aussi. A l'école primaire, où l'on devait chanter 'Maréchal! nous voila!. . .' de 1940 à 1942, tous les lundis, devant le drapeau, nous étions deux à garder la bouche fermée sur une classe de trente. Moi, et le fils d'un premier maître breton de la marine nationale. Nous nous étions vite repérés: 'tu ne connais pas les paroles?' – 'non, pas bien'. Et puis, rapidement: 'moi, je suis *pour les Anglais,* et toi, tu es *pour les Anglais* ou *pour les Allemands?'* – 'pour les Anglais aussi!' On disait en effet 'pour les Anglais' ou 'pour les Allemands', chez les enfants. Nous étions donc deux bretons républicains pour les Anglais. Les petits pieds noirs, il faut bien le dire étaient en général 'pour les Allemands'. Il y avait aussi trois camarades algériens musulmans qui ne se prononçaient pas, travaillaient comme des brutes avec des sourires exquis et prétendaient que ce débat ne les concernaient pas, ce qui nous laissaient perplexes. Le vichysme des pieds-noirs fit que je ne me fis guère d'amis pieds-noirs et que j'entrepris seul d'apprendre l'arabe maghrébin. Les enfants sont très sectaires. Mais quand, de retour en France en 1944, je connus de nouveau les rentrées d'octobre pluvieuses et glacées, je sentis que j'avais perdu une sorte de patrie, la patrie de mes années entre 9 et 13 ans, l'âge le plus adulte de la vie. J'ai donc perdu l'Algérie à la Libération. Faire une guerre pour la garder, garder l'odeur des mandarines et du jasmin, le bruit des cigales, le ciel d'or des aubes printanières, la mer bleue, le souffle brûlant du sirocco, cela m'apparut toujours comme une entreprise criminelle et sans issue.

d) *De la guerre froide*

Quand la bombe atomique larguée sur la Japon mit fin à la guerre dans un frisson d'horreur en été 45, je fus immédiatement contre cet engin. Je n'avais certes aucune sympathie pour les Japonais, qu'on imaginait comme un mélange de samouraîs fanatiques et de jolies verseuses de thé, difficile à apprécier, mais il me sembla – et je n'étais pas le seul – que ce dénouement bizarre, voulu par Truman, otait à la victoire son caractère de triomphe sur les forces du mal, pour lequel tant de gens avaient donné leur vie. Il n'y eut pas de *fête.* Je comparais avec les souvenirs de la génération antérieure. La victoire de 1918, ce fut autre chose. Quel délire! quelle joie! du moins dans les récits. Cette capitulation en queue de poisson n'était gu'une violation de la règle du jeu. Evidemment, si on pouvait détruire une ville entière avec un avion et une bombe, ce n'était 'plus de jeu'. L'Empereur avait dit 'pouce !' Mais ce n'était pas la fin de la guerre. Etait-ce la fin des guerres? On n'y croyait pas, alors. La bombe, c'était la guerre. Mon premier engagement politique fut d'entrer, à 16 ans, dans un groupuscule qui s'était pompeusement intitulé 'Internationale des jeunes contre la guerre' et avait pour insigne une bombe en aluminium estampé barré d'une croix rouge émaillée vengeresse. Ce groupe s'aliéna le PC dans ses premières

Assemblées Générales, car son leader charismatique, certainement trotskyste, fit adopter une plateforme qui dénonçait à la fois 'le gangstérisme du capital américain et le messianisme sanglant de la Russie des camps'. A cette époque, l'existence du Goulag qui était évidemment connue, n'était pas considérée comme un argument direct concernant les fondements de l'épistémologie marxiste.

La lutte contre la militarisation nucléaire du monde fut lancée sous Staline avec 'l'appel de Stockholm', évidemment pour protéger l'URSS par des mouvements idéologiques pendant la période assez brève de rattrapage du monopole américain. Ce n'est pas l'appel de Stockholm qu'il faut mettre au nombre des crimes de Staline. Il n'a rien empêché sans doute, mais pour autant, on ne peut pas dire que la bombe atomique à des centaines, puis des milliers puis aujourd'hui des dizaines de milliers d'exemplaires soit un bienfait pour l'humanité ni un monument de l'histoire de l'intelligence. Ce n'est pas non plus parceque les Américains ont contraint les Soviétiques à placer le meilleur de leurs ressources économiques et humaines dans cet effort militaire absurde que nous devons nous abstenir d'attaquer le Stalinisme même s'il est devenu un produit pervers de cette contrainte originelle.

e) Du neutralisme armé

Sur le désert de la guerre froide, l'affaire yougoslave joua un role fondamental pour conserver à l'idée socialiste révolutionnaire une certaine authenticité en Europe. Malgré les glissements inévitables auxquels la révolution yougoslave fut conduite, dans l'isolement où la réduisait la déclaration du Kominform de 1948, nous sommes tous redevable à son existence d'avoir incarné de façon concrète l'idée qu'un peuple, uni dans l'épreuve de la lutte armée contre le nazisme, pouvait faire, face aux pressions inoüies du système de Yalta. Les yougoslaves ont maintenu une légitimité populaire marxiste indépendante de Staline; ils ont inventé la théorie d'une transition particulière, autogestionnaire, au socialisme, ils ont défié le soi-disant sens de l'histoire dicté par les Superpuissances. J'ai fait partie en 1950 des brigades de travail qui ont construit la cité universitaire de Zaghreb et l'autoroute Zaghreb-Skoplje. On trouvait dans ces équipes, dont la préparation, en France, était animée par Claude BOURDET, des Trotskystes, des anarchistes, des socialistes et même des protomaoïstes. Un des personnages les plus populaires chez les jeunes communistes yougoslaves de base, à l'époque, qui venaient tous des maquis partisans, c'était Mao Tse Toung. Lui aussi avait fait sa révolution sans les Russes et par les armes. La plupart des responsables plus âgés étaient des anciens des Brigades internationales d'Espagne, et ces survivants, vieux militants exemplaires n'ont pas tous disparu ni sombré dans les honneurs bureaucratiques. Pendant cet été 50, les Américains furent presque rejetés à la mer en Corée. Entassés dans le réduit de Pusan, au sud-est de la péninsule, leur défaite paraissait une question de jours. Chaque victoire était affichée sur le journal mural de la brigade. En même temps, cet été là, Staline caressait sans que nous le sachions, l'idée d'envahir la Yougoslavie et de mettre fin, une bonne fois pour toutes, à ce vilain petit canard du camp socialiste. Des divisions blindées soviétiques faisaient pouvement et se déployaient, une par une, le long de la frontière. Tito vait décidé de passer ses vacances à l'île de Brioni, car l'été était très chaud et pendant tout le mois d'août, il fit des conférences de presse anodines, torse nu, dans lesquelles il annonçait son intention d'inaugurer en septembre la foire aux cochons de Zaghreb. Bebler, alors secrétaire général du ministère des Affaires Etrangères, raconte qu'il le suppliait tous les jours de rentrer à Belgrade, ce qu'il refusa. Quand la crise fut passée, il expliqua que si, par son attitude, il avait pu donner à Staline la moindre impression d'inquiétude, Staline en aurait déduit l'existence de déchirements internes et aurait donné l'ordre d'invasion. 'Il m'observait, je sais comment Il est, ne fallait pas que je cesse un instant d'avoir l'air insouciant'.

f) De la guerrilla et de la liberté

Ouvrier de choc en béton armé (je soupçonne que les normes étaient basses) je franchis la frontière barbelée et minée qui séparait la Yougoslavie de la Grèce Monarcho-fasciste. Il y avait encore, cette année là, quelques 'Andartès' isolés dans les montagnes, ou plutôt, le peuple le disait, selon la vieille tradition balkanique qui veut que certains pallikares ne peuvent pas réellement être battus. Le mythe de leur résistance et de leur survie était plus vrai que la réalité de leur écrasement. La Grèce était submergée par les dons incohérents du plan Marshall. Certains villages, où le labour par l'araire était seul adapté à la minceur de la couche arable et à le pente, transformaient philosophiquement des tracteurs lourds en petites centrales électriques. Partout la guerre civile et la répression policière posait sa marque. Cependant, lorsque j'arrivais à pied dans les villages, voyageur étrange (le concept de 'touriste' n'existait pas), la curiosité insatiable des Grecs transformait le devoir d'hospitalité en une sorte d'énorme Assemblée présidée par le Pope, l'instituteur ou l'ancien ouvrier émigré en Allemagne ou en Australie et le thème principal des questions était alors la Yougoslavie. 'Est-ce vrai qu'ils ont la bas un régime socialiste qui ne doit rien à personne?' 'peut-il y avoir à la fois communisme et démocratie?' 'combien gagne un ouvrier, combien vaut le pain, combien vaut l'huile?'

Le gendarme local essaya plusieurs fois, faiblement, de m'emprisonner, mais il en était empêché par le droit supérieur de l'hospitalité, ou par le pope qui voulait en savoir plus long sur le sort des orthodoxes serbes. Le camp de concentration de Makronissos où on déportait les 'communistes' et en fait les anciens résistants, ou l'équivalent de bons jeunes instituteurs radicaux socialistes pesait sur le peuple mais ne l'empêchait pas de parler. Il y avait comme un point d'honneur, dans cette population qui avait le plus souffert de l'occupation nazie puis de la répression britannique et fasciste, de comprendre à quelle sauce elle était mangée. 'La liberté chez les Grecs', m'a dit un vieux paysan, 'c'est de savoir toujours bien clairement comment ils sont esclaves. Ce droit nous le payons avec notre sang'.

g) *De l'Empire Universel*

En Crète, où des guerriers en turban noir racontaient volontiers les exploits récents contre les Allemands en buvant un vin épais, l'accord se faisait sur le fait que la deuxième guerre mondiale avait été gagnée par les Crétois et les Yougoslaves, que les Grecs appellent les 'Serbes'. Devant la carte du monde, toujours épinglée en bonne place au fond des cafés, on faisait le compte des divisions allemandes qui avaient été fixées par les Crétois et les Serbes réunis, et on les réinjectait, par hypothèse, sur le front russe ou en Libye, dans l'Afrika Korps. A tous les coups, la contre-offensive soviétique était stoppée, les troupes de Montgoméry refluaient en désordre sur le Caire, et Hitler prenait le canal de Suez, le Moyen-Orient, le Caucase et l'Inde, 'etcetera' concluait le Crétois avec un geste immense. J'avais connu dans un hotel de Skoplje une vieille femme de chambre, Russe blanche de Stamboul, qui m'avait donnée une lettre pour une cousine grecque originaire de Smyrne qui habitait Salonique et avec qui elle n'avait pu correspondre depuis 1939. Cette famille de Salonique m'avait donné des lettres pour des cousins crétois. Et dans cette communication fluide et solidaire, à travers le temps et l'espace des communautés dispersées, je découvrais les restes de l'Empire Ottoman mort. Sur le bateau qui me ramenait dans les Europes, comme on dit en grec, je conversai longuement avec un jeune étudiant Chypriote membre de l'AKEL (le PC Chypriote) qui m'expliqua pourquoi l'AKEL souhaitait, d'une part, la réunification avec la Grèce, parceque c'était la mère Patrie, mais la redoutait d'autre part, parceque le régime monarcho-fasciste allait immédiatement tous les pendre haut et court. 'C'est pourquoi nous aimons encore mieux les Anglais pour l'instant. Le jour où les Anglais partiront, nous serons pris entre les fascistes grecs et les Turcs, c'est à dire des deux côtés, les

Américains'. Et, penché sur le bord du vieux paquebot qui nous ramenait à Marseille, il désignait les vagues indigo et concluait: 'Si une Sirène sort de l'eau et te demande: «où donc est passé le Grand Alexandre?», si tu ne veux pas qu'elle t'entraine au fond, répond toujours: «Ζῆ καί βασιλεύει καί τόν Κόσμον γυρεύει».

('Il vit et il régne et dirige le Monde.')

Conclusion

Telle est la fin de mon apprentissage politique personell, celui qui se fait dans l'enfance et l'adolescence. La suite est de l'histoire générale collective. Par cette présentation, j'entends démystifier, à ma manière, la personnage du chercheur, en rappelant qu'il n'y a pas de pensée abstraite, désintéressée, qui ne s'accroche à quelque souvenir passionné et juvénile, et que je n'ai pas appris depuis beaucoup de choses fondamentales sur la Guerre et la Paix que je n'aie sues quelque part depuis longtemps, sauf la fraternité patiente des luttes militantes.

Les axiomes irréductibles que je tire de mon bagage enfantin et que j'appuie sur la parabole du dragon sec et de la grande pyramide, c'est que l'Antiquité n'est pas morte avec la chute de Constantinople, que le moyen-âge ne s'est pas terminé en 1789, que le fascisme n'a pas été écrasé en 1945, ni le Stalinisme en 1954. Que la guerre n'a jamais cessé d'être le meilleur moyens pour les Puissances, les Classes, les Empires de mater les peuples qu'elles exploitent, mais qu'elle ne peut les rendre idiots. J'ai vu fonctionner l'Antiquité, le Moyen-Age, le fascisme, le stalinisme et la guerre entre 1938 et 1950 sous des déguisements divers, et je les vois encore aujourd'hui rythmer les catastrophes, les génocides et les famines. Les nazis de 1980, les rois, les seigneurs les esclavagistes, massacrent ou laissent mourir de faim des millions de personnes. Le camps ne sont plus comme naguère seulement des lieux fermés. Il en reste sans doute, mais ils sont plus là pour la terreur que pour la production. Les camps de la mort de notre époque, ce sont les régions paysannes où les équilibres économiques ont été détruits et où, en une génération, on peut passer d'une civilisation traditionnelle agraire florissante à une communauté de famine. Ce sont aussi les quartiers immenses de misère qui entourent les grandes villes des pays sous-développés. Les camps de concentration *rentables,* ce sont enfin ces fameuses enclaves asiatiques où les gens travaillent dans des conditions d'exploitation dignes du XIX° siècle. Mais ce modèle tend à se répande ailleurs. Le nazisme moderne, c'est donc ce qui permet de dissocier les camps de la mort et les camps de super-exploitation, de rendre les camps de la mort 'libéraux' et même 'autogérés'. C'est ce qui permet de réintégrer dans le mode de production capitaliste tous les systèmes précédents d'extorsion, depuis l'esclavage et la galère jusqu'à la robotisation des travailleurs par l'électronique, en passant par des formes de servage, moderne ou pas du tout moderne. Aucune des formes de violence qu'ont pu engendrer les sociétés disparues n'ont étéréellement éliminées. Et au sommet de toute cette mosaïque trone et s'étale la Grande Pyramide militaire. La recherche sur la paix doit donc faire preuve d'imagination.

C'est pourquoi, nous qui, comme chercheurs, avons la privilège inouî d'être payés par la grande pyramide pour visiter sans cesse ses abords où règnent les souvenirs des jeux aquatiques et pour tourner insolemment autour en mimant le vol des oiseaux, à nos risques et périls, nous devons tant à Johan GALTUNG, même et surtout si nous sommes marxistes. Sans renoncer aux pompes du matérialisme historique et à ses oeuvres, la critique des jeux galtungiens obligera peut-être un jour les marxistes à devenir de nouveaux poètes.

Thirty Lessons from My Professional and Political Work in Iran

M. TAGHI FARVAR

Before getting into this subject, I must explain a bit about who I am. Not an easy question to answer. Even professionally, I guess I can claim to be a student of development alternatives – having come to this field from that of environmental sciences and engineering/mathematics.

Social or natural science – it is all a part of the rational methodology for systematically studying observable phenomena. So in this sense I am very much a social scientist, for I try to study systematically observable social phenomena, and to draw conclusions and lessons from all this, regarding how things might – or even ought to – look in the future.

So I will begin at the beginning! From the time I returned to Iran after having studied and researched the issue of development alternatives for some years in the US and in Latin America, I was hired by the Iranian Department of the Environment to help set up a division of human environment affairs, which I did. This enabled me to get a close look at how the public sector functioned in Iran, and the role of interest groups in running the country. In fact, the whole country was run by a number of high level foreign advisors, mostly Americans. They were everywhere: in the Planning and Budgeting Organization, in every ministry, contracting and consulting firms, and, of course the military. It was scary the way they literally ran the country. Native expert opinion did not count. If one had a valuable opinion or policy proposition to make, one usually had to find a prominent foreign spokesman to put it forward. It became a matter of standard strategy to keep on line a large number of international sources who were in favour of what we did.

In fact, our system before the revolution of 1979 could appropriately be called a *xenocracy*.

The whole show was a well-rehearsed play in which everyone knew his or her role and proceeded to act it. The Shah reigned supreme, in name only. He did run the show. But he himself rarely dared take any action without the approval of his own xenocrats – in this case the American Ambassador, who was the ex-chief of the American Central Intelligence Agency (and don't think they had sent Mr. Helms here for nothing!)

79

One Development and Resources Corporation (chaired by David Lilienthall), which had done the major water resources planning work for Iran in the 1950s and 1960s, was asked by none other than 'His Imperial Majesty' to come and redesign the entire public sector in the American image. So they did. Each sector report (education, agriculture, local government, etc.) that was confidentially completed, was immediately followed by major reshuffling in the public sector. Ministries came and ministries went, as DRC pleased.

I had a chance encounter with the supervisor of the DRC 'Iran Public Sector Project' in 1977 and 1978. When I asked him what was their top priority in the agricultural sector, he said unabashedly: 'to eliminate the small producers'. Wow! That is ambition, I thought, since it requires the elimination of some 60–70 percent of the population. They are a nuisance to the cancerous growth of agribusinesses and foreign capital that insist on their dominant development model: 'The growth of others in us'.

I soon realized the basic laws governing a xenocratic system:

1. The priorities are not set by the people directly affected; they come from Washington, London, Paris, Bonn, Brussels, Rome, Tokyo . . . ., in approximate descending order of significance!
2. The system of government is vertical and anti-participatory. There is an absolutely pyramidal structure, with a sharp clan structure (although no caste system).
3. New ideas and people are rapidly coopted into the system, integrated and neutralized. The mechanism used is temptation: offer of power and money. Those who refuse to be coopted are outcasts and discarded. If they insist, they are punished in varying degrees.

Fig.: 1. Royal family. 2. Military, aristocratic, financial, technocratic, bureaucratic top brass. 3. Middle technocrats & bureaucrats, military, capitalist strata. 4. Office workers, skilled labourers, rich peasants, shopkeepers. 5. Poor peasants, unskilled labourers, lowest echelon of public & private employees.

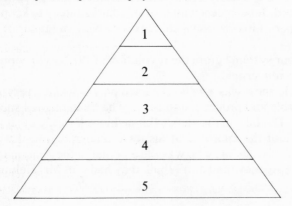

4. The whole system is made so that it internalizes foreign values. An elaborate legal and bureaucratic system is set up to do this directly, and a vast infrastructure of cultural penetration is established to accomplish the same tasks more indirectly.

5. The public sector is not taken seriously in this system. It serves two main funtions: a) to channel public funds as quickly as possible into private pockets, and b) to divide the spoils so that fewer people will complain.

6. There is corruption at every level of the system. Those who refuse to be corrupted are sifted out and punished.

7. Outside of the public sector with the characteristics just described, there is no room for anyone to operate, except in the private sector. There is, for all practical purposes, no such thing as a private non-profit enterprise.

8. There is no room for criticism. No opposition whatsoever is tolerated. The secret police controls everything. Fear and insecurity keeps everyone in line.

9. The system is not entirely monolithic. Within it there are interest spheres that are in competition with each other (always within tolerable limits). Each sphere is presided over by a member of the royal family (brothers, sisters, wives, mothers, children, and of course the monarch himself). Each of these demi-gods is in turn inspired by a respective foreign government or even 'wing' of a foreign intelligence agency.

10. Every public institution is ultimately under the umbrella of one of these demi-gods. Each institution or sector is thus relatively autonomous, as if they all had a mutual non-intervention treaty within proper limits.

The overall system was not therefore entirely watertight; there were minor cracks in the system.

As an example of the latter, we can take the case of the fate of the nomads. While the Shah himself and some of the other demi-gods believed in their total elimination and annihilation, his wife and twin sister considered them picturesque and attempted to preserve their culture and even to provide them with some needed mobile services (schools, health and veterinary workers), although their efforts never reached below the surface.

One corollary was that if one fell from grace within one institution through resistance or non-cooperation, there might still be some breathing room within a different institution which operated under the aegis of another demi-god – provided one's 'sins' were not cardinal (cardinal sins included armed opposition, organization of political nuclei, and sometimes possession or reading of anti-regime literature).

When I reached the end of the road in the Department of the Environment, I had accumulated a number of sins, which included non-cooperation and refusal to integrate myself into the system. One specific instance was helping to subvert the Department's plans for a huge game park, which would have denied some 80 000 nomads and villagers access to vital resources and routes and so spelt an end to their subsistence.

So I left the Department and went to work in a remote rural/tribal region to experiment with new patterns of development. Of course, this new venture operated ultimately under a different demi-god!

Here we were able to gather together a good group of people who were also searching for alternatives. We had access to people, and a budget to work with. So we began to put most of our emphasis on training local villagers. We found the experience quite stimulating. Although we could not solve the main problems of inequitable ownership and distribution of resources, yet we were able to help bring about a feeling of self-reliance, and critical consciousness of our and their predicament.

Here it only took about six months to reach the system's limits of tolerance. One by one we were threatened by the secret police. Some were called in for 'question and answer' sessions. Others, including myself, were threatened with 'trial for political crimes'! Soon after that, most of us (about 15 or 20 out of 25) were kicked out of the project. Only a few trusted souls were kept, of course, the foreign advisors! (Most of the foreign advisors, however, happened to be unofficial types who received equal pay with their Iranian collegues and were probably political misfits in their own country of origin.)

This experience taught us the following:

11. The cracks in the system can sometimes permit very worthwhile opportunities for social experimentation, research, and even action.
12. These opportunities, however, dry up as soon as one begins to kill sacred cows (such as the holy division of labour or the principle of private ownership of the means of production).
13. All these interesting experiments are ultimately tolerated only as showpieces and 'pet progressive minor projects'.
14. The more positively people respond to innovative programmes with a progressive social content, the more the whole project is in jeopardy.
15. If a project is people-oriented and not profit-motivated, especially if it succeeds in arousing popular consciousness, it will either be stopped or diverted.
16. The most one can expect from such projects within an anti-popular regime is: a) a bit more bread for the people (meeting some of the physical needs); b) raised consciousness – or at least the beginning of

such a process – and c) an intensive and worthwhile learning experience for all participants in the process.

17. It is not possible to undertake such projects without some official support in a totalitarian/authoritarian regime.

18. It is possible for both social and natural scientists to apply their science and technology in a socially liberating way. But they must be careful about the dangers of cooption, not only for themselves, but also for the dispossessed people whom they intend to serve.

19. The basic rule of the regime's game is to preach all the good things, but not to practise what they preach.

20. The most threatening situation for the regime happens when what they preach is taken seriously. In this rural project they were preaching that the 'pyramid of decision-making' should be inverted and people should manage their own affairs (the endogenous approach). But as soon as we began to implement these ideas, we were stopped.

The third experience involved another change of demi-gods. This time it was a new and innovative university, which claimed to be a 'university of development'. I was asked to become the Dean of its college of environmental sciences and natural resources – ie. to start it from scratch.

Right from the beginning we decided to reverse the normal academic process. Iranian universities are machines that recruit students on the basis of 'academic' criteria, put them through courses, and crown them with degrees before turning them loose on society. They may, if they are lucky, do a little research, usually of an irrelevant and isolated type. But they almost never touch social problems.

We would do things otherwise! We would begin with a rural development process: identify an appropriate region, learn about its needs, and then help the population solve their problems. Research and development (R & D) would come in immediately as we did technical and social research to find solutions for economic, managerial and technical problems. Only then would we begin to recruit students at various academic levels, and integrate them immediately into both the community work and the research process.

So we started. Initially we were able to recruit mostly young and enthusiastic people who accepted that their priorities would be the reverse of the usual academic ones. I shall not go into details here, for they are described elsewhere.

Eventually, it turned out that here, too, we rapidly reached the limits of the system. First, the financing promised by the government for the village work did not come through. Second, university high-ups began to oppose the project once it went beyond the usual 'show-case' status. Third, the rural police began to harass project-workers in the area.

83

Fourth, the government forced us to take on students one or two years sooner than we were ready to do. And what was left of the project finally distintegrated during and after the 1979 Iranian anti-Shah revolution. The final disintegration was due, on the one hand, to the disintegration of this new university itself. It had no firm university-like structures to protect it from opportunism and power politics. On the other hand, the rural project itself had not yet reached the level of self-reliance.

What can be concluded as lessons from this third try include the following:

21. The universities can play a very successful role both in the development of their surrounding environment and in research and development of appropriate technical and social solutions to the problems of society, even in a dependent third-world country. This is necessary in order to begin to be liberated from technological and socio-economic dependence on imperialist centres.

22. To do this they must abandon virtually all established academic criteria and habits and start (or start again) with the problems and needs of rural and/or urban communities around them. Only this will help them apply their technological or social knowledge to finding alternative solutions that are socially relevant. Student training must come only after or in conjunction with the two steps.

23. This 'academic revolution', however, needs it own preconditions. In our case, we found them to be reflected in the Charter of the National Association of Iranian Academic Workers: a) independence of the university system; b) democratic management in universities; c) academic freedom, and d) job security in the academic community.

24. The development of the community must rely on the endogenous efforts of the people. The university's role is to act as technical backstop for the community. The ensuing dialogue between academia and the community will dialectically enrich and transform both.

25. Academics, by their very class characteristics, will resist this revolution of social relevance. They prefer to act as armchair philosophers who know what is best for society. Institutional mechanisms based on 'encounter' with the community are needed to get them out of their neat and tidy armchairs and laboratories and into the untidy, real world.

26. Here, too, the ruling structures will attempt to impose the rule of not practising what they preach. This seems to be a fundamental law of both liberal and populist regimes which holds equally true in dependent dictatorships.

27. When the revolution finally comes, academics still prefer to remain in their armchairs and theorize about it, expecting the masses to come

to them with outstretched arms, shouting; 'Come, O supreme intellectual and eternal wise-man! Lead us to victory! Carry out, on our behalf, the Holy Dictatorship of the Toiling Masses!' During the long months of the revolution, no one from this 'university of rural development' bothered to go back into the villages to find out what the peasants thought about it all. Nor did they encourage the peasants to come and establish their presence in the university, and to share its problems. This was perhaps the fatal blow to the field project, and to the university alike.

28. What happened in this tiny neonate of a university provides, in fact, a microcosm of society at large. Everywhere the universities remained largely aloof from the rest of society, although participating in their own right in the revolution. For the most part, the intellectuals, especially those on the left, remained out of touch with the masses. Their lack of communication with the peasant, the worker, and the urban marginal dweller meant that their share in conscientizing the masses was minimal.

29. All this left the door open to plenty of opportunism. Those academics who were able to get themselves close to the social strata that availed itself of the leadership of the revolution, came to power immediately after the fall of the dying regime. Most of these opportunist individuals were themselves members of the 'National Association of Iranian Academic Workers'. But this did not prevent them from violating the very principles of the charter they had signed a few months earlier.

30. Again, as a result of this distance from the masses that we intellectuals like so much to talk about, even after the revolution there is no guarantee of the four basic principles we so much struggled to get. University professors are being fired en masse – a thing even the previous regime would not have dared to do. There are, no doubt, quite anti-revolutionary elements among those being sacked: professors who cooperated too closely with the political purposes of the imperial regime. But many people fear that authentic revolutionaries are being sacked as trouble-makers.

The Iranian revolution is not yet finished. There is much conflict of interest and ideology even in the new ruling class. There are surely many surprises in store for us yet. Will what the masses fought for materialize? Will even the conditional liberties granted in the new constitution be respected? Will the new regime be able to lead the nation to even higher levels of development with social equity and freedom? Will a social order finally emerge that will permit all Iranian people and institutions – including the universities – to reach their full human and social potential?

I realize I may not have answered too specifically the issues raised by the theme of this *festschrift*. But the fiftieth birthday of Johan Galtung – this exceptionally humane social scientist – has at least given me the opportunity to summarize some of my observations in over seven years of professional and political work in Iran. I hope these thirty mini-lessons hold the seeds of the answer to the important issues raised about the role of the social sciences and the social relevance of the scientist.

On Writing a History of the Future

RICHARD FALK

Johan Galtung's work, vitality, and commitment make him a vivid, enabling presence among social scientists. He does more, better than anyone else I can think of anywhere in the world. His range is astonishing, and none of his numerous inquiries are without their particular merit. In the end, however, what I find most inspiring about Johan's work is the degree to which his intellectual (including methodological) interests invariably flow from his normative commitments – for instance, how to make the world less violent, less imperialist, less racist, less sexist, and so forth.

At the same time, Johan's investigations are 'scientific' in at least two senses: first, the social scientific sense of concern for evidence and empirical validation, and secondly, the Marxist sense of attentiveness to the constraints of social, economic, political, and cultural structure. I believe it is this dual conception of empirical and structural rigor that gives Johan's remarkably disparate work its coherence and freshness of tone, as well as its genuine originality of content and method.

My own approach to social scientific inquiry has evolved in a similar direction, partly reflecting Johan's influence. My substantive focus has, of course, been much more restricted, and here, in these pages, I will discuss briefly my evolving efforts to participate in a program of research in the area of world order studies. To do this, it seems helpful to locate the kind of inquiry I support in a broader intellectual and political setting in which the term 'world order' is centrally deployed.

There are, at present, two principal varieties of international relations theorists who orient their work in relation to 'world order'. The first, here labeled Type I, reflects the view that international relations have become more complicated in significant interactive respects, causing a pervasive, dynamic, and intensifying circumstance of *interdependence* to exist. The character of this interdependence is especially relevant to the functioning of the capitalist world economy. Type I thinking does not question the traditionalist view of statism with regard to issues of security (war and peace), but it argues that this view is not sufficiently rich to capture the shifting character of international relations.

In effect, Type I world order thinking corresponds to the shift of foreign economic policy from the margins of 'low politics' to the core concerns of 'high politics'. Because the nature of foreign economic policy is itself segmented into concerns about money, trade, investment, resources (especially energy and ocean minerals), and markets, there is a sense of multiple arenas or 'chessboards' (in Stanley Hoffmann's phrase). For Hoffmann, traditionalists confine international relations to one main chessboard of security concerns based on alliances, balances, and relative capabilities, especially military capabilities. Type I inquiry, in contrast, depicts 'multiple chessboards', seeking to grasp the intricacies of their interrelationship. Characteristic of Type I inquiry is the work of the interdependence theorists who have, at times, adopted the rubric of 'transnational politics' to identify the distinctiveness of their efforts. The transnational dimension is associated with the rise of non-state actors (especially, banks, multinational corporations, and specialized international institutions, most prominently, international economic institutions) and from the breakdown of the boundaries between foreign and domestic spheres. The Type I worldview stresses the interpenetration of the domestic sphere by transnational forces.

It should be observed, also, that Type I inquiry is Western, non-socialist, non-Marxist; it is associated with the ideology of liberal internationalism as it is expressed in the Trilateral domain of world capitalism, especially in the United States. The normative quest, explaining the focus on 'world order', relates to ways to handle this complexity of international society in a moderate way that benefits mutual interests without ignoring the antagonistic elements of a basically competitive international order. For Type I thinkers these competitive aspects become destructive unless better procedures of coordination are evolved, and rapidly. The essence, then, of the Type I normative quest is managerial, nicely summarized by the notion 'the management of interdependence' (a phrase aptly adopted as the title for an influential study at the Council on Foreign Relations, a study that was the precursor to the Council's 1980's Project, a charasteristic Type I venture). This Type I approach to world order underlies Stanley Hoffmann's *Primacy or World Order* (1977), a book in which the managerial approach to the various issue-areas of world politics is contrasted with both the traditionalist preoccupation on power (that is, 'primacy' in the Hoffmann title) or, at best, with stability through alliances and balances and the allegedly utopian insistence on transcending the state system.

The Type I approach by its stress on world order is seeking principally to adapt statist orientations to economic interdependencies. The main resistance to Type I thinking comes from neo-Hobbesian analysis that underscores the factual and normative persistence of an anarchic system of states vis-à-vis international security. Such Type Zero thinkers ('Zero' because there is no pretension that more than international order is possible in a fragmented world of states; the 'world order' focus makes some minimal claim that the world, as well as actors in it, serves as a unit of analyses) as Hedley Bull (author of the influential *The Anarchical Society),* Kenneth Waltz, and Robert Gilpin argue that statist tendencies prevail, and that either economic policy is not so important as to alter this image or that, even if important, a new variant of neo-mercantilism will subordinate international economic policy to the priorities of the state. In effect, Type Zero thinkers dismiss Type I reformulations of international politics as trendy, diversionary.

My own work concentrates on Type II approaches to world order. The essence of Type II thinking is to start from the view that a Type Zero world, even if modified along Type I lines, is neither sustainable nor decent and that, therefore, on both moral and self-interested grounds it is necessary to study the possibilities for an alternative framework of world order. Type II posits images of preferred worlds not as mere manifestations of a lively imagination, but as projects to be realized in the world.

To get a clearer sense of this Type II endeavor it seems helpful to distinguish three stages, which are partly suggestive of an evolutionary sequence and partly revelatory of complementary tasks for social science in this setting. Type II, Stage 1, is characterized by blueprints for the future, often built around advocacy of world government in some form. These blueprints (e.g. Grenville Clark and Louis B. Sohn, *World Peace Through World Law,* 3rd rev. ed., 1966) rest their claims for adherence upon appeals to reason and self-interest. That is, if the intelligent leader would consider his/her interests, then it would be obvious that regardless of present wealth/power/prestige all actors would be better off in a world stabilized by a centralized constitutional authority. Stage 1 blueprints and proposals tend to be utopian and apolitical in the sense that not much attention is given to how various forms of resistance to their recommendations might be overcome. Also, this type of thinking seems culturally provincial, coming mainly out of such countries in the North as have enjoyed long periods of moderate rule on the domestic level.

Type II/stage 2 represents an effort to overcome Stage 1 deficiencies. Perhaps, the most concerted Stage 2 effort is that of the World Order Models Project (WOMP) (for depiction see Saul Mendlovitz, ed., *On the Creation of a Just World Order* (1975)). WOMP, as a transnational academic exercise started in 1968, seeks to combine the notion of a preferred world with the promotion of specific world order values (peace, equity, social and political justice, ecological quality, and as a cumulation, humane governance) by means of serious concern about transition from a Type I to a Type II world (that is, to a world system in which the five world order values are substantially realized). WOMP's Stage 2 effort consisted of inducing a series of scholars from different parts of the world to work out their Type II version of a preferred world, including transition scenarios, to the extent possible, for crossing the bridge from here (Type I) to there (Type II). A series of books emerged out of this work including Rajni Kothari, *Footsteps into the Future*, Johan Galtung, *The True Worlds: A Transnational Perspective*, Ali Mazrui, *A World Federation of Cultures*, Gustavo Lagos and Horacio H. Godoy, *Revolution of Being: A Latin American View of the Future*, and my own, *A Study of Future Worlds*.

This process of generating diverse images of Type II solutions to the world order challenges of the present was a stimulating experience. It shattered the illusion of Stage I that there was 'a right answer' with respect to a Type II approach that derived from a kind of rational, universal humanism. Instead, it illuminated the extent to which moving beyond the statist constraints of Type Zero involves challenging its imperialist and managerial elements; that is, the politics of transition are, above all, a matter of resistance to the Type I reformist managerial strategies associated with a group such as the Trilateral Commission. This anti-imperial element of transition also emphasized the critical role of the Third World in setting the priorities and the agenda for a program of global reform. It was in the Third World, despite its many diversities, that one encountered the most assured constituencies of struggle, committed to changing the present world order system in specific ways that corresponded with WOMP values.

Type II/stage 3 is a continuation of Type II/stage 2, except that it goes deeper into the idea of listening to the voices of the oppressed to gain insight and leverage in relation to transition. WOMP has since 1977 devoted its attention to the task of writing a history of the future from the viewpoint of oppressed peoples. The reorientation implicit here is that both normatively and politically the most attractive prospect for breaking the hold of the Type Zero/I world upon our destinies is through an understanding of and, then, an alignment to the struggles of the oppressed for liberation and justice. In these struggles against imperialism, racism, sexism, social forces with a stake in normative change exist.

The conception of 'oppression' is also being extended in this WOMP work beyond the neo-Marxist domains of the visibly oppressed. The conception of 'invisible oppression' is central to this new stage of Type II world order thinking. Especial emphasis is placed upon the extent to which a Type Zero/I World by *its very structure* and *operating procedure* has become oppressive for all people regardless of race, class, sex, or ideology. The spectre of nuclear war and the experience of an array of environmental hazards epitomize invisible oppression.

A main task of WOMP is to awaken the oppressed, to end their 'alienation', and to make, in effect, their circumstances more visible, as well as to point toward a direction of liberation (that is, non-oppression). This imagery of liberation on a global scale involves the prefiguring of a preferred future, not in the form of a blueprint for a new world order, but in the shape of a value-realizing process that improvises institutionally as its capacity to exert influence grows.

Social science in this mode is macro-historical journalism of the highest possible order. It seeks to align knowledge with the flow of history, and it accepts the interpretation of our epoch as one in which the struggle against oppression is the central drama. Accordingly, the pursuit of Type II/stage 3 world order gives me my identity as a social scientist. Simultaneously, because of the concreteness of the struggle and the universality of its aspirations, such inquiry allows me to add the identity of planetary citizen to those more traditional bonds of loyalty to family, neighborhood, and nation. Ultimately, then, this kind of social science is a battlefield in the wider ideological war about the nature of knowledge, and its proper connections with feeling (as validation) and action (as manifestation). Social science can contribute to our prospects for the future only if it is willing to engage in subversive activities, especially to mount an assault on claims of legitimacy presupposed on behalf of existing power-wielders at all levels of governance. In this sense, the attuned social scientist is a critic of 'the old' and a prefigurer of 'the new', relying on a mixture of analytical skills and imaginative outpourings. Such a mixture is not alien, but rather insists that social science is 'a humanity' as well as a species of 'science.'

Intercultural Relations: New Field of Study in the Social Sciences?

ROY PREISWERK

Tribulations of a concept

In the development of every science, problems arise which, owing to conventional divisions among disciplines, find no scientific status. Concepts of main importance because they refer to fundamental human issues often appear as 'homeless' in the labyrinth of disciplines. Thus, for instance, in 1973, the prevailing lack of discussion on an essential *problématique* such as the individual and social identity of man, led an author to entitle her paper on this subject as follows: 'Psycho-social identity, a concept in search of a science'.[1] She could have said the same of cultural identity.

After G. F. Klemm had outlined, in 1843, the concept of culture in its widest sense to express a reality as old as mankind, it was at first entrusted to ethnologists and anthropologists.[2] The latter had great fun with it and went around the world to report how the others out there were behaving. This in itself is quite all right. Soon disciples of other disciplines also discovered how helpful the culture concept could be. Many historians, psychologists, sociologists or political scientists could not stay in the dark any longer about the need to conceptualize the great number of institutions, value scales, or behaviour patterns in different human societies. Even some economists tracked the anthropologists down to see if they could use the concept of culture to their benefit. Thus, the cultural identity of different populations came to be recognized as a scientifically relevant fact. This again, is quite all right, but it made the concept of culture 'homeless', leaving it drifting around in the social sciences under a variety of forms and under various flags.[3] UNESCO, which, at the level of international organizations, officially supervises culture, takes this into account insofar as in its documents at least five different kinds of definitions are used, so that adherents of different academic tribes or members of various diplomatic missions may underline with satisfaction the one which is convenient to them.

An epistemological problem

How do we get further? Is there a possibility of assembling under one roof the findings in various scientific fields concerning culture? To define a problem-area of 'intercultural relations' may be a temporary answer. This is not a new discipline delimited from the existing specialized fields. On the contrary, its aim is to reduce existing barriers between recognized sciences such as anthropology, psychology, social psychology, history, and every kind of comparative studies (comparative law, comparative politics, cross-cultural studies, etc.). Modestly this means: intercultural relations, a field of study in search of an epistemological basis. Less modestly, it raises the question: just how necessary and lasting are in fact conventional delimitations between various disciplines?

A similar question arises in another field with which a great many social scientists have already identified themselves decades ago: international relations. Attempts were made to bring together certain aspects covered by disciplines such as history, economics, law, political science. The question here is not whether these attempts were successful. There is a deeper reason for considering intercultural relations as a new field of study in the social sciences than just bringing separate disciplines closer together. Epistemology should not be self-serving, and it is not our intention to raise a particularly difficult epistemological problem only to create job opportunities for intellectuals.

A social reality

Intercultural relations are of interest mainly because they deal with a social reality that has been insufficiently considered up to now. The classical study of international relations, biased by the primacy attributed to the concept of the state, precisely neglects differences in cultural identity. Major human aspirations thus remained unconsidered for a long time. Intercultural relations, as a historical fact, have existed since the origins of mankind, that is from the time when human groups began to meet which prior to that had independently developed a specificity of their own. International relations, as a historical fact, only appeared in more recent times, when the nation-state became a particular form of social organization. The fact that the study of these two phenomena in the social sciences was interverted is significant, but not untypical.[4]

Nowadays, intercultural relations are mainly of interest when looking at micro-cultural revolutions and macro-cultural confrontations.

Micro-cultural revolutions appear in various forms, mainly in attempts of ethnic minorities to break away from centralized states

(Basques, Bretons, Scots: the list has no end) and in the struggle of oppressed minorities against ruling powers (Eritreans, Kurds, Palestinians and many others). Most of today's violent conflicts are cultural conflicts in the widest sense (e.g. economic and political factors included). This is true as well for the problem of Kashmir, the Biafra War and Bangladesh's secession from Pakistan, as for the situations in Northern Ireland, the Middle-East and Cyprus.

Macro-cultural confrontations mainly appear in the huge field of so-called 'development' of the so-called 'Third World'. This is often seen as a harmonious process of balancing out economic and technological differences between poor and rich countries. In fact, it is the most tremendous cultural conflict of world history, following Europe's expansion since the 15th century.

The shock – since 1947 – between different conceptions of values and ways of life in development cooperation seems less spectacular than the one between colonial armies and armed forces of conquered countries in the past centuries. But this is so only at the surface. The process of worldwide cultural uniformization, starting with expansion and continuing with scientific and technical means, encounters opposition. Let us just mention briefly: in 1949, and more evidently so from 1960 to 1977, China withdraws and pursues an autonomous development policy. The rest of Asia and the Arab region proudly refer to their traditions, but, at the same time, look for massive assistance from industrial countries. Africa, with completely demobilized social structures, desperately searches for a new identity. In 1977, the Indians, from Alaska to Chile, after nearly complete extermination in the nineteenth century, assemble to bring together the remnants of their culture and to think of a future of their own. The re-emergence, with Khomeiny, of a certain Islamic resistance to a Western-type of 'modernization' has dramatized the issue most forcefully in a long time. Last but not least, more and more people are interested in movements for a new life-style in industrial countries. The industrial countries' development style, considered as the only way to go, is seriously questioned from many different angles.

Relevance to the ongoing development debate

In the present debate about future international development strategies, two main points of view are opposed.[5] On the one hand, Third World representatives at the UN claim for a New International Economic Order (NIEO) to have faster industrialization, increasing exports, better raw-material prices, more financial aid and technology transfers. Taking a closer look, it becomes obvious that the international distribution of labour could be modified to a certain extent, but that basic premises of the Present International Economic Disorder (PIED) remain untouched. Adaptation of the 'new' strategy to different peoples' cultural specificity was never mentioned in the UN meetings, even by the Third World. This is highly interesting for development sociology, since nowadays one really has to wonder whom representatives from these countries actually represent.

For the other side in the development debate, this is an essential point. They see that very little is done for the poorest classes in the Third World, even worse: that independent initiatives for local development based on self-reliance mostly encounter repression on behalf of national governments. Foreign development organizations are obliged, often unfortunately, to work together with such governments, while such governments, equally unfortunately, work only for themselves. For some time now, various organizations, mainly the World Bank, therefore favour directing the development process towards the satisfaction of basic needs among all segments of the population, if necessary by bringing pressure to bear on the ruling class. But how to define basic needs? The World Bank 'solved' the problem rather simplistically by picking out five of them: food, employment, health, habitat and education. Viewed from a culture conflict angle, this is already problematic. Indeed, some somatic needs are vital to everyone: air, first of all. But for food, the question is already different, since the way of satisfying this need is culture-bound. Even more complex are the non-somatic needs. Not only the question how to satisfy, but how to define needs, vary from one culture to the other. Security, dignity or justice obviously do not have the same meaning everywhere. It is not easy to find out which values and forms of behaviour such concepts involve in various culture spheres, according to which priorities they can be classified, and how they must be related to somatic needs.[6]

A double challenge is presented here to the study of intercultural relations. On the one hand, it is necessary to deal with basic needs in their macro-cultural as well as in their micro-cultural dimension. Value systems and behaviour patterns of the larger cultural sphere are as relevant as local, historically specific influences, as well as ecological and geographical factors. On the other hand, a methodological problem arises of a complexity rarely faced in the social sciences. Are the poorest populations in the world able to express their needs? Who registers their statements? To what extent are politicians, officials or traditional chiefs, who speak for 'their people', culturally representative? What allows research institutes and international organizations to work out their own priority lists for other people?

One thing is sure: research methods worked out in Western cultures, for instance opinion polls, can only be applied restrictively to other culture spheres. A large enquiry is necessary, but cannot be done with uniform questions. The researcher must have considerable advance knowledge of the culture he is going to study, which makes it impossible to use him in too many different parts of the world. It would therefore be necessary to have an enormous number of researchers for prolonged periods of time all over the world. The better these researchers approach their task, i.e. if they succeed in sorting out the authentic and specific needs amongst the declared and general ones, the harder it gets to compare results cross-culturally. This makes the operational use of research by development organizations very difficult. Some institutions have been confronted with such questions for a certain time, and we already have tentative answers.[7]

The culture conflict between the Third World, representing today nearly 80 percent of the world population, and the industrial countries, as well as within all national entities, is a reality. It is of main significance in the field of development studies, and consequently also for the future of industrial nations, whether one merely describes the present misery or also states normative postulates for the future. Beyond this, it is perhaps up to futurology to find out prospectively what is to be expected. Futurologists may have an advantage insofar as they are not a sect linked to a single classical discipline, but try to handle our society's future in its totality. Let us hope that in this totality intercultural aspects will take their appropriate place.

NOTES

1 Marisa Zavalloni: 'L'identité psycho-sociale: un concept à la recherche d'une science', in: Serge Moscovici (ed.), Introduction à la psychologie sociale, Larousse, Paris, 1973, vol. II.

2 G. F. Klemm, Allgemeine Cultur-Geschichte der Menschheit, Leipzig, 1843–1852, 10 Bde.

3 A. L. Kroeber and Clyde Kluckhohn: Culture, A Critical Review of Concepts and Definitions, Vintage Books, New York 1952. P. Bohannan: 'Rethinking Culture: A Project for Current Anthropologists', Current Anthropology, 14, October 1973.

4 To a certain extent, historians have dealt with cultural encounters over millenaries. However, certain essential concepts for intercultural relations such as cultural identity, cultural distance, assimilation, acculturation, identity crisis, empathy, ethnocentrism, or ethnocide are usually missing in the writing of history. For more details, see: Roy Preiswerk, 'The Place of Intercultural Relations in the Study of International Relations', The Yearbook of World Affairs, London, Stevens, 1978, pp. 251–267.

5 By this opposition we only consider two opinions raised against the existing world economic disorder. The strongest position still belongs to rich industrial countries, who wish as little change as possible in the existing system. See Roy Preiswerk, 'Le nouvel ordre économique international est-il nouveau?, in Etudes internationales, 1977, 4.

6 Johan Galtung has paid particular attention to all these intricate issues in his 'The Basic Needs Approach' in a forthcoming book edited by Katrin Lederer, Berlin, 1980.

7 Amilcar Herrera et al., Catastrophe o Nuevo Sociedad? Modelo Mundial Latinoamericano, Buenos Aires, Fundacion Bariloche, 1976.

The Study of World Society: Some Reasons Pro and Contra

PETER HEINTZ

I have my personal stake in the study of world society: I did a lot of thinking and writing about it and I also try again and again to motivate students to study this subject. Thus, there is no doubt that I am inclined to justify my own endeavour.

Let me first, therefore, give a few reasons in favour of the study of world society:

(1) If I study world society I am concerned with the only truly global society, and I do not submit to the social pressures impelling me to study other societies, which are socially defined as global in spite of the fact that, in structural terms, they are not, for example national societies.

(2) If I study world society I study a subject that is common to all social scientists wherever they are located, whatever the culture to which they belong, etc. Thus, doing so I can define myself as a member of a very loose kind of world-wide community of social scientists.

(3) If I study world society I investigate a subject that has been highly neglected by social scientists. The marginal utility of such studies may be high even if they are carried through on a modest scale.

(4) If I study world society I am studying a very particular type of society, the knowledge of which promises to be fruitful for theory construction. This society has no identity, and it is not perceived by most of its members. In other words, I am studying a stateless society of immense complexity.

There are also many reasons that argue against studying world society; I mention only four:

(1) Nobody has ever asked me to study world society. World society seems to be no social problem at all. Thus, I am not justified by trying to answer questions that other people have formulated and put to me.

(2) If I study world society only a very small elite who, for professional reasons, are interested in the topic (foreign policy makers, managers of multinational corporations) may be interested in my findings. But I may not like to strengthen the power of this elite by providing them with additional information whose usefulness is not perceived by anybody else.

(3) If I study world society I act as if I could overcome all kinds of perspectives that are inherent in the loci I occupy in this society. There may be few social scientists who believe that this is feasible at all.

(4) If I study world society I investigate a subject that produces a lot of information, but I know that this information is very biased. Such information, as for example government statistics and mass-media news, has not been produced for the purpose for which I am using it, and no other information is available.

The coexistence of some strong reasons for and against the study of world society may reveal the existence of incompatible goals. Once the existence of some major incompatible goals has been established, we may then ask why the study of world society is accompanied by such an incompatibility.

One major incompatibility I shall analyse is the following: Reason pro: World society is something which is, at the same time, highly relevant and widely ignored.

Reason contra: Most people (with the exception of some small elites) are not interested in world society. It may be that those who are directly concerned with world society are deflecting the attention of others from what is important to them.

Having stated this incompatibility it seems quite reasonable to say: the discrepancy between the relevance of and the interest in an object is extremely large with regard to world society. I should like to go still one step further and formulate the following proposition: this large discrepancy is a distinctive feature of world society. Thus, I postulate that world society is as it is because it is widely ignored.

If in spite of the reason contra I insist on studying world society, I should also investigate this feature and compare this society with other ones (which by definition are part of world society) taking into account the causes and effects of this particular feature.

Now, the fact that I include in the study of world society one of the major reasons for not studying it may be seen as an additional justification for doing so. I try to explain why people do not ask to know more about world society even if they feel that this society is highly threatening.

However, I do not pretend that I study this feature of world society only as a means of justifying my own investigation. There are other reasons for doing this. It seems to make just very good sense to study the reasons for some widely shared ignorance.

If we look for reasons that explain why world society is widely ignored, we will certainly come across an extremely trivial hypothesis: people are only interested in knowing the time spaces within which they can act. For most people world society is no action time space. Why should they then be interested in world society? I believe that this most trivial hypothesis underlies many of the questions concerning the action relevance of empirical research in social sciences. Today, scientists are, indeed, very frequently asked to justify their activities in terms of the action relevance of their findings.

But this hypothesis has, to my view, a very serious implication: it takes the existence of limited action time spaces for granted. If, on the contrary, we are not willing to take it for granted we will not be satisfied with the answer: people ignore world society because it is no action time space for them. This answer may be true but it is, at the same time, most superficial. The question now is: Why is world society no action time space except for some very small elites? This question can also be phrased in the following terms: What are the action time spaces that prevent people from looking at world society as such a space, and, of course, why? If we answer this question we may add something substantial to our knowledge about world society.

In other words, if we study world society as well as the discrepancy between its relevance and its being ignored, we do not study what people are concerned with but what are the societal areas of social knowledge and ignorance. Thus, I am especially interested in knowing more about the mechanisms implied in the barriers that prevent people from looking at world society. I even believe that one of the most important principles that govern world structure is the systematic limitation of action time spaces, and that taking this fact for granted prevents us from making use of some important possibilities of inquiry. If one accepts this kind of reasoning one may state the following theoretical question: Is ignorance of relevance a major factor contributing to the reproduction of the structure of world society in terms of limited action time spaces? If one argues like this, one implicitly criticizes all those social scientists who are convinced or feel obliged to justify their own scientific activity in terms of the usefulness of their findings for action within given action time spaces.

At this point, my case for studying world society seems to have become quite good, because one of the major reasons against ('nobody is interested') now looks quite different. But my argumentation depends on the assumption that world society is, in fact, a self-reproducing structure of ignorance and knowledge. There is a very long way to go to prove this.

As we have suggested before, social problems (as one of the reasons for justifying research) are defined within existing action time spaces as a guarantee for the action relevance of the findings. However, even if one accepts the above-mentioned assumption, one may still object to our analysis by observing that there is a set of social problems which are in fact formulated on the world level, for example the problems of war and hunger. This is perfectly true. But the action time spaces to which these problems are referred are almost exclusively those of governments and intergovernmental organizations. And this fact again is in perfect agreement with the postulated world's structure of ignorance and knowledge. World affairs are mainly seen as government affairs, and we guess it is the governmental elite (besides other ones) who have a vital interest in maintaining this structure.

Let me finish by saying: I tried to take up the questions raised by the editor: How to justify what I am doing. In terms of my personal history, I certainly did not start my thinking about world society by looking for justifications. In particular, I did not start by searching for problems in order to have a good reason for studying world society. If I had done so I would probably not have turned to this kind of study.

There actually exists a strong trend among social scientists to look for problems in order to justify their activity. This process of selecting problems previous to research is necessarily highly restrictive: the major choices are delegated to society. There may be good reasons for doing so. But there may also be some disadvantages, the major one being the loss or lack of scientific imagination. I cannot help but think that if Johan Galtung had always felt obliged to justify in advance his research, he would not have engaged in the extremely stimulating work he has produced.

Towards a Human Social Science

PATRICK HEALEY

In his novel *Island,* Aldous Huxley presented a personal vision of utopia.[1] This utopia contrasted starkly with the prophetic distopia he had written about in *Brave New World,* and it demonstrated a view that, in order to achieve even a half-decent world in which to live, it is necessary to bring together a powerful moral vision and a perceptive social analysis. The moral vision is to provide the social and human goals for a good society, and the social analysis provides the basis for the structural and institutional arrangements that will be necessary if these goals are to be achieved.

If Huxley had used such language (perhaps thankfully he did not) he might have said that the truth of Sociology is praxis. In fact he said the same thing in a more accessible way in *Island* in the form of the title of the philosophical work that was the intellectual inspiration of the members of the utopia. The work was titled: 'Notes on What's What, and on What it Might be Reasonable to Do About What's What'.

Discovering 'what's what' is the purpose of all scientific work. The training of the scientist provides him with a set of perspectives and tools for finding out 'what's what'. The thing that is missing from most science is consideration of what it might be reasonable to do about 'what's what' once you have discovered it. And not only absent from traditional models of science but actively excluded from them is the possibility of deliberate involvement by the scientist in what's what in order to bring about what might be: in other words purposive action for change. Such considerations are defined as being outside science, which deals with what 'is', and lying in the ethical and moral realms of what 'should be'. Science we are told is positive, statements of goals and values are normative, and to mix the two is bad science.

The problems raised by the separation of the positive and the normative in the scientific endeavour have been dealt with in many places.[2] The issue that interests me here is that this separation takes no account of the *social product* of science. All human activity, of which science is just one part, derives from social life and has implications for that life. There is in this sense no neutral acitivity in human affairs, everything has some effect, even inaction; not to attempt to intervene when the strong threaten the weak, for example, is not to stay outside the struggle but is rather to favour the strong.

The work that we undertake in Social Science should be grounded in a purposeful framework rather than being a series of unrelated and ad hoc programmes and activities. The question of the social product of our work provides such a framework. In general science encourages us only to consider the individual or professional product of work. This is reflected in academic papers published, institutional honours received, and career advancement flowing from these, all individual products of a very seductive kind.

Given that all work is rooted in concrete social situations, however, choosing to emphasise the individual product of one's work does not make the social product disappear; it merely puts it outside our control.

In natural science, for example it was realized only too late that the development of equations which led to the unleashing of nuclear energy was not just a mathematical issue, but a social and a moral one too. Indeed the social and moral significance of the development were, in human terms, of far greater importance than the mathematical. Discovery and innovation are not good in and of themselves considered outside of their social context. The social product of science has therefore to be a criterion for the evaluation of the scientific endeavour and for the results that it derives.

Human activity is actually or potentially a *resource,* and resources are always *directed.* The direction of a resource may be *implicit* or *explicit,* but it can never be absent. If the direction remains implicit, this means no more than it is uncertain, arbitrary, or in the control of others. In each of these cases the direction of the resource will benefit some individuals or groups rather than others. This benefit or disbenefit is one aspect of the social product of the resource, and is always present in the consequences of human activity.

I would argue strongly in favour of the conscious direction of the resource of our work as social scientists, and also, assert that the social product of our work should be a central criterion for evaluating it. The social product as anticipated in advance of the work should constitute part of the goal of the work. To extend this further, the desire to produce a certain social product should be the purpose of our work. Of course here the traditional scientist finally shakes his head and leaves us, for the ultimate desecration of the scientific method is to intervene in situations under scientific scrutiny. Even if the scientist produces an analysis of what's what, and adds to this a studied statement on what it might be reasonable to do about what's what, to then go ahead and do it is scientifically unacceptable. Of particular unacceptability is to intervene in situations in such a way that the outcome of the situation becomes different to that which would have occurred had the scientist not been present. Much of the scientific method in social science is designed precisely to prevent the scientist from influencing the social situation under examination.

It is interesting but disturbing to note that the preceding observations about the professional work of the scientist, would be considered absurd if applied to his private life. Indeed, to suggest that private life would not be guided by quite contrary considerations would be taken as a slander of the first order, impugning the very status of the scientist as a human being. This can be demonstrated very clearly by the use of the concept of the *family*.

The social scientist in his private life sees himself as a member of family groups defined by reference to personal relationships and other fundamental social ties. These ties may be of many kinds: class, race, sex, age, even nation. I use the term *family* in describing these relationships deliberately, rather than some other categorization such as interest group, reference group and so on. In an increasingly privatised world where the nuclear family is growing in importance as the social unit of primary social and personal identification, the term family conveys, for me at least, the deep attachment that I wish to emphasise about these relationships. The concept of the familiy while based upon our common and shared understanding of the term, is being used here, therefore, not merely as a kin-oriented conceptual category but as a normative and generalizable model of human relationships.

The responsibility of any human being (including the social scientist) in his family relationships is clear and unambiguous: it is to establish the just demands of the members of his familiy and then put his energies at their disposal in achieving those demands. This responsibility is, indeed, seen as axiomatic: if family members are in need, that need must be met in any way possible. The further the action is removed from the actual family based on kinship, the less likely is this axiomatic loyalty to be so completely binding, but it will extend for all of us in many directions and for varying distances. The archetype of the isolated and dehumanized person is thus precisely he for whom there are no binding loyalties of this kind, the man who is without a family.

When the scientist enters his professional role he is required to put aside loyalties and ignore family ties. If family ties are of particular significance to his work he must declare his family 'interests' in advance of conducting his work, or risk having his work rejected as distorted and partial afterwards by his professional peers.

Of much greater importance, when the social scientist enters his professional role he is not only required to renounce his family but also to treat all those he deals with in his research and other work strictly as *non-family*. The requirement to treat the subjects of our professional work as non-family extends to aspects of the relationships we establish with them, the methods we use to examine them, and the legitimate lengths to which we may go in our involvement with them.

Johan Galtung indicated something of the nature of the relationships we are required to establish with non-families in professional work when he asked if any of us would use the survey method in order to get information from members of our own families.[3] The answer is of course no, for the survey method is based on the building of a distance between the researcher and the subject that would be unthinkable in a family. The social scientist might respond by claiming that the survey method is necessary because he deals with larger numbers of people than one usually does in the family and other methods cannot get the same volume of data. The survey method is an indicator of the type of relationship the scientist wishes to establish, however; it does not derive from the requirements of research. This is seen clearly if one considers that the researcher even when operating in small scale situations will still set up relationships designed to establish distance between him and the subjects and to destroy intimacy and involvement in the interests of 'objectivity'.

The treatment of the subjects (objects is in fact a term closer to the truth) of social science work as non-family can be linked to the treatment of *non-families* as *non-human*. A matrix of these dimensions illustrates some interesting points. The variables in the matrix are shown below.

	Family	Non-Family
Human	1	2
Non-Human	3	4

Type no. 1 presents no problems for our analysis; it is the type we are all familiar with, and the requirements of the relationships are known after a fashion to us all. This type is the truly human mode of personal relationships. It requires closeness, intimacy, creative dialogue, loyalty, and love. It does not require an uncritical attitude to everything the family does, but it does require that criticism be directed to the building of better relationships and situations, not exercised for its own sake. Truth is not totally sacrificed to loyalty within the family, but it is put at the service of constructive development. Above all one does not use information gained within the family for purely personal ends

104

outside it. Information is not defined as neutral, but as having actual or potential consequences for the family, and these consequences have to be taken into account when considering what to do with the informa-tion. The goal of family action is therefore to promote, develop, and advance the family.

If type 1 is that which is truly human, based as it is upon some of the highest ideals of interpersonal relationships, it follows that types which diverge from it do so in the direction of increasing degrees of dehuman-ization both for the social scientist (or any other person), and for the objects with which the scientist has his working relationships. The movement away from type 1 is in the direction of increasing 'profes-sionalization' of behaviour, increasing 'quality' of scientific work, and increasing object status of the persons and groups the scientist studies. Only type 1 involves the meeting of equal subjects; the other types reduce one or both parties in the relationships to objects. The nature of subjects is active, autonomous and creative, and the status of objects is passive, subordinate, and re-active.

Type no 2 occurs when the scientist is dealing with non-families that are sufficiently familiar to his family understanding for him to treat them as human, but not as subjects. When the scientist studies non-families from his own culture or country this will be the case. While the intimacy and involvement of the family relationship is abandoned in the search for scientific and professional objectivity, there may be nonetheless limits on the lengths that the researcher will go to in order to obtain information, and certainly there will be limits on the conse-quences for the non-family that the researcher will be willing to accept responsibility for.

What is totally missing, however, is any commitment on the part of the social scientist to do anything about the situation of the objects of his study. Even if he discovers suffering, poverty, and exploitation, his sense of responsibility may extend no further than to report what he finds. There is no requirement for him to report his findings to those who may be best able to change the situations, and it is in fact in his interests in promoting his work as objective and scientific not to be-come involved in political issues of this kind. Certainly if he is seen to be actively engaged in political action to change the situations he finds, it is likely he will be redefined as a lobbyist rather than an academic, and his work will be treated with caution and indeed suspicion.

Type no 3 consists of those who are putatively members of a family, but who through choice or circumstances cannot be accepted as hu-mans, given that 'humanness' is a social category based on the nature and potentiality of relationships between persons. An example of this would be the extremely mentally disturbed such as depressives, who while accepted formally as family in a general sense are considered to be so far from the truly human that the normal rights we admit for humans do not apply, and the accepted loyalties and relationships we give to family members are suspended. One function of defining others as non-family and/or non-human is to allow us to treat them in ways that would be otherwise unacceptable. In this type 3 case the family relationship is waived because of extenuating circumstances, and the disturbed person can be shipped off to special prisons called asylums, given treatment identical to the more sophisticated techniques of torture employed in the world today (electroconvulsive therapy), and otherwise dealt with in a manner appropriate to non-humans. The intention in this case is benign, of course, which is to return the non-human to a human form, whereupon he can be readmitted to the family. In the type 4 case the intention is simply to eliminate the non-humans in the most effective and most painful way possible.

Type no 4 illustrates by the extreme case the dehumanizing tendencies built into the scientific enterprises, and it has profound implications for both natural and social scientists.

It can be demonstrated by the example of the treatment of enemies in times of war. In order to be able to kill and mutilate our enemies during a war it helps enormously to destroy any impression of similarity between them and us. This is achieved by propaganda, atrocity stories, and all the techniques of distorted communication available to governments for the systematic redefinition of other human beings as evil, destructive, cruel, and so on. This whole exercise is greatly assisted by enemies being of a different racial type and colour. If the enemy does not look like members of our family and we can be convinced that he behaves in ways that we cannot consider to be truly (or even marginally) human, then we can slot him comfortably into the non-human/non-family box, and proceed to bomb, napalm, and starve him to death in the assurance that we are not really doing it to human beings, let alone to human beings like ourselves and our family.

To do 'science' in its traditional form is for both the scientist and his objects of study to move along a continuum of dehumanization as defined by the family model.

The scientist is required to adopt relationships and methods with the objects of his study that he would find repugnant with his family. In order to do this effectively he has to make up some interesting fictions about the social world and then construct methods consistent with those fictions. The positivist seeks causal relationships in the social world, and in order to keep those relationships untainted he builds distance between himself and the social world with his techniques of investigation. Such techniques include the better known ones of stealing peoples' insights (known as conducting social surveys), lying to people (known amongst other names as participant observation),

106

manipulating peoples' natural trust and credibility (known as constructing experimental situations), and worst of all, keeping people in ignorance in order not to distort the experimental or research situation.

Keeping people in ignorance is necessary because the nature of social reality militates against the fictions and the methods of the scientist. As Galtung has observed, there are few social laws that are causal to the extent of being automatic.[4] This is a truth we accept within the family without question: if we find a certain situation to be other than we wish it, or to be to the detriment of the family, we do not speak of the lawful necessities of social structures, we simply set out to understand the situation, and then attempt to change it. It does not occur to us to ask if change is possible, because we know that it is, within the limits set by our understanding and the constraints within which we work. The purpose of seeking understanding is to make us aware of the nature of the constraints and possibilities, so that our action for change is better informed and therefore more likely to be successful. Similarly, we do not ask if change is desirable, or if our accepting a role in it is required, because the very fact that it is a family matter we are considering provides the moral imperative for both change and our involvement in it.

This formulation gives a model for sociology that is praxis-oriented and has three interrelated aspects:

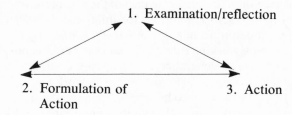

1. Examination/reflection

2. Formulation of
Action

3. Action

A sociological understanding of the world provides formulations of action which produce action. The whole of this triangle is social science; social science does not consist of only examination and formulation, even less is it a matter of simply applying to the real world the insights gained in the process of examination. The model is not linear and sequential but holistic and continuous. The three elements proceed simultaneously and interact in a way that both advances and modifies all three at the same time.

Such an approach to sociological work demands involvement and participation. It is therefore the approach best used in family situations;

it is indeed nothing more than the translation to the general sociological sphere of the relationships and objectives of the family model, and as such it provides a general model for a humanized social science.

The particular role of the trained sociologist in this model is to put his insights and knowledge at the service of the family he seeks membership of. The intellectual can contribute a great deal to the examination of and reflection upon the issues confronting the family, as well as to the formulation of action. His involvement in the action itself then feeds back into the reflection and formulation, insights born of the engagement with the real world. An important function of the intellectual is to use his skills to provide appropriate strategies for achieving the desired changes in the situation of the family. By taking a full sociological account of possibilities and constraints, and examining them dynamically in the struggle to meet needs and achieve goals, the intellectual helps to create a solid basis for change and avoid a naive utopianism which posits goals but neglects structural realities of social situations. No actions benefit all persons equally at all times. Social systems are highly stratified vertically and distribute benefits and opportunities differentially, usually according to the relative power positions of the social actors. The social scientist has to use his skills in the service of his family to ensure that conditions are being created by which their needs may be met, if necessary in opposition to others who may seek to prevent this.

This model of social science therefore neither seeks nor assumes consensus, although a further aspect of the role of the intellectual in this model will be to seek resolutions to situations of conflict that may not be readily apparent to non-sociologically trained family members. In this direction a working rule would be that as far as possible attempts should be made to generalize the model by treating others as if they were family. Two corollaries of this are to work out the consequences of actions as if they were to be visited upon the family, and to consider what the result would be if the family were treated in the same way as non-family.

I would therefore urge a human role for the social scientist based upon a model of the most humanizing social environment any of us experience, that of the family. The work of social science as advanced here has the following characteristics: 1. it is to be seen as a resource; 2. it is to be a consciously directed resource; 3. it is a resource consciously directed to the achievement of a specific social product; 4. the social product to be achieved is the understanding and advancement of the interests of the family; 5. all methods and procedures must derive from the model of human relationships provided by the family.

When we as social scientists have achieved the translation of the family model to our professional work, I believe we will have achieved the beginnings of a human social science that will give a new dedication both to our consideration of what's what, and to our understanding of what it is reasonable for us to do about what's what.

NOTES

1 Aldous Huxley (1962): *Island* (Chatto & Windus Ltd, London).
2 See for example: Johan Galtung (1977): *Methodology and Ideology*. (Christian Ejlers, Copenhagen).
3 Johan Galtung (1978): *On Dialogue as a Method* (Mimeo).
4 Johan Galtung (1977), op cit, page 94.

Visions of Desirable Societies

ELEONORA BARBIERI MASINI

In 1977 I was with Johan Galtung in Dubrovnik and the ideas of 'Visions of Desirable Societies' emerged. Societies which are seen in visions by the people of today and which are desirable, hence with a force of change in themselves. Visions are in people who are not captured by the social system in which they live, or at least they do not help the system to be built and to be maintained.

The search for visions of desirable societies is really future research where it is linked to the possibilities in the process of historical change; hence not visions that are separated from the process of listening, but ones that are linked with the process. Moreover the seeds of the visions are in the process of change.

In this framework the search for the people who are able to have visions of desirable societies and at the same time are capable of finding seeds of change in the process of the history of humankind, is crucial. I believe, and I think it is in line with Johan Galtung's thinking, that the people whom one could call creators of visions and capturers of the seeds of change are the ones who, as we said, do not build the social system: the politically persecuted, women and children. I shall not speak of the first but of the second and third categories.

Women have not built the social system in which they live and do not help, generally, to maintain it and are better capturers of the seeds of change as well as better creators of visions of desirable societies. They have not built societies themselves; they are not, usually, if not captured by the system, maintainers of the system. They are capable of sensing the seeds of change which need not only rational capacities but intuitive capacities. This intuition has not been developed by centuries of searching for better productivity, more profit, hence more consumption, which is what men do. Women instead have capacities that are of help in capturing seeds of change that are still alive, such as:

a) capacity to grasp the wholeness of a situation other than the details, such as the feeling ill or well of a family;
b) capacity to act rapidly after rapidly grasping whole situations, such as stopping a child from falling out of a window;

110

c) capacity to change from one' interest to others almost at the same time, ironing, reading, watching the child at play, etc.
d) capacity to sacrifice herself for the good of others. This capacity has very often been ill used.

All such capacities make a better audience for the seeds of change and better creators of visions. Children are also better capturers of seeds of change and hence better creators of visions. They too are not builders of the social system in which they live, and they are not maintainers of the system itself. They are watchers; they are not called to responsibility, although they have responsibilities in watching younger children and in many societies in helping in the economic production.

Children's images of the future, if one does any research in it, is staggering. I have done some research in Italy, and the view of children of the future is, in the short term, one of refusal of the present and of desire for a different future; for a future where jobs are stable if the present is one of uncertainty, a future where fruit is available and not expensive, a future where marriage is one of one's choice in a society where marriage is still not of one's choice.

In the long term, the future is one of more solidarity among people, rather than hunger; one of love and understanding rather than one where the atomic bomb is present; one of peaceful living in big towns, rather than one of violence which the children experience every day.

Such visions of societies are a big accusing finger for adults who have built a world in which children do not like to live. Why not call all this to the attention of adults and make them search in the present for possibilities to realize the desirable societies children envisage? Why do not adults bring to the fore their decisions which should be responsible for the visions of children? Why do not adults try and save such visions so that children will be able to keep them until they too are old enough to be decision makers, but ones who are carried by visions of such societies, desirable societies rather than societies of war, of exploitation, of profit and consumption?

This I believe is future thinking. The analysis of such visions and the transformation into tools of action are the real aims of social services.

In this way the present is linked to both the past and the future; in this way there is no separation between them but a continuous flow, which derives from the vision of the future, which is in the seeds of change in the process of the history of humankind. A process that is past, present and future. In these terms there is no separation but a continuum.

The importance of visions is hence that of capturing this continuum and at the same time of building an antithesis to the present, which people like women and children reject. The thesis-antithesis dialectics brings about change and a different future. Hence this double function

111

of visions must be stressed, builders of change bringing about change and at the same time understanding of the continuum of the process of humankind's history, which is a flow. This brings about a different future.

In these terms we can speak of a diverse and different future of social science research – a research geared to change and action, or rather a research geared to innovation rather than to maintenance. In this, I believe, Johan Galtung believes.

Human Life as 'An Art' and as 'A Craft' and the Role of Social Sciences

ANDRZEJ SICINSKI

I should like to approach here the problems of science and its functions – a constant subject of reflection accompanying any scientific activity – using a certain analogy, namely, the analogy between *creative* activity in all spheres of life (individual, as well as societal) and a *reproduction* of existing established patterns, on the one hand; and between *art* and *craft,* on the other. In fact, the basic difference between the latter two can be reduced to the distinction between the creation of new values, important rules, or forms, and a more or less accurate application of known rules, i.e., the multiplication of accepted schemes.

In the field of art the illegitimacy of an expectation that a theoretician or critic can provide artists with reliable recipes for particularly valuable, outstanding, works has, by and large, been acknowledged; even less could the theoreticians and critics be expected to create such works by themselves. Their role is different; it consists in making a critical analysis and drawing theoretical conclusions concerning the existing pieces of work. The theory of art interprets what has been created, and that is no mean feat; but it can do nothing more, particularly not provide a collection of rules and prescriptions for the creation of new artistic values.

The same is true, in my opinion, for all other spheres of human creativity, including individual and collective creation in the field of shaping societal and personal life. Human creativity consisting in designing fundamental changes in social organization, in the division of labour, in the distribution and functioning of power, in constructing legal systems, or principles of distribution of goods, privileges, etc., does not, and can not, result directly from scientific knowledge. Also, scientific knowledge does not provide any satisfactory basis for shaping our life-style or our relations with other people. Science, and I mean here first of all social and humanistic disciplines, can undoubtedly be instrumental in such creativity by analysing and generalizing past experiences; however, to the extent to which human actions are really of a creative character, it would be unreasonable to expect science to provide recipes for that creativity. So vain are the claims and hopes raised from time to time in this respect. The art of living, òur individual

113

or societal life, is not reducible to a series of effective technological operations connected with our functioning in the reality of the empirical world. It also comprises our relation to metaphysical problems of human existence, in particular those connected with a quest for the meaning of the world.

The scientist, however, may be, and very often is, a very successful adviser or expert on such sorts of human activity as consist in the reproduction or improvement of certain existing patterns, or which are an extension of experiences gained in one domain or situation to others, etc. So, going back to the proposed analogy, the scientist can put forward recommendations and suggestions or instructions dealing with what is 'craft' in our life activity. And that is no small part: the 'craft' activity probably consumes much more of the time and energy of people and societies than the really 'creative' activity, the 'art', does. So, social policy that aims at the improvement of an existing social system can, and should, take as full advantage as possible of the resources of science. As an example we may mention those domains where scientific reflection and research have been particularly useful: work, education, administration, etc.

Our discussion leads to the following conclusions:

i) Aristotelian 'utility', i.e., a practical efficacy, is undoubtedly an important function of science, particularly in social sciences, as far as a vast area of human activity of a 'craft' character is concerned. For example, technological achievements, for many decades a source of pride of the Euro-American civilization, have obviously been due to an intensive development of science.

(ii) It would also be difficult to overstimate that function of science which, again in terms of the Aristotelian distinction, consists in an enrichment of human 'wisdom', i.e., in satisfying our curiosity, in developing our understanding of the world and of ourselves. First, it plays an important role in relation to the way we make use of the 'utilitarian' function of science. It is clear nowadays that it has not always been in our best interest, in the interest of our societies, or of our species. Hence, a contemporary disillusionment with the achievements of technology.

Second, science, through its critical analysis of people's actions, their forms and results, systematizes previous experiences of individuals and of societies, and, in particular, it makes us aware of unsuccessful solutions (one could say, it falsifies them). In this way science helps to shape our social imagination; it makes us aware of the scope of our freedom, and of the limitations of our decisions; it makes us sensitive to by-products, unintended consequences of some ideas, solutions, or actions; therefore, it makes it possible to work out some strategies of development.

(iii) However, to the extent to which our life is a form of creativity, or 'an art', it extends beyond suggestions and recipes originating in science: particularly when axiological problems of individual or societal life are concerned, when decisions not on strategies but on goals are involved. (Of course, this does not mean we are questioning here the scientist's right to, or, in same circumstances, even responsibility to participate in the process of formulating such goals.)

I believe, it would be an illusion, sometimes even a dangerous one, to advocate an opposite point of view.

Justification of Social Science

HÅKAN WIBERG

It is a courageous as well as a demanding thing to ask anybody what is the purpose of social science research, with what arguments he justifies the present direction of his work and, in short, why he is engaged in social science at all. And it is both, because any interesting reply will have to strike a balance between different modes of interpretation, avoiding likewise introspective psychologizing and proclamations so general that it is difficult to see what concrete implications they would have for any research enterprise.

One first and obvious thing to do is to question the questions, by asking how it comes about that social scientists seem so much more preoccupied with them than, e.g., humanists or natural scientists. Part of the answer might be found in a collective status anxiety. After all, other branches of learning have had so much longer in which to trim the arguments in their self-justifications and get them accepted by a wider public, whether phrased in instrumental terms or in terms of knowledge as a cultural and psychological value. Moreover, whereas few outsiders would imagine that they understand Greek philology, quantum mechanics or biochemistry without having devoted a long and arduous study to the field, this is not so with much of social science. Here, the researchers have had to convince politicians and others that there is more to social phenomena than meets the eye of the ordinary citizen, who may often have the attitude that 'an expert is somebody who arrives to find out, and departs before he is found out'. Nor have cascades of elaborated terminology always been very successful as camouflage, since in some cases it has been revealed as a way of saying trivial things in an oracular way, and in any case there are many sceptical onlookers who have in mind Einstein's quip that 'you have really understood a theory when you can go out and explain it to the man in the street'.

So the problem of self-justification is certainly there, and very broadly speaking, one may discern two main tacks that have been tried: knowledge and understanding as a value in itself, and the promise of instrumentality. The case for the social scientist is more difficult than the others, whatever tack is chosen – and they are also more difficult to reconcile with each other. The more humanistically oriented social scientist will find that whereas students of Lydian coinage or other galaxies may be accused of sitting in ivory towers in respect of their choice of topics, that accusation is rarely coupled with a request that the students *do* something about them, while he himself may become the target of both criticisms. The social scientist who tries to emulate natural science both in methods and in claiming instrumentality, whether in the service of social reforms or revolutionary class struggle, will often find that control of man tends to be regarded as a more questionable achievement then control over nature, and that in an era of receding optimism about the future he is just as suspect as physical scientists of creating a Leviathan that threatens to devour us all.

I would say that any good (in terms of argument) and successful (in terms of reception) justification of social science will have to reconcile the two lines of argument, whatever significant role the social scientist attempts to lay claim to. Yet it is only in Utopia that this reconciliation is comparatively easy; for there we find not only consensus, but also a 'true' consensus, in the sense that it is based on common interests rather than on successful exertion of power. Hence, the promised instrumentality of social science consists in coordination, in which everybody has an interest, rather than in control, which some have an interest in establishing and others in undermining.

For the social scientists of various observances who manage to believe that the particular society they live in approaches Utopia (in this sense), there is then no great problem in combining the lines of argument and donning the white mantle of the experts. For the rest of us, seeing fundamental differences of interest in all present societies (although not necessarily the same ones), the only non-controversial way of doing that is to retreat from instrumentality into a scientistic position – or to gladly accept and even strive to be controversial by taking sides between the interests, whether in terms of defining our research as being in the service of some value and/or of some social category or actor.

To say 'and/or' is easy; but this logical conjunction covers a very concrete dilemma, as many practitioners have discovered. One horn of the dilemma is illustrated by the value-committed social scientist without a constituency; and the other by him who hands over the responsibility of defining worthwhile research issues to some social actor under increasing doubts as to whether the choices made make sense from the point of view of the values incurred.

And to continue the creation of ideal types, the perfect committed social scientist must have achieved perfection in at least two ways: on the one hand, he must be such an accomplished social analyst that he is certain that he has correctly identified the most important cleavages of interest, and on the other hand he must command such an expertise in *Wissenssoziologie* that he can confidently assert what knowledge will in reality serve which values or interests.

In the world we live in, matters are of course not so simple, nor demands so absolute. Institutional loyalties will have to be conditional, and a matter of more or less complicated judgment. Identification of interests will have to abandon claims to 'objectivity', rely on value premises, and anyhow be preliminary, approximative, and open to revision. The attainment of perfect knowledge will be seen as a hindrance to, rather than a necessary precondition for, research and other forms of social action.

Yet it should be underlined that the epistemological problem does define a problem, or ought to define it. For if we remember the classical 'definition' of social science as the study of unanticipated consequences of purposive social action, there is no intrinsic reason why research activity should be an exception. *Defining* the search for knowledge as being value-oriented is no guarantee that the knowledge, once attained, will have that effect. The findings from the framework of rank disequilibrium theory may be useful in the process of social mobilization – but perhaps just as useful in attempts to avoid social change by preventing the creation of potentially rebellious groups, by coopting them or by controlling them (one might wish that governments in South Africa had known less). Findings about mechanisms of penetration can be used to reveal and delegitimize them – but conceivably also to bring them to increasing perfection.

The lover of paradoxes might even add that in order to be able to predict the consequences of a specific search for knowledge we will have to be able to predict with certainty the results of the search – in which case the search would be superfluous.

Yet again it makes little sense to ask for perfect knowledge when all we can get is more or less well-founded intuitions, and where they are often sufficient to serve as a basis for decision. So let us try to sketch some rules of thumb, rather than arguing a case of paralysing scepticism.

To the extent that there exist crystallized social actors around the interests or values to which one has committed oneself, their expressed demands for research may be a good indication of what is worthwhile, even if the social scientist may in some cases think (and sometimes have good reasons for thinking) that he knows better how to define the problems in research terms. The problem, of course, becomes more complicated when there is more than one social actor purporting to be on the same side as the researcher, and where they have conflicting opinions. Again, he must use his own judgment.

Likewise, to the extent that the powers that be make efforts to

118

prevent or hinder some types of research, that may also be a good indicator. Again, it is not infallible. When the production of statistics on the mother tongue in Belgium or religion in Lebanon has been suppressed for a long time, that does not necessarily mean that it would serve the interests of peace, negative or positive. On the contrary, it might serve to reinforce the ethnic definitions of conflict and thereby stalemate further social change tied to other and more fundamental conflict dimensions.

In some cases, the existing distribution of knowledge or pre-knowledge may give important hints. When knowledge might, at least in principle, be used to serve opposite purposes, but the topdog has, or appears to have, it already, then one may generally assume that the underdog is better served by getting access to it, too. In this sense, spying will be a legitimate enterprise for the social scientist; one might also put it in terms of reversing the traditional direction of the social scientist's common activity of spying downwards on behalf of the topdog. Secrecy must generally be assumed to be suspicious, whatever official arguments are given for it – which, again, does not mean that we have an ironclad rule that relieves the researcher from using his judgment.

The content of the knowledge sought will often in itself indicate the effects of finding it. We may safely assume that many kinds of mechanisms for exertion and preservation of power operate more efficiently when their nature and perhaps even existence are unknown to both sides, or at least to those that are ruled. Likewise, different forms of exploitation may also be taken to suffer from closer scrutiny. And, again, this does not mean a case for suspension of judgment: increased knowledge can conceivably lead to paralysis just as well as to mobilization, at least as long as knowledge about the resources of the topdog is not supplemented by finding out more about the latent power bases of the underdog.

So much about general principles. What are their implications for research orientation, and in particular, how would I justify my own? How much is left of any general tendencies, when a number of accidental impulses, studies for specific conferences, anthologies, etc. have been subtracted? It is not so easy to see, especially if one wants to avoid giving an exaggerated impression of a rational process, but some trends might perhaps be discerned.

First, a gradual movement from more basic to more applied research. Here, the dilemma might be spelled out thus: if there is too much emphasis on basic research, at least in a value-oriented area like peace research, then the risk is that there is no one left to apply it, and that in the end it proves to be research for its own sake. And if too much emphasis is given to applied research, then it ultimately may risk becoming starved of the fertilization for which basic research is crucial. The former risk appears to be the greater one, and hence it becomes necessary for the social scientist to devote some energy to spelling out the implications of his findings, rather than trusting that somebody else will do it.

Second, a gradual movement from highly actor-oriented research, whether game theory or opinion studies, towards more structure-oriented, e.g. studying arms races, world trade, etc. – and then a growing insight that the two types should be synthesized rather than opposed: in order to find 'deeper' textures in a confusing stream of events, actor-oriented research will have to combine itself with structure-oriented – and in order to have any practical implications, results from the latter must somehow be translated back into the former, in order to avoid some new form of scholasticism.

Third, a movement away from theorizing before research in order to conform to traditional criteria of hypothesis-testing, and towards doing more of the theorizing in the course of research. One argument for this may be that it seems more reasonable that the research matter should determine what theorizing is relevant than vice versa. The dilemma might be formulated as one between rigorous testability and relevance.

How sure must the researcher be of what he is saying in order to allow implications to be drawn, by others or by himself. If the criterion is set too low, he ceases to be a researcher and becomes just another opinionator; and if it is set too high, he will be doomed to political impotence by forbidding himself to say anything at all.

This dilemma also occurs in the fourth development, from fairly limited pieces of research, attempting to piece together a few variables of rather similar type, to attempts at finding patterns in the interplay between several different types of social phenomena, usually treated by specialists of different kinds – or not treated at all. The obvious risk here is amateurism and superficiality – but some of that risk will have to be taken in attempts to get broad perspectives. Still, there seems to be some arguments for the view that interdisciplinarity tends to become undisciplined. But then, this should also be modified, since what the criticism often means is that it does not conform to the established criteria in the traditional specialized disciplines, and this is not necessarily something to be afraid of. When the accusation goes on to add that few new criteria have been developed either, it becomes more serious indeed, and has to a considerable degree to be granted, even if criteria in this context do not necessarily mean entirely codified and explicit criteria – after all, very few disciplines have that, when we go beyond mechanical rules for testing hypotheses and checking logical consistency.

Here, as in so many other of the dilemmas and choices mentioned above, it is not possible to formulate any hard and fast rules, whose application allows us to suspend our judgment and discretion – nor does that mean that it is not important to search for preliminary and tentative rules, or to exercise a stern and suspicious control over that judgment as long as nobody has presented solid proof to the effect that social scientists are less susceptible to the Baconian idols than others.

Reopening of the Cold War and the Crisis of the World Order

HIROHARU SEKI

On 21 January 1980 President Carter announced in his State of the Union message to Congress a policy giving priority solely to the selfish security interests of the United States. This was a far cry from the type of policy desired by the non-aligned states that had supported the US in its call for the immediate withdrawal of foreign troops from Afghanistan a week earlier in the United Nations. By turning the Soviet invasion of Afghanistan to his own advantage, Carter began to revamp the old US alliance network by taking the path of military expansion. The US attempt to take a firm stand against the USSR under the banner of the 'Carter Doctrine' may produce fear in the Third World of again being exposed to a military threat from the US. In fact Iran, which supported the US in the UN General Assembly, is growing more hostile to the US – despite the overtures being made to the post-revolutionary government – because it suspects the US may be using the invasion of Afghanistan as a pretext for joining hands with pro-American governments in Israel, Egypt and Saudi Arabia in order to regain the control of the Persian Gulf region it lost after the collapse of Shah Pahlavi's regime.[1]

The most salient feature of the Carter Doctrine as seen in the State of the Union address is that the location of Soviet troops within striking distance of the Indian Ocean and the Persian Gulf is one of the gravest threats ever faced by the US. In short, the Soviet intervention in Afghanistan does not simply expose Pakistan and Iran to Soviet political threats; it also leads to possible Soviet control of an area of vital strategic interest to the Western world, the Far East, and ultimately to the very existence of the US. Carter has firmly pronounced that the US should boost military power and adopt a posture of military confrontation with the USSR by stepping-up aid to Pakistan and other peripheral countries. As pointed out in the 21 January issue of *Newsweek*, this was the start of a second Cold War.

This issue of *Newsweek* even goes so far as to suggest that the conditions presently faced by Carter are the same as those faced by Truman at the outset of the Cold War in the late 1940s. Likewise, in the 28 January issue of *Time*, American international relations specialists characterize the Afghan problem as marking a 'crossroad', 'watershed', or 'turning point' in US-USSR relations. Such expressions as these were quoted by *Time* in a policy of strong support for the Carter Administration's new measures for arms build-up and its tough stand against the USSR. The quotes were used to objectively emphasize that the Soviet invasion of Afghanistan had heightened international tension to the most serious level in the post-Vietnam era or even before. Nevertheless, the Soviet invasion of Afghanistan in and of itself is hardly enough to create a crisis in US-USSR relations – it is only when the US response to Soviet action sets in motion an escalation in action-reaction that the danger of nuclear war arises. In this sense, 'crossroad', 'turning point', 'watershed' and so forth were being trotted out as symbolic expressions of legitimization for the US decision to reopen the Cold War. It will moreover become clearer as time passes that, in comparison to other countries, the US overreacted to the USSR's invasion of Afghanistan. If this does not become clear, then the lessons of the absurd history of the first Cold War will have borne absolutely no fruit. Although excellent researches on the origins of the Cold War point to and criticize the overreaction of the US at the time, the same kind of overreaction has again occurred. Even Japanese weekly magazines have published articles on the possible outbreak of World War III.[2]

The problem with the discussions of World War III in Japanese magazines, however, is that any analyses that are carried out of the actual historical and societal factors leading up to World War III demonstrate absolutely no interest in the destructive consequences of the nuclear war resulting. Such types of discussions can blunt a critical perspective on the reopening of the Cold War. It is at the point where international and domestic politics meet that the possibility of choice for the future exists: scenarios that gloss over this possibility share characteristics in common with war game scenarios modeled on the process of war. In war games, for example, a predetermined course calling for military action is set as though the rules cannot be altered and an 'evil logic' of geopolitical imperative is similarly regarded as being unalterable. An attempt was made to inculcate in Japanese politicians who participated in the exchange program with US politicians under the auspices of the Japan-US International Exchange Center, an ideology supportive of this logic. The US participants in the program sought Japanese cooperation in line with their expectation that World War III may possibly erupt in the event of a stand-off between the US and USSR in Iran or Pakistan. Japan cannot possibly cooperate in regard to these stupid demands if we take into consideration Japan's own national interest. The program ought to have been used to make this plain to the US. In any event, along with the overreaction of the US to the Soviet invasion is this concomitant attempt to inculcate in the people of other countries an ideology supportive of the reopening of the Cold War.

Of course, in defense of Carter it can be said that he did not go so far as to announce in the State of the Union message the complete abandonment of detente, as had been feared by the Western Allies. This is because Carter considered SALT II to be of benefit to US security interests. Still, the logic of the Cold War is clearly given precedence over the logic of peaceful coexistence. Even though the Western Allies were thereby relieved, the danger of the US alone following the logic of the Cold War still remains.

The reason for this can be found in the fact that a cold war type of hawk ideology has already gained ground in the Western Camp, and a 'death march' has started-off in the direction of strengthening the cold war content of the Carter Doctrine. In some cases, the ideology is not unfolding systematically as a theory of power politics or a strategic theory, but simply as criticism of the US's potential enemy. What can be seen here is the net result of a self-fulfilling prophecy that strengthens the hawk's logic. It is only in the process of building up a belief in the prophecy that a nuclear war can occur. In any event, what is of particular concern is that Kissinger's concept of power balancing is being revived and is permeating the Carter Administrations foreign policy.

Originally, Kissinger's diplomacy aimed to set up a tri-polar relationship between the US, China and the USSR in line with the necessity to supplement the relative decline in US power, and to break away from the former ideologically based bi-polar diplomacy. In this way the US enlisted the support of China, a 'half-power', and expected to be able to gain a position of superiority vis-à-vis the USSR by playing this 'China card' and gaining the voluntary backing of Japan and the EC. Nixon referred to this tripolar international order favoring the US as a floating 'peace structure'. However, this 'peace structure' only had a peaceful character for one or two years, from the time of the US's defeat in Vietnam, to the period of detente between the US and USSR topped by the July 1975 Helsinki meeting. This was linked to the attempt under the Nixon Doctrine to stop to some extent the global deployment of US military force.

Even under the Nixon Doctrine, however, Kissinger's diplomacy did not relinquish the pursuit of US supremacy in this tri-polar structure. It was simply that immediately after the end of the Vietnam War the US concentrated its efforts on pursuing those objectives that seemed indirectly or easily attainable either through building up arms sales to Iran and Saudi Arabia or by improving relations with Japan and the EC. This is why the US's pursuit of supremacy did not clearly surface. Kissinger continued to advance into what were considered 'grey areas' in the SALT negotiations in a way that did not make the US stand out more than the USSR. The US's giving way to the USSR in Angola illustrates this point.

President Carter initially stirred-up the domestic political environment surrounding Kissinger's diplomacy, broke away from this kind of diplomacy, and attempted to develop a new world order diplomacy. In his May 1977 speech at Notre Dame University Carter emphasized that the US had at last become free from the abonormal fear of communism, and expressed strong faith in detente. Against the background of detente Carter attempted to make human rights diplomacy the basis of his foreign policy. However, diplomacy aimed at building a new peace order did not last long. This is because the hawk Brzezinski gradually consolidated a position of power within the Carter Administration. In the background to the ascendency of Brzezinski is the strong opposition to Carter's initial championing of disarmament and human rights diplomacy expressed by periphery countries the US had militarized. In the first place, through the establishment of a linkage system between hawks in the peripheral countries and traditional hawks in the US, efforts began to be made to try and roll back Carter's policy. These efforts were carried out surreptitiously at first, but before long a grouping similar to a global hawk coalition was informally set-up in allied countries. Through an increase in contact between these hawks pressure was exerted to try and amend the Carter diplomacy; in the process, however, a warning was served to the hawks in the USSR, this in turn strengthening hawkish logic. As a consequence, hawks within the USSR were able to increase their political power. The above can be chronologically described as follows.

In the first place, along with the progress in reconciliation between Israel and Egypt, the power of the US in the area, which had been built-up in the post-Vietnam era along Kissinger's line of providing military aid to Iran and Saudi Arabia, began to weaken. The reason for this can be found in the fact that, by ignoring the Palestine problem, the partial peace between Egypt and Israel created a new bi-polarity in the Middle East.

In February 1979, US power, which had supported the Pahlavi Regime and infiltrated the Iranian domestic order, was suddenly overturned when the Shi'ite Muslims took over control of Iran. In this can be seen the failure of modernization aimed at making Iran a military big power and the existence of increasing, domestic economic disparities. What cannot be ignored, moreover, is that the PLO forged links with Iran after the Iranian Revolution took place. Furthermore, in early 1978 President Carter visited Teheran and met with the Shah, followed by the visit of China's Hua Kwo-fêng in August and Japan's Fukuda in

September. We can see from this that in 1978 an attempt was indirectly underway to form a coalition between the US, Japan and China in order to prop up the Pahlavi Regime as the policeman of the Middle East. Until the end, Iran under the Shah was simply a strategic pawn of the US. During the visit of Prime Minister Fukuda to Teheran large scale mass demonstrations against the Shah erupted and the collapse of the system became imminent. Since the Sino-Japanese Peace and Friendship Treaty was signed in August 1978, the attempt of Japan, the US and China to prop up the Pahlavi Regime shaped the conditions for the normalization of relations between the US and China as the Iranian situation became more critical. Again, after the signing of the Sino-Japanese Treaty a similar treaty was signed in November between the USSR and Vietnam. Through the treaty's opposition to the establishment of normal relations with China it was linked to the real confrontation between the US and USSR. At the final stages of the decision to normalize relations with China both the US and the USSR warned against interference in Iran's domestic affairs; and in the end, the US had to withdraw from Iran during the last hours of the Pahlavi Regime. This was a major shock for the US.

The US-Chinese link-up on the level of diplomatic relations has also been accompanied by talk of establishing a military alliance between the two countries. Along these lines Brzezinski opposed the SALT-II Agreement pushed by Secretary of State Vance, who is backed by Marshal Schulman, a dove in respect of the USSR. Agreement was at any rate reached on SALT II in May 1979; however, since the Vance policy line only plays second fiddle to the Brzezinski line, the domestic ratification of the SALT Treaty will not be easy. The signing of the Sino-Japanese Peace and Friendship Treaty in 1978 and the normalization of relations between the US and China produced fear in the USSR of being encircled by an anti-Soviet combine made-up of the US, China and Japan. The final attempt at a relaxation of tension was made by the USSR when it offered to limit the deployment of the SS-20 in exchange for the halting of the West's modernization of nuclear weapons, but the plan aborted due to the refusal of the West.

The Hawk Coalition

Glancing over these events we can only discover developments in inter-governmental diplomatic relations showing the dynamic transformation of international politics. In the background to these developments, however, is the existence of a hawk coalition that had already been spreading an ideology supportive of an increase in international tension. Even in the USSR, this resulted in attention simply being focussed on the causes for the increase in international tension

126

lying behind the development of diplomatic relations. In short, by a kind of self-fulfilling action-reaction linkage the hawks in the US and USSR mutually supported each other.

For instance, Western military analysts and their political ideologues criticised Finlandization and stepped up activities in order to draw together an anti-Soviet hawk coalition. They forged a link with the tough stand taken by China against the USSR, and the influence from this extended to the anti-Soviet hawks in Japan. The military alliance-building measures between the US and China were born out of this kind of environment. In the USSR, in contrast, no hawkish pronouncements surfaced; in fact, only dove activities surfaced in 1979, such as the preparations for the Olympics or the holding of the 12th Congress of International Political Science Association in Moscow.

It is certainly true that in the moves for the normalization of relations between the US and China the domestic dove groups in favor of economic cooperation with China were juxtaposed with militarily oriented hawk groups favoring a strategy against the USSR. However, conditions developed for the easy acceptance by the USSR of the latter's actions and ideologies. This cannot be denied. In short, the despatch and receipt of information is carried out by hawks who are strategically opposed to one another. The process of the hawks increasing political power on the home front in the midst of new developments in international relations progresses somewhat separately from other international relations. Ironically, the hawks in the US and USSR have cooperated in boosting each other's power within their respective countries. For instance, in the Carter Administration the power of Brzezinski has increased vis-à-vis that of Vance. The same situation also developed in the USSR in the sense that the hawk-oriented group like Gromyko and Andropov increased their power more than the dove-oriented group like Chernenko and Romanov.

The myth that policy decisions in the US are in Carter's hands or that in the USSR they are in Brezhnev's hands has, in a sense, been nothing more than a cover-up for the true nature of recent developments in US-USSR relations. The problem is that the political situations in allied and peripheral countries are connected to the unfolding of US-USSR relations. The global hawk coalition's strategically hostile logic on the ideological plane is penetrating into allied countries and peripheral countries.

This has the potential to undermine the logic concerned with the problems of demilitarization and development on a global scale, because of the holding power of the logic of traditional international politics in the background.

For instance, the Nobel Peace Prize winner, Andrei Sakharov, was stripped of all Soviet honors. This was the USSR's response to the reopening of the Cold War by the US. In this sense, the suppression of Sakharov can be said to be the result of the joint pressure of the global hawk coalition, which began pushing the world toward the reopening of the Cold War. It was Sakharov who emphasized in a message to the 25th Pugwash Conference in Kyoto (he was personally unable to attend) the necessity of announcing the non-use of nuclear weapons in order to bring about disarmament. His stand was surely different from that of the official Soviet line. Those who are protesting to the Soviet authorities about the problem of Sakharov's human rights should emphasize the fact that Sakharov called for the non-use of nuclear weapons and take a clear stand in opposition to the reopening of the Cold War. A dramatic shift has occurred in the Carter Doctrine in response to the Sakharov incident; that is, the Carter Administration has suggested reinstating the draft, abolished by the Nixon Administration in 1973.

This is clearly linked to the Carter Administration's recognition of the build-up in Soviet strategic power, fully reappraised as a result of the Soviet intervention in Afghanistan. It is not to be denied that this includes an awareness of the Soviet Navy's advance into the Pacific Ocean, Indian Ocean and Persian Gulf. At the same time, however, the Soviet Union's recognition of being encircled by the US, China and Japan and the US's recognition of a build-up in the strategic position of the USSR can be located in one stage of a positive feed-back loop. The common sense of purpose held by members of the global hawk coalition is being strengthened in the development process of this feed-back loop. However, we are now entering an era when new politics on a global scale should possess the power to go beyond a sense of purpose centering on military strategy. Of course, the old type of politics has the opposite effect of strengthening the possibility of a new Cold War. This is represented, for instance, by the political immaturity in the logic of political change in peripheral regions which have embroiled the US and USSR and in political ideas centering on security guarantees.

In fact, the reopening of the Cold War between the US and USSR has its origins in the interference of these powers in nascent political change in peripheral regions. The ensuing hegemonic struggle created the opportunity to promote a major change in the classic balance of power policy. In the background to the reopening of the Cold War is the influence arising from combining the application of a Kissinger type classic balance of power policy to relationships between the US, China and USSR with the existence of a wide 'grey region' as a result of the delay in the SALT negotiations. The intervention of the US and USSR in various conflicts developing in peripheral regions is clearly a result of the combination of both these factors. In addition, in the world of the 1980s, the result of progress in developmental politics on a global scale will tend to produce new conflicts in the peripheral regions. The same prediction is made in this respect by Westerners and Third World Marxist scholars like Samir Amin. Along with the successive outbreak of new conflicts in the peripheral regions is the danger of a vicious feed-back loop worsening the Cold War situation.

The USSR came under fire in the UN for its intervention in Afghanistan. Even non-aligned countries that had usually supported the USSR voted in favor of the motion calling for the withdrawal of foreign troops from Afghanistan. In the Islamic Foreign Ministers Conference in Islamabad, Pakistan, moreover, it is said discussions took place on applying economic sanctions against the USSR. Nonetheless, the Carter Administration is not learning anything from the drift of non-aligned conferences such as this. The Carter Administration continued to investigate the possibility of employing military force against Iran – albeit never realized – even before the Soviet intervention in Afghanistan. Since all-out use of force was impossible given prevalent political conditions, the Administration continued to hint at the possibility of limited military action against Iran. In the end, however, the Carter Administration continued to talk of the possible use of force, but did not use it; on the other hand, the USSR never even mentioned the use of military force, but invaded Afghanistan like a flash, taking the offensive over the US. The strategic interaction between the US and USSR in their struggle to take the first initiative can be clearly seen on the dimension of the hawks' strategic logic.

In this regard, it is first necessary to compare the different political conditions faced by the US in Iran and the USSR in Afghanistan; next, it is necessary to examine in what way Iran and Afghanistan were connected, and finally to examine how the confrontation between the US and USSR developed in regard to the relationship between Iran and Afghanistan.

In Iran, the 1978 anti-Shah demonstrations were on a nation-wide scale and centered on the Shi'ite Muslims. The demonstrations were neither isolated nor dispersed; rather, they developed as typical broad-based demonstrations involving lower class and middle class Iranians, irrespective of any distinction. The Pahlavi Regime was thus forced to face the largest mass demonstration in the post-colonial period. In the end, the Regime collapsed, bringing with it the collapse of an outpost of US political power that had been of central strategic importance. The energy produced by the Iranian Revolution became the high mark of the non-aligned movement. And this created the world conditions making the military intervention of the US in Iran almost impossible. Still, it seems Kissinger was seeking an opportunity to reinstall Pahlavi even after he was forced to flee Iran in February 1979.

This was nothing more than an out-dated tactic to try and oppose the strength of the non-aligned movement. It was Kissinger, too, who was behind the policy of allowing the Shah into the US. It is still not clear why he did this; in any event, it kindled the hate of the Iranian masses who toppled the Shah. This is a historical fact. So long as the fear of the CIA again planning to reinstate the Shah is alive, the possibility of this hate exploding cannot be discounted.

Kissinger's ideas, which had infiltrated the Carter Administration, were challenged in this way. The flippant way in which the US treats the history of other countries was clearly shown by the US's attitude towards granting an entry permit to the Shah. At the same time, this marked the collapse of the peace structure and the concept of an international order centering on the superpowers, both of which Kissinger had championed. The use of military force hinted at by the US proved to be impossible. In short, the mass movement in Iran can be said to have contained enough hate to be able to make the military option untenable.

The Structure of the Afghanistan Crisis

The political situation in Afghanistan was quite different to that in Iran, although the Islamic ideals that had spurred on the Iranian Revolution had some impact on developments in Afghanistan. Most Iranians are Shi'ite Muslims, whereas Afghans are Sunnis Muslims. Moreover, leaving aside the problem of increasing disparities in Iran, the per capita GNP in 1975 had already reached $152, whereas in 1978 Afghanistan's GNP was only $89, indicating the tremendous difference in the level of industrialization in the two countries. Afghanistan also belongs to the LLDC group and was severely affected by the oil crisis.[3] Clearly, Afghanistan was far less politically developed than Iran.

President Daüd came to power in Afghanistan in July 1973 in a republican revolution which abolished the monarchy. This revolution had the character of a palace revolt and was a long way from being based on mass support. The coup d'état of April 1978 can be considered the first time the people gained power, but thereafter the Taraki government swung back and forth due to factional rivalries between the rather weakly based Khalf (people's faction) and Parsham (red flag faction). The former faction could not preserve unity and its internal conflict resulted in divisions. Taraki, who was himself a member of this faction, lost power and was killed in a military clash with Amin, who also belonged to the same faction. It was in this way that Amin came to power.

The Amin government gradually narrowed its base of power. The land reform started under the Taraki government had already met with

130

strong opposition from old tribal land owners and religious leaders represented by clergy. The Taraki government had feared that this kind of opposition might be reinforced by guerilla action by foreign powers through Pakistan. It was because of such fears that the Taraki government entered into a Treaty of Friendship, Good-Neighborliness and Cooperation with the USSR in December, 1978 and sought military cooperation. Article 4 of the Treaty, stating that on discussion and mutual agreement appropriate measures will be taken to ensure the independence and territorial integrity of Afghanistan, in fact contravenes the nominal position of Afghanistan as a member of the non-aligned group. Through this treaty the Taraki government opened the way for agreement on the despatch of Soviet troops to Afghanistan in certain cases. Afghanistan thus became similar to other non-aligned nations that already had cooperative military arrangements with the US; in other words, while nominally speaking these countries may belong to the non-aligned group, in fact they are not non-aligned. In the case of Afghanistan, it was the Taraki government that put Afghanistan in this treaty relationship with the USSR. Moreover, approximately five thousand military advisors cooperated in the land reform in Afghanistan. The existence of military opposition to the land reform promoted a division on the policy level regarding pushing forward with the reform. This division over the land reform created severe factional in-fighting, this in turn making relations with the USSR more complicated.

In 1979 the Amin government tried to push through an even more radical land reform than the one proposed under the Taraki government. The result was the narrowing of the base of power to the point where the government faced the possibility of collapse of political power as a whole. Unlike in Iran, where the revolution was based on mass opposition to the Shah's regime, the case of Afghanistan was characterized by broad-based guerilla opposition to the land reform. The conditions which brought about a set-back in pushing forward with socialist policies in Afghanistan should be compared with the conditions which brought about a set-back in the white revolution carried out through capitalistic modernization in the Shah's Iran. What is common to both is Islamic culture and social structure, despite the differences resulting from the fact that Iran is made up largely of Shi'ite Muslims and Afghanistan, Sunnis Muslims. What is different about the movements that developed in opposition to the two governments is that the violent guerilla movement in Afghanistan was a far cry from the mass, non-violent movement in Iran. In the case of Afghanistan, therefore, a vicious cycle of violence and counter-violence was started. So long as Afghanistan maintains the Treaty of Friendship, Good-Neighborliness and Cooperation with the USSR, and this vicious cycle continues, the conditions for the despatch of Soviet troops will also continue to exist.

Afghanistan had the weakness of being non-aligned and the weakness of a political, military struggle; in contrast, Iran had the strength coming from the move towards non-alignment and the strength of mass political participation. In Afghanistan the Amin government, which the USSR originally recognized, at least to all appearances sought Soviet aid, but was nevertheless brought down by Soviet forces. This is the ironic result. If US forces had been sent to Iran on the formal request of the Pahlavi Regime, and the Shah had been brought down by these US forces, the military action of the US in Iran would have been the same as the USSR in Afghanistan. However, even when faced with the collapse of the Pahlavi Regime in 1978 and 1979, the US was unable to use military force, despite Kissinger's recommendation to the contrary.

By making the US intervention in Iran impossible, the 1979 Iranian Revolution advanced the global autonomy of Islam. The PLO's challenge to the US can be seen in this light, since the PLO is in solidarity with Islam. Such movements for mass autonomy contained the potential to push the strategic conflict between the US and USSR onto a completely different level. From the time of the peak of anti-American demonstrations in 1978 the US government was forced to recognize this and make a gradual retreat. In the end, however, Carter succumbed to Kissinger's pressure. The occupation of the US Embassy and the taking of hostages by radical students in November 1979 was the direct response of the Iranian people to the fact that the Carter Administration succumbed to Kissinger's pressure.

This proved to be the second occasion on which the US was thrust into a situation of all-out confrontation with Iran. It was the second time the US had investigated using military force against Iran. Quite clearly, the toughening of Carter's policy toward Iran was against the background of the forthcoming presidential election, although it is not certain to what extent it was aimed at the presidential election and to what extent it was rooted in a unified US policy. So long as the US's tough stand against Iran includes the possibility of US troops occupying Persian Gulf oil fields, then the US's foreign influence may exceed its own expectations.

The US's response to the Soviet invasion of Afghanistan was clearly an overreaction. The problem is, however, that the US lost Iran without being able to employ military might. This was not because of a Soviet invasion, but because of dissolution within the Western camp. Through military invasion, the USSR was able to avoid losing Afghanistan; in contrast, the US was not able to avoid losing Iran. In this sense, it is only the truly non-aligned countries that have a legitimate base from which to raise objections and criticisms of the Soviet invasion of Afghanistan. The US attempted to carry out economic sanctions against Iran as military sanctions were impossible. Yet with the sudden invasion of Afghanistan by the USSR, the US was forestalled, and gradually relaxed sanctions against Iran and shifted them to the USSR.

What was the significance of the US sanctions against Iran? Certainly Iran was the political enemy of the US, but the USSR was the strategic enemy; hence, the explanation that the US switched from Iran to the US's main enemy, the USSR, is plausible. But if this is so, then what has been learned from an East-West conflict, going back over 35 years, from which we were just graduating into an era of detente? Now is the time when we should be searching for a solution to the North-South problem; instead, an attempt is now underway to reverse detente and bring back a 1950s mode of East-West conflict. This is nothing other than stupidity. It is perfectly clear that without successful detente between East and West the North-South problem is impossible to solve. In the 14 January 1980 issue of *Time* Brzezinski spoke of a second cold war from a geopolitical, classic power political point of view. In the article, Brzezinski mentioned areas of 'an arc of crisis' for the geopolitical encroachment of the USSR, furthermore emphasizing that the expansion of Soviet influence to an area previously outside the Soviet sphere was one aspect of the USSR's desire for control of this arc. Brzezinski concludes that this is a direct threat to the security of countries in the region – Pakistan and Iran – which are of vital US interest.

It is clear from the above that major contradictions exist in respect of the security policy pursued by the Carter Administration in the Middle East. Formally the US follows the principle of only intervening in a country that has been attacked on the request of that country's government. The US has started negotiations on the possible use of bases in Kenya, Somalia, Oman, Saudi Arabia, Egypt, Israel and Turkey. In the case of Saudi Arabia, however, the government is opposing the use of bases by the US. Even so, the US is adopting a posture of being prepared to intervene in Persian Gulf countries in order to secure a stable supply of oil. Compared to the Truman Doctrine this posture is even more dangerous.

First, the security network constructed under the Truman Doctrine, although starting from the danger in Greece and Turkey, was actually centered on Europe. The central focus of the Doctrine was the creation of the Marshall Plan and the formation of the North Atlantic Treaty Organization. In the Europe of the late 1940s this was certainly possible; however, the Carter Administration faces a completely different set of circumstances. The Middle Eastern countries follow the principle of non-alignment and express strong opposition to control by either of the two superpowers. A security policy which envisages the possibility of setting-up US military bases against Middle Eastern Islamic states or the possibility of military occupation by the US may be regarded as a US attempt to regain the territory it lost on the pretext of a Soviet threat.

Second, at the time of the Truman Doctrine, the conflict with the USSR took place in the context of a bi-polar structure. At the present time, however, the world is undergoing multipolarization. China stresses that even with a defense pact with the US, it is still necessary to oppose the major hegemonic power, i.e. the USSR. In contrast, Western Europe and Japan have opposed the attempt of the US to strengthen the Cold War structure; moreover, these countries are tending to decide on their policies towards the USSR independently. The US demanded of Japan and the European countries strong measures against Iran; however, the US itself relaxed sanctions against Iran and switched to applying sanctions against the USSR, the US's number one objective. Since 1980 is an election year, there is no telling when the US demand for sanctions against the USSR will again switch, particularly as the US's policy of reopening the Cold War is an overreaction. Brzezinski is deciding policy against the USSR along the lines of a 1950s type of Cold War ideology. By not admitting the bankruptcy of Kissinger's ideas, moreover, Brzezinski is being unrealistic. To revert to a Cold War type of ideology at a time when even Kissinger's ideas are bankrupt is nothing more than anachronistic.

Third, compared to the Truman Doctrine, the Carter Doctrine has been formulated at a time when there has been a relative decline in the power of the US. Economically, too, the role of the US is in relative eclipse. So long as this continues, an increase of what amounts to more than five per cent in defense spending (boosting expenditure on arms to over 20 per cent) will spur inflation. With aid to Pakistan and Egypt and the halt to grain exports to the USSR, the pressure imposed on the US economy will be more than anticipated. The economic situation today is completely different to that at the time of the Truman Doctrine when the economic power of the US accounted for half of world GNP. If the economic power of Japan and Europe further weaken a US economy stressing a boost in military spending, then the world economy may enter a crisis period.

Fourth, the voice of the Third World was hardly audible at the time of the Truman Doctrine; it is completely different now. If we accept that the tough stand taken by the US against the USSR is in line with the reopening of the Cold War, then the Third World, centering on the non-aligned countries, will view this as a challenge to the demands being made for the creation of a new international order. The Third World will not accept any attempt to roll-back these demands on the

134

pretext of the SU's invasion of Afghanistan. The Third World possesses the legitimate strength to setback an US attempt to reconstruct a Cold War structure inside any peripheries of the Third World.

Fifth, at the time of the Truman Doctrine the US held the monopoly on nuclear weapons. It is different now. The unlimited competition in nuclear weapons currently underway increases the danger of nuclear proliferation along with the reopening of the Cold War. The *Bulletin of the Atomic Scientist* pointed to the increasing danger of nuclear war by moving the minute hand on the nuclear clock closer to midnight. The time now stands at seven minutes before all out nuclear war, having been moved forward two minutes. It should be emphasized that the time had been at nine minutes before all out nuclear war since the Indian nuclear explosion in 1975. The need to build up awareness of the possibility of nuclear war is a major task to be carried out now and in the future.

Options for Japan

The attempt of the US to reopen the Cold War is not only a challenge to the demands for a new international order made by the Third World; it also brings closer the danger of the collapse of the old order. The reason for this lies in the fact that, through the reopening of the Cold War, the US leadership capability for strengthening an economic and military order centering on the US will continue to decline and the position of the US will be rapidly undermined. Although the reason for the decline of the US can be found in the Cold War type of military economy, the US is again boosting military expenditure. This may temporarily revive the economy, but in the long run it is bound to exert a negative influence.

The role of Japan, in contrast to the US, will rapidly expand. Given that Japan is second to the US in economic power in the Free World, the role that Japan plays should be in the context of a theory of international relations that is realistic and can fully take account of the workings of international politics. In developing such a theory it is necessary to go beyond the old mode of thinking in examining the political reality of power politics and at the same time to positively and normatively examine the reality that is not included in the framework of power politics. It is at this point where these two realities cross that the possibility exists to create a theory which goes beyond the classic type of power politics. The framework of power politics has been far too optimistic concerning the possibility of nuclear war. Strategic theoretists, because of a major defect in their method of grasping the reason for the outbreak of nuclear war, have also been too optimistic, and have in fact shut their eyes to the most important point – the actual result of a nuclear war. In any event, the strategic logic of the hawks creates mutual interaction, and it is only in the process of this interaction that the danger of a nuclear war increases in a self-fulfilling way. In analysing the process of the reopening of the Cold War this becomes perfectly clear.

What is of foremost importance in the case of Japan is that Japanese diplomacy opposes the attempt to reopen the Cold War. The Indian Ocean and the Persian Gulf belong to neither of the two superpowers. Japan's peace diplomacy should be carried out bearing this in mind; Japan should not submit to US pressure or inducements to reopen the Cold War. This is entirely different from criticizing the military action of the USSR. In short, Japan should criticize the US and the USSR in line with its own independent position.

We must next turn to what must become the base for criticism of the superpowers – Japan's economic strength. At present, mutual interdependence and interaction are increasing between countries. This is the unique feature of a multi-polar world. Moreover, the possibility of using this enormous economic strength – not for military purposes, but for building a peaceful, new order – is increasing. Furthermore, now is the time to firmly unite the principles of peace which are able to tackle the 1950s type of thinking behind the moves to reopen the Cold War with the use of economics, *per se*, as the base of economic strength. If such a union could be brought about, then a new vision of peace stretching beyond the 1980s to the 21st century can certainly be achieved. The historical development of Japan's peace economy during the past 35 years can provide mankind with an extremely valuable experience in this regard. It is as a result of Japan's past 35 years of economic growth that Japan's economic strength has been fully recognized around the world, as has Japanese technology and other factors at the base of Japanese economic power.

In Middle Eastern countries, for instance, they are rapidly pushing ahead with improving the people's life environment in city development plans undertaken in place of investment in industry. Since Japan leads the world in the development of alternate energies, energy-saving devices and the micro-computer revolution, great expectations will come to be held about Japanese technology. In contrast to the US and USSR, Japan has not concentrated capital investment in military technology. As a result, Japan was able to develop technology for the improvement of the people's life and environment. A mood is building up in the Middle East to invest the enormous surplus of petro dollars in Japan, relying on its safety. The problem is whether Japan has the ability to transform purely cooperative, economic relationships into positive efforts for the creation of a new, peace order. At present Japan lacks political leadership prepared to strive for the creation of a peace order. The inability to overcome this problem has been the weakness of post-war Japan. Moreover, Japan has been also behind the times in internationalization.

In this weak position Japan comes under US pressure to cooperate in sanctions against Iran or the USSR. From the perspective of Japan's Third World diplomacy, however, it cannot follow the US. And even from the perspective of promoting peaceful coexistence and detente and creating a new, peace order, Japan should not follow the US but instead oppose the attempt to reopen the cold war by the positive use of Japanese economic power. From the perspective of promoting disarmament, for instance, investment should be built up in order to consolidate public opinion against the attempt to expand armaments by the US and USSR. Of course, such kinds of efforts by Japan may provoke criticism and make it more difficult for Japan to carry out its diplomacy. Moreover, efforts by Japan alone face limitations.

In order to overcome these limitations the United Nations University, local government diplomacy and functional diplomacy by specialized groups should all be promoted. These are of importance in order for Japan to carry out its role. Of course, the ultimate goal of promoting diplomacy on the local level is to make the role of the members of the World Federation of Local Governments on the prefectural level the same as the UN. What is required is the courage to make Japan into something akin to the EC. Positive decentralized independence is the ultimate objective of the much talked of 'local era' in Japan. This is because the creation of a high degree of unity, with internationalized individual units, can be directly linked to the building of a new, peace order.

The irony of unification through decentralization has already been emphasized even in the case of Marxist and Leninist theories. The modern nation state is presently faced with a basic re-examination of an international order centering on the sovereign nation state. At a time like this, those countries that are able to head in the direction of decentralization on their own initiative can be said to be countries with a high level of civilization. If a country decentralizes power, external pressure is divided; further, the potential for diplomatic activity rapidly expands.

For instance, if all of Japan's 47 prefectures joined the UN, then these 47 new countries, which would have transformed the concept of sovereignty, could join hands with the original state governments of the EC in pressing for disarmament. Further, it would be almost impossible for pressure from the superpowers to influence all 47 countries. If there were a number of unarmed neutral states among them, for instance, they could follow the path of Costa Rica, which is in reality an unarmed, neutral country. It would also be possible to more effectively criticize countries that employ military force through the expansion of voting power in UN bodies.

At the same time, in respect to creating a positive peaceful order, the power of group solidarity can be developed. All of the above are actually impossible to carry out without huge economic and financial support. Of course, in regard to the immediate task of halting the reopening of the Cold War, the only option is probably to rely on diplomatic action as heretofore. However, even at the present stage, it is possible to employ local government diplomacy and functional diplomacy through specialist groups. It is a fact demanding critical re-evaluation that these activities have not been fully developed. In the latter regard, for instance, it would be appropriate to invite to the United Nations University US Japanologists and specialists on the Middle East to carry out in depth discussions.

If activities of this kind were increased then one country could function as a plurality of countries, because influence could be exerted on multi-dimensional levels. It is now time to end the necessity for only the Prime Minister or Foreign Minister to come under pressure from the superpowers. Even if the Cold War is reopened, public opinion should be built-up in order to prevent the possibility of the central government conducting diplomacy alone. What we should remember is that mutual dependence and interaction have reached a stage where it is possible to achieve the above targets.

NOTES

1 *Tokyo Shimbun* (Tokyo Newspaper), 25 January 1980.
2 For example, the *Shukan Asahi* (Weekly Asahi), 1 February 1980 issue, included a semi-fictional article entitled 'The Straits of Hormuz Blockaded: The Outbreak of War between the US and USSR!' the *Shukan Yomiuri* (Weekly Yomiuri), 3 February 1980 issue, included a special article on 'The Terror of World War III in 198X'; the *Sunday Mainichi,* 3 February 1980 issue, included articles on 'The Soviet Invasion and World War,' included among them being an article from a French magazine entitled, 'The Scenario for the Outbreak of World War III'; finally, the *Shukan Diamond* (Weekly Diamond), 26 January 1980 issue, had a special issue on 'Japan's Life-Line' and included here was an article by the Modern Geopolitical Society entitled, 'Scenario for Catastrophe in 1983'.
3 Not only is Afghanistan included in the LLDCs, it is also one of the 42 countries designated by the UN in May 1975 as being severely affected by the Oil Crisis.

Überwundene Unterentwicklung im modernen Weltsystem. Eine historisch-unhistorische Betrachtung

DIETER SENGHAAS

Unsere entwicklungsgeschichtliche Betrachtung setzt in der Zeit zwischen den beiden Weltkriegen ein. Nehmen wir an, man würde das Jahr 1935 schreiben. Nehmen wir weiter an, der Betrachter würde mit einem in den vergangenen Jahren entwicklungstheoretisch geschärften Blick seine Umwelt sichten. In diesen vergangenen Jahren hat er nämlich gelernt, daß erhebliche Wachstumsschübe in der Dritten Welt Massenarmut nicht beseitigt hatten und 800 Millionen Menschen in absoluter Armut leben. Er kennt optimistische Schätzungen, denen zufolge sich bis zur Jahrtausendwende das Ausmaß solchen Elends kaum verringern läßt, wenn nicht erhebliche Eingriffe in die überkommenen entwicklungshemmenden Strukturen erfolgen. Befriedigung von Grundbedürfnissen, so lautet heute vielerorts das entwicklungspolitische Programm. Wie man es im einzelnen Fall verwirklichen kann, ist sicherlich umstritten; unumstritten ist, daß nur eine breite Erschließung menschlicher und natürlicher Ressourcen Entwicklung gelingen läßt. Erforderlich ist, was in der Dritten Welt sträflich vernachlässigt worden ist, eine Leistungssteigerung der Landwirtschaft und eine landwirtschaftsnahe Industrialisierung, weil nur die enge Vernetzung von Landwirtschaft und Industrie einen organischen Entwicklungsprozeß erlaubt.

Zurückversetzt in das Jahr 1935 wird unser Betrachter ein gutes Dutzend Länder feststellen, die damals noch typische «Drittwelt-Länder» waren, während sie heute, 45 Jahre später, wie selbstverständlich nicht mehr zu den Problemfällen nationaler und internationaler Entwicklungspolitik gezählt werden. Diese Länder zeichneten sich damals, wie die heutige Dritte Welt, durch bruchstückhafte Wachstumsprozesse aus: Nur ein Teil der Landwirtschaft, meist der exportorientierte, entwickelt eine bemerkenswerte Leistungsfähigkeit; der Aufbau der Industrie orientiert sich an der kaufkräftigen Nachfrage, und da die Einkommen extrem ungleich sind, erschließt die Industrialisierung nicht die potentiellen Massenmärkte; wie Landwirtschaft und Industrie, so ist auch die Infrastruktur verzerrt – das weite ländliche Hinterland bleibt unterversorgt, während in den städtischen Zentren sich Bildungs- und Gesundheitseinrichtungen zusammenballen; dramatische Folgewirkungen hat das Fehlen technologischer Fertigkeiten und die daraus sich ergebende Abhängigkeit vom Maschinenpark und den Technologien der hochindustrialisierten Länder.

Im Jahre 1935 gehörten nach heute gängigen entwicklungstheoretischen Maßstäben die folgenden Länder unbestreitbar noch zur Dritten Welt: in Osteuropa Ungarn, Polen und die Slowakei innerhalb der Tschechoslowakei; in Südosteuropa Bulgarien und Rumänien; auf dem Balkan Jugoslawien und Albanien; und außerhalb Europas China, Korea und Kuba. In diesen Gesellschaften kam es auf unterschiedliche Weise zu politischen Umbrüchen, die den Weg für eine sozialistische Entwicklungspolitik öffneten. Diese Umbrüche hatten verschiedene Ursachen: die Zuspitzung sozialer Konflikte in der Zwischenkriegszeit; gesellschaftliche und wirtschaftliche Zerrüttungen, die durch den Zweiten Weltkrieg bedingt waren; erfolgreiche Befreiungsaktionen von Partisanen-Bewegungen; militärische Besetzung; echte sozialrevolutionäre Umbrüche – und oft war eine Mischung von diesen Ursachen bestimmend.

Wie die heutige Welt aussehen könnte

Es ist nicht schwierig, sich einen hypothetischen Entwicklungsweg der genannten Länder in den vergangenen 40 Jahren ohne erfolgten politischen Umbruch und ohne sozialistische Entwicklungspolitik vorzustellen.

Beginnen wir mit dem größten, China, weil dieses allein heute ein fünftel der Weltbevölkerung beherbergt. Wäre es zu keiner sozialistischen Umgestaltung dieses Landes gekommen, so müßten, allein Chinas wegen, bei konservativer Schätzung die Statistiken der Weltbank über die Größenordnung von absoluter Armut in der Welt von 800 Millionen Menschen auf ca. 1,2 Milliarden erhöht werden. Angesichts der ländlichen Struktur im vorrevolutionären China – sie zeichnete sich durch Bodenknappheit, Zerstückelung der Betriebsflächen, stagnierende Produktivität und ländliche Armut aus – wäre ein höherer Schätzwert realistischer.

Es gibt plausible Gründe zu unterstellen, daß China sich, ohne politischen Bruch 1949, in der Tendenz wie Brasilien entwickelt hätte. Bekanntlich zerfällt Brasilien in große verstädterte Industriekomplexe, den Wachstumspol, mit einer nach Millionen zählenden Slumbevölkerung um diese Industriezonen herum, dann in riesigen Großgrundbesitz (Latifundien), der für nationale und internationale Märkte produziert, und in eine wachsende Zahl von landarmen Kleinbauern und Landlosen, die entweder wie in der Landgebieten vor allem des Nordostens an der Grenze zur chronischen Hungersnot leben, oder aber resigniert aufgeben und an den Rand der städtischen Zentren drängen, um dort die Elendsviertel weiter wachsen zu lassen. Die industrieträchtigen Ballungszentren Chinas lagen, mit Ausnahme der Mandschurei, immer schon in Küstennähe. Die Durchdringung dieses Gebietes von seiten westlicher imperialistischer Mächte seit der Mitte des 19. Jahrhunderts hat diese Region erst recht zu den Wachstumspolen Chinas werden lassen. Sie hätten, wie überall in der Dritten Welt, Millionen von Menschen aus dem stagnierenden ländlichen Hinterland angezogen, und die Landflucht hätte sich angesichts der Hunderten von Millionen von Menschen in diesem Hinterland in eine Slumbildung von dramatischen Ausmaßen in diesen küstennahen Städten übersetzt. So wening wie in anderen Ländern der Dritten Welt heute, wären die überkommenen Übel und die sozialen Nöte des ländlichen Raumes in China beseitigt worden. Wenngleich im ländlichen Raum Chinas niemals lateinamerikanische Zustände – nämlich riesiger Grundbesitz, gepaart mit parzelliertem Kleinbauerntum und einer sich ausbreitenden Landlosigkeit – herrschten, hätte sich die überkommene Ungleichheit hinsichtlich der Verfügung über Land, Wasser, Kredite und Vermarktungswesen zugespitzt; eine deutlichere Schichtung zwischen reichen, mittleren und armen Bauern und Landlosen hätte sich herausgebildet, weil die Ausweitung der Geldwirtschaft, wie überall in der Dritten Welt, größere Betriebe begünstigt. Auch in China hätte man mit der Grünen Revolution experimentiert, und die für solche Experimente typischen Folgen wären unausbleiblich: Ertragssteigerungen und soziale Verdrängungseffekte, weil unter Bedingungen von ungleicher Landverteilung die neuen Saatsorten der Grünen Revolution Landwirte mit guten Böden, viel Wasser und dem nötigen Geld für den erhöhten Einsatz von Düngemitteln und Maschinen begünstigt hätten. Der Masse der Menschen wäre im wahrsten Sinne des Wortes der Boden unter den Füßen entzogen worden, zum Teil auf Grund solcher Verdrängungseffekte, zum Teil auf Grund einer in der Dritten Welt allenthalben beobachtbaren Schwächung der Selbstversorgungslandwirtschaft der Kleinbauern (Subsistenzwirtschaft), denn auch die Subsistenzwirtschaft benötigt Investitionen (und seien sie noch so kärglich), um als Subsistenzwirtschaft aufrechterhalten werden zu können; andernfalls führt eine laufende Überbeanspruchung natürlicher Ressourcen zur ökologischen Zerrüttung und zu Produktionseinbrüchen bei schon geringsten klimatischen Schwankungen.

Die küstennahen Wachstumspole und die städtischen Ballungsräume wären in China beliebte Investitionsbereiche multinationaler Firmen geworden, die, wie in Brasilien heute, die Erzeugung von dauerhaften Konsumgütern (wie Elektrohaushaltsgeräte, Autos usf.) in eigene Regie übernommen hätten. Demgegenüber wäre die Erzeu-

141

gung von nicht dauerhaften Konsumgütern wie Textilien, Schuhen, die Verarbeitung von Nahrungsmitteln noch in den Händen eines nationalen chinesischen Kapitals. Die seit dem späten 19. Jahrhundert sich herausbildende peripher-kapitalistische Gesellschafts- und Wirtschaftsstruktur hätte sich nach dem Zweiten Weltkrieg zugespitzt. Die inneren Zerklüftungen zwischen dynamischen und wachstumsintensiven Teilregionen und einem stagnierenden Umfeld, in dem die Masse der Menschen leben würde, wäre größer geworden. Wie in Brasilien, so bestünde auch in China der Kern des Entwicklungsproblems nicht in einem Mangel an Wirtschaftswachstum; problematisch wären die ausbleibenden Breitenwirkungen des Wachstums und damit die mangelnde Erschließung der binnenwirtschaftlichen Räume.

Auch in China hätte ein solcher Entwicklungsweg den sozialen Sprengstoff steigern helfen. Und was könnte einen dazu verleiten anzunehmen, daß nicht auch in China eine Militärdiktatur, ähnlich wie in den meisten Ländern der Dritten Welt, das für solche Regime typische Entwicklungsprogramm verkündet hätte: weitere Wachstumssteigerung vermittels einer Konzentration der Einkommen an der Spitze der Gesellschaft und Realeinkommensverluste bei der Masse der Menschen, langfristig Hoffnung auf eine Verteilung des wirtschaftlichen Kuchens, nachdem dieser gewachsen ist, während gleichzeitig internationale Organisationen und karitative Hilfswerke sich mit punktuellen inselhaften Hilfsprojekten um die Grundbedürfnisse eines Bruchteils der städtischen Slumbewohner sowie der Landlosen und kleinbäuerlichen Bevölkerung in den ländlichen Räumen bemühen würden. Der allenthalben beobachtbare Fehlschlag eines solchen Entwicklungsweges ist heute offenkundig; China wäre keine Ausnahme. Hätte es heute noch peripher-kapitalistische Strukturen, so würde es allein auf Grund seiner Größenordnung einen großen Teil der international verfügbaren Entwicklungshilfemittel auf sich ziehen, und die übrige Dritte Welt würde noch weniger derartige Mittel erhalten, als dies heute schon der Fall ist.

Dieser hier hypothetisch unterstellte Entwicklungsweg, der angesichts der Größenordnung Chinas besonders dramatisch erscheint, ist hinsichtlich der anderen erwähnten Fälle nicht weniger brisant. Der nördliche Teil Koreas, der während der japanischen Kolonialherrschaft nur als Bergbaugebiet (Exklavenwirtschaft) erschlossen wurde, würde auch heute noch im wesentlichen Exporteur von mineralischen Rohstoffen für den Weltmarkt sein. Die Landwirtschaft des Nordens Koreas, deren Entwicklung von der Bewältigung schwieriger topographischer Gegebenheiten abhängt, würde wie vor 1945 darniederliegen. Die Entwicklungsplaner würden den Süden Koreas als Reiskammer definieren und deshalb keine Veranlassung für forcierte landwirtschaftliche Entwicklungsprogramme im Norden sehen. Insofern mit dem Export von Bergbaurohstoffen Devisen erwirtschaftet werden, würde eine beschränkte gehobene Nachfrage entstehen, die wie in Lateinamerika nach 1930, zu einer ersten Stufe der Industrialisierung führen würde (Import-Ersatz-Industrialisierung). Die dafür erforderliche Technologie käme aus dem Ausland, und die eintretenden Engpässe wären, wie in der übrigen Dritten Welt heute, dieselben: wachsende technologische Abhängigkeit, finanzielle Verschuldung, Rückkopplung der lokalen Wirtschaftsdynamik an die Entwicklungsdynamik der Industrieländer. Aufbauend auf frühe Regungen eines koreanischen Nationalismus, wäre der Versuch eines betont nationalen Entwicklungsweges nicht unwahrscheinlich; das Ende solcher Bemühungen wäre in Korea jedoch nicht anders als in fortgeschritteneren Fällen der übrigen Dritten Welt: Sicherung des status quo durch Machtübernahme von Seiten der Militärs (Lateinamerika, Indonesien, Philippinen usf.)

Kuba würde mit Korea das Schicksal teilen, weiterhin Exklavenwirtschaft und damit abhängig vom Zuckerexport zu sein, vergleichbar allen übrigen Exklavenwirtschaften in der Karibik und ohne Chance, den monokulturellen Charakter von Gesellschaft und Ökonomie zu überwinden. In gleicher Richtung würde Rumäniens Entwicklungsweg zielen. Wie nach 1820 würde es sich auf die Produktion von Getreide spezialisieren; seine Agrarstruktur wäre trotz erfolgter Agrarreform in den zwanziger Jahren eine Mischung von Großgrundbesitz und Zwergbetrieben; die ländliche Armut wäre, wie in der Zwischenkriegszeit, immer noch erheblich; ein Teil der städtischen Bevölkerung, insbesondere der Verwaltungsapparat, würde an den Einkünften aus den Ölexporten teilhaben, allerdings nur, solange die Ölvorräte reichen. Bulgariens Entwicklungsproblem läge vor allem in winzigen landwirtschaftlichen Zwergbetrieben begründet, weiterhin in einer exklavenförmig erschlossenen Bergbauproduktion. Für weitergehende Industrieinvestitionen wäre, ähnlich wie in Jugoslawien, kein Anreiz vorhanden («Binnenmarktenge»). Aus Albanien würden die auf dem Weltmarkt vermarktbaren nützlichen Rohstoffe herausgesogen werden, während die ländliche Bevölkerung sich in dem schmalen, ökologisch nicht gefestigten Küstenstreifen (Malaria!) zusammendrängen würde, wo sie wie in dem gebirgigen Hinterland nur ein kümmerliches Leben auf immer brüchiger werdender Grundlage fristen könnte. In der heutigen entwicklungspolitischen Diskussion wäre Albanien sicherlich (wie auch Bulgarien und wahrscheinlich weite Teile von Jugoslawien) ein Land der Vierten Welt («Least Developed Countries»).

Demgegenüber hätte Ungarn, und in der Tendenz auch Polen, ein Gesellschafts- und Wirtschaftsprofil erreicht, daß demjenigen lateinamerikanischer Länder sehr nahe kommt: Eine latifundistisch-organisierte, exportorientierte Landwirtschaft würde für eine Minderheit der

Bevölkerung ausreichende Einkommen schaffen, die Grundlage für eine erste Welle von Industrialisierung wären. Das Ausmaß an Analphabetismus wäre geringer als in den südeuropäischen und Balkanstaaten, und es wäre nicht ausgeschlossen, daß ein Land wie Ungarn ähnlich wie Südkorea oder Taiwan spezifische Entwicklungschancen in einer exportorientierten Industrialisierung suchen würde, zumal schon in der Zwischenkriegszeit bemerkenswert breite Bildungs- und Fachqualifikation in der Bevölkerung vorhanden war.

Von den genannten Beispielen wären China, Korea, Kuba, Rumänien, Jugoslawien, Bulgarien und Albanien auch heute noch eindeutige Problemfälle. Ungarn und Polen würden höchstwahrscheinlich zur Kategorie jener Länder gezählt, die als teilindustrialisiert gelten, ohne daß sie gravierende interne gesellschaftspolitische Probleme wirklich bewältigt hätten. Den heutigen teilindustrialisierten Ländern vergleichbar (Mexico, Argentinien, Brasilien, Indonesien usf.), wäre in ihnen die innere Ressourcenverteilung zu ungleich, als daß Wirtschaftswachstum sich in einen breiten Entwicklungsprozeß übersetzen könnte.

Wenn in den genannten Ländern eine sozialistische Entwicklung nicht stattgefunden hätte, und wenn man (wie der *Weltentwicklungsbericht 1979*) unterstellt, daß die Volksrepublik China allein schon 886 Millionen Menschen beherbergt, dann kämen zu den 1,9 Milliarden Menschen, die heute in der Dritten Welt leben, noch einmal etwas mehr als eine Milliarde hinzu. Von unserem Argument her gesehen könnte diese Zahl durchaus um 250 Millionen erhöht werden, wenn man die Sowjetunion und die Mongolei, die schon vor 1935 einen sozialistischen Entwicklungsweg einschlugen, zahlenmäßig zu den späteren Fällen hinzuaddiert. 650 Millionen Menschen in den hochentwickelten kapitalistischen Gesellschaften würden dann wenigstens 3,2 Milliarden in der «Dritten Welt» gegenüberstehen – ein Begriff, der sinnlos wäre, weil eine «Zweite Welt», also der Bereich, in dem eine nachholende Entwicklung auf sozialistischem Wege erfolgte, nicht existieren würde.

Nachholende sozialistische Entwicklung

In all den genannten Fällen hat eine nachholende sozialistische Entwicklung zur Überwindung der krassen Merkmale und Krisensymptome von Unterentwicklung geführt. D.h., die grundlegenden Maßnahmen, die nach allgemeiner entwicklungspolitischer Ansicht notwendig sind, wurden eingeleitet. Brachliegende Produktivkräfte in allen Bereichen der Wirtschaft wurden mobilisiert, und es wurde versucht, die innere Zerklüftung der überkommenen Wirtschaftsstruktur zu mildern und ein ausgeglicheneres Verhältnis der Wirtschaftssektoren (Schwerindustrie, Konsumgüterindustrie, Landwirtschaft) zueinander zu schaffen. In der Mehrzahl der Fälle Heiß dies: Mobilisierung der landwirtschaftlichen Ressourcen, u.a. durch Bodenreform und eine schrittweise Kollektivierung, die zu größeren Betriebseinheiten führt; weiterhin Aufbau einer Schwerindustrie als Grundlage für eine eigene, insbesondere landwirtschaftsnahe Ausrüstungsgüterindustrie, Ausbau von Infrastruktur, Mobilisierung von Arbeitskräften, Bereitstellung von öffentlichen Dienstleistungen, vor allem im Erziehungs- und Gesundheitsbereich. In allen Fällen hat die sozialistische Entwicklung zu einer sehr frühzeitigen Bewältigung jener elementaren Probleme geführt, deren Lösung in der heutigen entwicklungspolitischen Debatte als Ziel der sogenannten Grundbedürfnisstrategie angegeben wird: Beseitigung von Analphabetismus; Überwindung von Arbeitslosigkeit (wenn auch nicht immer von Unterbeschäftigung), Gesundheitsvorsorge und Alterssicherung, schrittweise Weiterqualifikation von Arbeitskraft im Rhytmus der immer differenzierter werdenden Agro-Industriegefüge.

Die Tatsache, daß sozialistische Führungsgruppen in unterentwickelten Gesellschaften und nicht (wie es die traditionelle Sozialismustheorie erwartete) in hochkapitalistischen Gesellschaften zur Macht kamen, hat ihnen nicht nur die Bewältigung einzelner derartiger Aufgaben aufgebürdet, sondern die Summe aller, die es im Grunde genommen gleichzeitig zu bewältigen galt – eine schiere Unmöglichkeit. Denn womit soll eine solche Entwicklung in allen Bereichen finanziert werden, wenn es in der Regel keine potente Finanzierungsquelle gibt, weder im Innern der Gesellschaft, noch außerhalb ihrer. Die Industrie war in der Regel nicht entwickelt oder zu defekt entwickelt, als daß eine problemlose Selbstfinanzierung aus dem industriellen Bereich hätte kommen können. Die Landwirtschaft gehörte in all diesen Ländern zu den strukturschwachen Sektoren, gerade auch dort, wo sie sehr exportorientiert war (wie in Rumänien, Ungarn und Polen). Seit 1914 hat es in den letzteren Ländern in der Landwirtschaft kaum Produktivitätsfortschritte gegeben. Solche können, außer durch Veränderungen in der Agrarstruktur, (Bodenreform usf.) langfristig nur durch entsprechende industrielle Mittel zustandekommen (Landwirtschaftsmaschinen, Dünger, Schädlingsbekämpfungsmittel usf.). Aber gerade diese konnte die Industrie noch nicht zur Verfügung stellen, da eine schwerindustrielle Grundlage fehlte und der Maschinenbau erst zu entwickeln war. Zwar lassen sich manche Entwicklungsprozesse im Bereich der öffentlichen Dienstleistungen und der Infrastrukturmaßnahmen durch unkonventionelle Maßnahmen, die nur geringe Kapitalmittel verschlingen, zu Wege bringen. Zu denken ist z.B. an den massenhaften Einsatz von Arbeitskraft beim Bau von Deichen, bei

Terrassierungen usf., was vor allem von China her bekannt ist. Aber neben solchen unkonventionellen Maßnahmen sind sehr frühzeitig auch in diesen Bereichen «harte» Kapitalinvestitionen erforderlich. Die Fülle solcher Aufgaben macht einsichtig, warum eine nachholende sozialistische Entwicklung immer unter extrem autoritären Bedingungen stattfand. Diese Tendenz wurde noch dadurch zugespitzt, daß die politische Machtfrage weder im Innern noch in der internationalen Umwelt zugunsten der neuen politischen Führung wirklich eindeutig geklärt war. Oft kamen noch wirtschaftspolitische Auflagen hinzu, die die Sowjetunion von anderen sozialistischen Ländern nach 1945 verlangte, was in Fällen, wo es nicht zum Bruch mit der Sowjetunion kam, die lokale Autonomie zur Gestaltung eines eigenständigen Entwicklungsweges massiv einschränkte.

Was haben Länder wie China und die übrigen vorgenannten entwicklungspolititsch anders gemacht als die übrige Dritte Welt? Die Inhalte der alternativen Entwicklungsstrategie lassen sich hier nur kurz aufzählen. Der politische Umbruch führte zur Beseitigung der überkommenen krassen Ausmaße von Ungleichheit, die zu den grundlegenden Entwicklungshemmnissen der Dritten Welt gehört. Diese Beobachtung bestätigt übrigens eine historische Erfahrung, der zufolge Länder mit vergleichbarer Eingliederung in die Weltwirtschaft nur dann einen erfolgreichen inneren Entwicklungsprozeß durchlaufen konnten, wenn ihre Binnenstruktur eher durch eine milde als durch eine krasse Ungleichheit sich auszeichnete (bemerkenswerte Fallpaare sind Finnland - Rumänien, Schweden - Spanien, Dänemark - Portugal, Australien - Argentinien usf.).

Der politische Umbruch zwingt zur Herstellung neuer institutioneller Rahmenbedingungen, innerhalb derer Entwicklungsprozesse stattfinden. Obgleich diese in allen Bereichen der Gesellschaft von Bedeutung sind, kommt der Erschließung des ländlichen Raumes besondere Wichtigkeit zu. Maßnahmen wie die Kollektivierung, der Aufbau von Volkskommunen, die Ansiedlung von ländlicher Industrie, die Verbreitung ländlicher Gesundheitsvorsorge und von landwirtschaftsnahen Erziehungsinstitutionen gehören zu diesen Aufgaben der ersten Stunde. Viele der dabei getätigten Investitionen machen sich nicht unmittelbar bezahlt; sie erhöhen, wie die Investitionen in die Schwerindustrie, das Produktionspotential einer Wirtschaft, das zu einem späteren Zeitpunkt sich in ein höheres Konsumgüterangebot übersetzen soll. Vor mehr als 150 Jahren sprach Friedrich List schon von der entwicklungspolitisch erforderlichen «Produktion produktiver Kräfte», die für den Aufbau einer lebensfähigen Gesellschaft und Wirtschaft wichtiger sei als eine an kurzfristigen Interessen orientierte Wirtschaftspolitik. Dieser Überlegung liegt die Beobachtung zugrunde, daß die Schwerindustrie die Grundlage für die Entwicklung der

Landwirtschaft und der Leichtindustrie ist. Wenn mehr Landwirtschaftsmaschinen gebaut werden, kann auch mehr Getreide produziert werden; wenn mehr Ausrüstungsgüter für die Bauindustrie produziert werden, lassen sich auch mehr Häuser produzieren; und wenn mehr Schiffe zur Verfügung stehen, lassen sich auch mehr Fische fangen.

Natürlich hat eine solche Festlegung von Prioritäten auch Kosten. Nicht alles läßt sich gleichzeitig verwirklichen. Wenn, wie in allen sozialistischen Ländern, Nachdruck auf die Schwerindustrie gelegt wird, läßt sich, solange dies sinnvoll ist und praktisch betrieben wird, eine ausgeglichene Wirtschaft nicht herstellen. Konsumgüterindustrie und Landwirtschaft werden folglich zu kurz kommen. In diesem Zusammenhang ist interessant zu beobachten, daß die erste Phase sozialistischer Entwicklung, die ungefähr 20 ± 5 Jahre umfaßt, wichtige Strukturmängel der überkommenen vorrevolutionären Gesellschaften überwunden hat. Es kann auch kein Zweifel daran bestehen, daß Grundbedürfnisse in den genannten Ländern als verwirklicht gelten können, weshalb heute niemand mehr daran denkt, diese zum Gegenstand aktueller entwicklungspolitischer Diskussion zu machen. Natürlich gibt es auch in diesem Bereich Probleme. Solange in die Landwirtschaft zu geringe Investitionsmittel fließen, bleibt das landwirtschaftliche Potential unausgeschöpft und die Nahrungsmittelversorgung krisenanfällig. Dies Problem nimmt in manchen Fällen, wie in Polen, absurde Dimensionen an, da es sich um ein potentielles Überschußland handelt. Nicht zufriedenstellend ist in allen sozialistischen Ländern sicherlich die Wohnungssituation, und kritisch ist nicht nur unter allgemein menschlichen Gesichtspunkten, sondern gerade auch im Hinblick auf die Weiterentwicklung von Ökonomie der autokratische Charakter der politischen Regime und die Abwesenheit von Freiheitsspielräumen.

Die Probleme der heutigen sozialistischen Länder, die noch vor weningen Jahrzehnten «Dritte Welt» waren, sind nicht mehr vergleichbar mit denjeningen der Dritten Welt. Sie alle bewegen sich heute in einer Übergangsphase von extensiver zur intensiven Wirtschaftsweise. Während die extensive Phase auf der massiven Mobilisierung von brachliegenden Kräften beruht, wirken befehlswirtschaftliche Lenkungsmechanismen im Übergang zur intensiven Wirtschaftsweise entwicklungshemmend. Denn intensives Wirtschaften hängt, das zeigt gerade die kapitalistische Entwicklung, vom Einsatz und der Verbreitung technischen Fortschritts und der Erhöhung von Arbeitsproduktivität ab. Die vieldiskutierten Wirtschaftsreformen Osteuropas haben hier ihren Stellenwert, und auch der sogenannte Modernisierungskurs Chinas ist in diesem Lichte zu sehen. Alle Reformversuche waren bisher, vielleicht mit Ausnahme der ungarischen, zum Scheitern verurteilt, weil sie sehr frühzeitig die Grundlagen der neu aufgebauten

Herrschaftsstrukturen berührten. So gelangt man in der Analyse sozialistischer Entwicklung zu einer paradoxen Feststellung. Die Prioritätensetzungen der ersten Entwicklungsphase waren, gemessen an der peripher-kapitalistischen Entwicklung in der Dritten Welt, erfolgreich, während die dabei entwickelten Lenkungsmechanismen und politischen Strukturen sich auf die weitere Entwicklung in einer zweiten Entwicklungsphase blockierend auswirken. Der wohl schwerwiegendste Mangel besteht in der Abwesenheit von demokratischen Beteiligungschancen und individuellen Entfaltungsmöglichkeiten, ohne die intensives Wirtschaften gerade in sozialistischen Gesellschaften unwahrscheinlich ist. Was sozialistischen Gesellschaften bisher nicht gelungen ist, ist der Durchbruch zu einer offenen institutionalisierten Konfliktregelung zwischen unterschiedlichen Interessengruppierungen, die es selbstverständlich auch in sozialistischen Gesellschaften gibt, ohne daß sie offen politisch zum Tragen kommen dürfen.

Sozialismus im modernen Weltsystem

Entwicklung setzt Kapitalbildung voraus und diese ist ohne den Verzicht auf den Konsum eines Teiles der erwirtschafteten Güter nicht denkbar. Ist das Produktionspotential einer Ökonomie gerade auch angesichts einer noch durchschnittlich geringen Produktivität relativ klein und soll Entwicklung dennoch mit Nachdruck vorangetrieben werden, so spitzen sich die Zielkonflikte zu. Es ist im übrigen keine Besonderheit nachholender sozialistischer Entwicklung, daß in solchem Zusammenhang autoritäre/autokratische politische Regime jene Modernisierungsinstitutionen werden, die Konsumverzicht abverlangen, um vermittels produktiver Investitionen das Produktionspotential einer Wirtschaft insgesamt zu erhöhen. Ein Teil der Aufgaben, die sich einer nachholenden sozialistischen Entwicklung stellen, ist im Falle der kapitalistischen Frühentwickler während Absolutismus und Merkantilismus erfüllt worden, und selbst in diesen Fällen war die Entwicklung später keineswegs durch ein hohes Maß an demokratischer Beteiligung gekennzeichnet. Die Entwicklung kapitalistischer Gesellschaften, schon gar der Spätentwickler (wie Japan und Preußen-Deutschland) vollzog sich ebenfalls unter autoritären Vorzeichen. Es kann unschwer historisch nachgewiesen werden, daß es mehrer Demokratisierungsschübe auch in den hochindustrialisierten westlichen Gesellschaften bedurfte, um die autoritären Strukturen zumindest durch Herstellung der formalen politischen Gleichheit abzubauen. Mit Ausnahme von Australien, Neuseeland und Norwegen, die schon vor 1914 ein offenes Wahlrecht aller Männer und Frauen kannten, sind ein Teil der heutigen selbstverständlichen Demokratie-Elemente in etlichen Ländern erst aus den Zerrüttungen des Ersten und Zweiten

Weltkrieges hervorgegangen. Die Ineinssetzung von kapitalistischer Entwicklung und Demokratisierung ist eine historische Verfälschung, durch die weder die tatsächliche Aufeinanderfolge von kapitalistischer Entwicklung und Demokratisierung, noch die wirklichen politischen Kämpfe angesprochen werden, die zur Erreichung gewisser Formen von Demokratisierung erforderlich waren. Es ist zwar verständlich, aber dennoch abweigig, wenn die historische Betrachtung von Kapitalismus und Demokratie auf die Zeit nach 1950 verkürzt wird, wo in der Tat hohe Wirtschaftswachstumsraten *und* parlamentarisch-liberale Regime, wenigstens in den meisten hochindustrialisierten/kapitalistischen Gesellschaften des Westens, gleichzeitig zu beobachten sind. Doch eine solche Gleichzeitigkeit ist vor 1914 kaum festzustellen, und sie war vor 1945 keineswegs die Regel! Und worin bestanden, wenn Leistungen und Fehlschläge fair verglichen werden sollen, die *sozialen* Entwicklungsleistungen kapitalistischer Entwicklungsdynamik innerhalb von 3–4 Jahrzehnten, beispielsweise nach 1830 oder nach 1850 – und selbst noch nach 1900?

Die Probleme, in denen sich Gesellschaften nachholender sozialistischer Entwicklung heute befinden, sind nicht einfach zu lösen. Autoritarismus war eines der Mittel, eine schnelle Agro-Industrialisierung voranzutreiben. Abschaffung von autoritären Führungsstrukturen – oder positiv formuliert: ein erhebliches Maß an Dezentralisierung trotz bleibender zentraler Planung und die Ermöglichung individueller Entfaltung sind Voraussetzungen einer weiteren Entwicklung selbst in rein ökonomischem Sinn, wo sich heute die überkommenen hohen Wirtschaftswachstumsraten nur durch einen überdurchschnittlich hohen Einsatz investiver Mittel aufrechterhalten lassen; d.h. im Klartext, durch ein nicht mehr zu rechtfertigendes Maß an Ressourcenverschwendung. Nicht umsonst sind sozialistische Gesellschaften, die eine mehr, die andere weniger, in einem Gärprozeß, der immer wieder punktuell politisch nicht mehr steuerbare Kräfte freisetzt, während Unterdrückung die zugrundeliegenden Strukturprobleme nur noch einmal verschärft.

In der bisherigen Geschichte war Sozialismus ein Mittel, nachholende Entwicklung unter internationalen und internen Bedingungen zustandezubringen, unter denen sie normalerweise nicht mehr zustandekommt. Unsere Betrachtung hat aufzuzeigen versucht, daß sie kein problemloser Schlüssel zur Lösung aller nur denkbaren Probleme ist und daß, wenn einmal einige Probleme wie die Befriedigung der Grundbedürfnisse gelöst sind, andere schon wieder sich aufgebaut haben, die ganz andere Lösungszugänge erforderlich machen.

Im modernen Weltsystem gibt es ein Entrinnen aus drohender und faktischer Peripherisierung. Im 19. und zu Beginn des 20. Jahrhunderts war solches noch unter kapitalistischen Vorzeichen möglich. Im 20.

Jahrhundert ist Sozialismus das Mittel nachholender Entwicklung geworden, ganz anders, als es sich die frühen Theoretiker des Sozialismus vorstellten. Diese erwarteten Sozialismus als eine Stufe jenseits der «Fülle» des «reifen» Kapitalismus. Es ist paradox zu sehen, daß es in den oben genannten Fällen eines Bruches mit den Spielregeln der kapitalistischen Weltökonomie, überdies oft militärischer Interventionen und Embargos von Seiten kapitalistischer Gesellschaften bedurfte, um aus Peripherien des modernen Weltsystems in jeder Hinsicht kreditwürdige und attraktive Geschäftspartner entstehen zu lassen, wie das Osteuropa-Geschäft und neuerdings auch die China-Geschäfte zeigen.

LITERATUR

Dieter Senghaas (Hrsg.), *Kapitalistische Weltökonomie*. Kontroversen über ihren Ursprung und ihre Entwicklungsdynamik, Frankfurt 1979 (edition suhrkamp 980).
Dieter Senghaas, *Sozialismus*. Eine entwicklungstheoretische Betrachtung, In: Leviathan. Zeitschrift für Sozialwissenschaft, Nr. 1, 1980 (mit ausführlicher Begründung der hier vorgetragenen Beobachtungen und reichlichen Literaturverweisen).

Action Research as Part of Peace Making

ADAM CURLE

The aspect of peace research with which I have been most concerned might perhaps be best described as action research. It has grown out of practical efforts towards peace making; what I have learned in this context I have then attempted to apply, testing the validity of my concepts (hypotheses would be too grandiose a term) in the next round of peace-making activity. Obviously the context of peace making varies greatly, and this form of research (if that, too, is not too pretentious a word) can never be developed by controlled experiments. In any case, the practice is more important than the research, and the value of the research is only to be measured in terms of its contribution to practice. Nevertheless, it has potentially the same sort of validity as some aspects of clinical medicine: although the circumstances of every patient vary greatly as, usually, does the character of the disease, the experience of the physician gives him helpful and indeed reliable guidelines for treatment.

Before proceeding, I should explain what I mean by peace making. An unpeaceful situation, according to a definition I have found practicable, is a relationship between individuals, groups, or nations in which they are doing each other, or are likely to do each other, more harm than good (the harm being physical as in war, economic as through exploitation, social and political as through oppression, psychological as in an unhappy marriage, or a combination of all these and indeed other elements such as are often found in violent situations). Peace making is action to reverse the situation, to promote a relationship in which the parties involved do each other more good than harm. This is easily said. In practice it is very difficult, especially when the parties to the unpeaceful circumstances differ greatly in power. In an unpeaceful relationship between the oppressor and the oppressed, for example, there is little likelihood that the powerful oppressors, who profit from the status quo, will readily surrender any of their advantages. Peace making in such a situation is, therefore, different from how many might interpret the phrase. The emphasis is not so much on mediation or negotiation as on efforts to achieve social change.

If we consider peace making in this light, there are, it seems to me, three general types of peace-making action. Each is probably appropriate in all unpeaceful relationships but, as I just observed, the emphasis will vary. My enquiries and practice have focussed on attempting to obtain a better understanding of these three types.

1. *Awareness*. Lack of adequate understanding is a universal element in all unpeaceful situations. This may seem a bold generalization, but I feel it to be justified. There are very few human situations in which the participants can be said to have full understanding, and where there is any degree of fear, violence, hatred, resentment or anger, understanding is diminished. Where there is a sufficiently serious lack of understanding, efforts at peace making are inevitably impaired.

The most fundamental lack of awareness is a failure to appreciate the unpeacefulness of the situation or the possibility that it could ever be changed. Thus a bitterly oppressed people in a remote part of Asia have said to me: 'It has always been like this. The rich have victimized the poor and the poor have suffered. It is the will of God; there is nothing anyone can do'. In South Africa, about 20 years ago, there were high hopes that the Apartheid system might be brought down by, amongst other things, a massive strike by black workers. But on the appointed day, very few people withheld their labour, and the leaders sadly admitted that their people had not been sufficiently educated: 'they are not yet conscious', they said.

These are extreme examples, but it would be hard to find an instance of any situation in which those involved have a complete grasp of what is happening to them and of what they might do to alter it. This is especially true, paradoxically, of the most bitterly oppressed and of the most intransigent oppressors. The former, in a sense, conceal from themselves knowledge that might impel them to action that would lead to retribution. The latter forge a philosophy that makes them oblivious to the violence that their way of life does to their own natures.

I have mentioned that the strong and confused emotions evoked by violence constitute a reduction of awareness – about the nature and motives of enemies, the total situation – that seriously impairs the reasoned search for solutions. I have heard the leader of a nation at war angrily reject a perfectly sincere and and sensible proposal in the following terms: 'Those people are completely treacherous and unreliable, therefore any proposal they may make is just a trick. I won't give them the satisfaction of even looking at it'.

A constant and crucial component of peace making is, then, the attempt to raise the level of awareness of all concerned. This has two main components. The first is the presentation of information and ideas in an acceptable and comprehensible fashion. The second, and more difficult, is the creation of the right psychological climate for consideration of different points of view, including the most unpopular. The

152

ultimate purpose of both is to enable the parties to a quarrel to perceive their opponents without distortion. It is true that they may not like what they then see any more than what they disliked when seen through the distorting lense of prejudice, but at least they will be helped to act rationally. This always gives greater hope for an ultimate settlement than irrational action.

The attitude and behaviour of the peace maker, his/her ability to relate, respond, and listen to both parties with objectivity and good will, are of supreme importance. The peace maker must learn to recognize and understand the origin of moods, fears, hostilities, resentments, etc with sympathy, but must also be able to demonstrate that they may be based on misconceptions or faulty information. Basically the peace maker must put his/her feelings sufficiently into the background to emphathize profoundly with those he or she is talking to.

2. *Social Change*. Almost every imaginable type of unpeaceful situation needs to be changed if it is to be made more peaceful. People who, for whatever reason, are at odds with each other do not stop fighting unless the circumstances of their relationship alter. The peace maker must, therefore, be engaged to some extent in effecting social change, whether he or she is a Gandhi, Danilo Dolci, Helder Camara, Cezar Chavez or Martin Luther King leading a revolutionary movement, or a statesman readjusting the boundary lines of two nations engaged in a territorial dispute. However, since most recent wars have involved attempts by one group to cling to privilege and by another to gain their fair share, the work of Gandhi etc is especially important in the contemporary world; it is on this that I shall concentrate. (I shall not consider the changing of society by violence, although this may appear on occasion as a relatively easy short cut to better things. However, I have seen far too much of the uncontrollable miseries inflicted by war to believe that it can ever be condoned by anyone who claims to want to 'make peace'.)

Apart from non-violent involvement in one resistance movement (for which I paid a heavy price), my own experience in this field of peace making has largely consisted of attempts to get conflicting parties to change their demands and expectations, to accept compromises, and to consider means of persuasion or coercion other than shooting or threatening to shoot. But this is a particularly delicate role for an outsider, and I have learned that he or she will only be listened to if prepared to suffer the same risks and disadvantages as those he or she is talking to: if they are ready to be shot or imprisoned because of their opposition to an oppressive regime, so must be the would-be peace maker.

The problems of bringing about social change are manifold. Of particular importance in peace making are non-violent methods of effecting changes normally brought about by violence. I have little to add to the literature on the topic, except to stress the relevance of awareness.

3. *Mediation*. The aspect of peace making that might be termed mediation involves acting as a go-between in any type of unpeaceful relationship. It is, however, particularly important when the contestants are more or less equal in power and the essence of the conflict is tolerably clear, so that there is somewhat less pressure for social change or raising awareness. In fact, the role of mediator is what, to most people, is meant by peace making – the toing and froing, persuading, explaining, interpreting, suggesting compromises and face-saving formulae. Obviously the mediator must do what he or she can to raise awareness on both sides, but I have found it especially important to develop a relationship with each party that enabled me to be friendly with the other. Initially efforts are made by each party to win the mediator over to their side. The other side are portrayed as sinister, untrustworthy, dishonest, etc and when it becomes clear that the mediator is still determined to have dealings with them, he or she is in danger of being similarly characterized. It may take a long period to earn the right to be friendly with each side. One must be entirely consistent in both good will and impartiality, in refusal to take sides, while being warm and sympathetic with all the parties involved. It is also essential that the mediator should be seen to have no personal interest in the situation, to be acting solely in the interests of those suffering in the conflict, and to have no 'party line' about the manner of its resolution.

These three elements in peace making, raising awareness, effecting social change, and mediating, often overlap, fuse and merge. In some of my own activities I have not been able to separate them. Nevertheless, as I have suggested, there are also situations in which, at least for certain periods of time and until the situation alters, there is greater need for one rather than the others.

All three call for some combination of two types of competence on the part of the peace maker. The first of these is the skill of the political or, in a more general sense, of the social scientist who can analyse and interpret the situation in a convincing fashion; without this ability no one will pay him much attention. The second is closer to that of the psychiatrist or clinical psychologist who can identify the distorted perceptions, the exaggerated fears and the anxieties of the protagonists, and behave in such a way as to reduce them. This latter ability is much less well known and understood than the first and forms the principle focus of my own practical interests and the speculation that has followed from them.

Empowering People for Global Participation

CHADWICK F. ALGER

People everywhere are immersed in a sea of transactions that link them to people in distant places – as purchasers of food, clothing, automobiles, electronic equipment, and other consumer goods from around the globe. Distant producers even determine what people want to drink (Coca Cola), to wear (jeans), to watch ('Starsky and Hutch'), to listen to (Rolling Stones), and to eat (McDonald's hamburgers). Global economic processes determine the quality of life through their impact on inflation and unemployment. Global enterprises affect the quality of life by polluting fishing grounds and the atmosphere and by converting food-producing farms to manufacturing and cash crops. Some would say that these observations simply reflect the fact that we are living in an increasingly *interdependent* world brought on by the impact of new technologies for transportation and communication on manufacturing, marketing and investing. Actually, however, most people are increasingly *dependent* on global forces over which they have little control, which they don't understand, and which they often do not even perceive.

Why Can't People Cope with Global Issues?

Why cannot people cope with the global dimension of daily life? Two factors seem to be very important. *First* is the way in which people have been taught to perceive the world. They have been taught that the world is composed of so-called nation-states. They are the 'important' actors on the world scene. While there are a diversity of other global actors – churches, corporations, voluntary associations and non-state ethnic and nationality groups – they are difficult to perceive, and if they are perceived, their actual and potential significance is not understood. The so-called nation-state system then is the analytic screen through which the world is observed.

Second, people are taught *not* to participate in the nation-state system. Norms of the nation-state system dictate that only very extraordinary people – a small elite with very special knowledge and experience – participate in policy-making in the nation-state system. For this

155

reason no country in the world has a democratically controlled foreign policy, and in most countries people are not even aware of many major foreign policy decisions. It is their role to proclaim loyal support for policies formulated by others in pursuit of the 'national interest'.

Scholars are largely, although not completely, responsible for the inability of people to cope with a changing world. It is they who have permitted national state ideology to permeate research and teaching about the world. This ideology declares that nation-states are the most 'important' actors. Scholars have made this a self-fulfilling prophecy by using nation-states as an almost exclusive unit of analysis.[1] The ideology says that there is a 'national interest' that is discernible only by an elite with special knowledge and experience. Scholars have largely accepted the notion that only a few people in a politico-military bureaucracy distant from the people know what is in the 'national interest'. They have reinforced the power of this self-proclaimed elite by maintaining a gulf between the academic discipline of international relations and democratic theory.

In summary, people cannot cope with the increasing intrusion of global processes on their daily lives largely because they do not have an analytic perspective that permits them to perceive and understand the sea of global processes in which they live. They have been taught that important international things happen in distant places – primarily in national capitals. They do not expect to take part in foreign-policy-making because they have been taught that they are incompetent.

International Organizations Are Distant From Most People

Meanwhile, the agenda of global problems in which all people are involved is increasing – with respect to food, energy, resources, inflation and pollution; in the commons of the oceans, atmosphere and outer space; and in terms of conflicts generated by this growing agenda. National governments have responded by joining together in a growing multitude (some 300) of international governmental organizations (IGOs) in efforts to cope with these problems. Responsible to representatives of national foreign policy bureaucracies who are themselves distant from their people, IGO bureaucracies are even more distant. Most people in the world don't even know the names of these agencies – ICAO, IMCO, UNCTAD, UNEP, WMO, WHO, etc. How then can they hope to reflect the interests of the people of the world or to acquire legitimacy for their proposed solutions to global problems?

Some organized citizen groups have attempted to close the gap between the people of the world and IGOs through direct pressure on IGO bureaucracies, their decision-making bodies and their constituent national governments. A dramatic example has been the efforts of international nongovernmental organizations (INGOs) and their constituent national nongovernmental organizations (NGOs) in the context of global UN conferences on environment, food, population, habitat, water resources and disarmament. They have run parallel conferences, published daily conference newspapers, acquired media coverage for their activities, and sometimes established direct links between their conference representatives and governments and constituent organizations in their home countries. It should not be surprising that INGOs and NGOs have had difficulty mobilizing support because of the apathy of people back home. Like national governments, NGOs that comprise INGOs tend to be small elites that are for the most part located in the headquarters of national organizations – distant from most people. The foreign policy-makers for NGOs tend to be as distant from rank and file members of national organizations as are policy-makers in foreign offices of national governments.

While it is widely agreed that IGOs and INGOs are serving useful purposes, some people are concerned about the global distribution of opportunity for participation in them.[2] Participation requires money for travel and communication and necessitates the investment of time by skilled people. Because these resources are more abundant in industrialized countries than in the Third World, opportunity for participation in and influence of IGOs and INGOs is much greater in industrialized countries. Likewise, within all countries opportunity for participation is limited because only a small elite in the national office of most NGOs takes part in the formulation of NGO foreign policy and in participation in INGO meetings. Opportunities for participation in INGOs are also unequally distributed because some national governments are more willing to permit their citizens to participate in INGOs than are others. Thus most people are not only perceptually and organizationally detached from these international activities, they are also inhibited from participation because of lack of resources and the desire of many national governments to limit and control participation.

Demands for Decentralization Within Countries

While cosmopolitan elites are building IGOs and INGOs, most of their activity is unperceived by most of the people of the world. Frustrated by the impact of incomprehensible global processes on their daily lives, and feeling distant from efforts by national governments to deal with the social consequences of high technology, the reaction of many people is to demand decentralization of government and to focus their concern on local affairs. This demand for decentralization is not confined to industrialized countries but extends to the Third World, where most people are dissatisfied that Third World cosmopolitan elites have been the main beneficiaries of national development strategies. As a result there are increasing demands for satisfaction of human needs through local self-reliance.

Unfortunately, movements for decentralization tend to neglect the impact of global processes on local places, whether they be small communities, cities, metropolitan complexes or regions. If these movements are to satisfy the demand of people for more local control over their fate, they must acquire local control over global processes that impact local places. But this will require new analytic frameworks that will permit local people to perceive how they are related to the world. It will also require overcoming feelings that so-called foreign policy is too difficult and complicated for local people to understand and overcoming local deference to distant elites on foreign policy issues. This is no easy task because tradition has lulled most people into a cycle of apathy with respect to international affairs.

A Strategy For Empowering People

A plausible strategy for change is to begin by aggregating information on global links of local cities and regions – information on trade, investment, religion, science, education, agriculture, etc. This knowledge must then be shared with local people through a diversity of media – newspapers, television, radio, and educational programs of voluntary organizations, universities, and schools. This will create a new image of the place of the local community and region in the world and make people self-conscious about their involvement in global processes and that of other local people and organizations. Through time, as portrayed in Figure 1, this can lead to the competence of local people to evaluate their involvement in global processes which would in turn lead to responsible participation – in contrast to widespread non-perceived involvement. This participatory learning could provide the base for foreign policy agenda setting in local communities – in contrast to reaction to agenda set by powerful governmental and nongovernmental organizations in distant cities.[3]

Figure 1. Moving the Public From Perception to Self-Conscious Action.

Providing local people with information on their involvement in global processes would first require social scientists to put people in their paradigms for viewing the world – generally our research and teaching only tell people about elites in powerful centers. This would require scholars who study local communities and regions to include the global dimension of local life in their work. Likewise, people who study international affairs would have to take special interest in the international dimension of the lives of local people. Traditionally people who study local and regional affairs have ignored the international dimension of local and regional affairs and people who study international affairs have ignored the local dimension of their field of inquiry. Knowledge about their place in the world that this kind of inquiry would offer local people can be a source of power in global affairs. Presently international relations scholars enhance only the power of national governmental and nongovernmental elites by helping them to understand their place in the world and by providing knowledge relevant to their policy problems.

It would not be expected that dissemination of knowledge about global linkages alone would bring dynamic local participation in world issues. This would require organized support within local organizations – political, religious, labor, professional, women, service, etc. Presently specialized competence for approaching global affairs in these organizations tends to be aggregated to their national offices, through a braindrain of people most informed about global issues to national centers. It is necessary that this talent either be returned to local communities or regions or that new local talent be developed. This dispersion of talent would make it possible for a variety of local organizations to develop education and action programs with respect to the global dimension of local and regional affairs. For example, local and regional labor organizations should have staff for global issues. Development of this talent presents new challenges for local educational institutions. They must train specialists who can cope with global issues in local contexts and who are attracted to this vocation. This would slow the braindrain of trained talent in global issues to national government, IGO and INGO centers.

Widening Participation in the Design of Future Worlds

People in local communities can be empowered to take part in the design of future worlds in which they will have a meaningful role through a process of participatory learning. This process could be spurred by: (1) procedures for gathering information on actual and potential linkage of the local community to external organizations, (2) procedures for making this information comprehensible to local people

159

– through a variety of easily accessible and easily understood media, (3) procedures for local evaluation of actual and potential external linkages, particularly with respect to their equity in contribution to local needs, and (4) procedures for local representation in decisions of external organizations that affect the local community.

It is difficult to speculate on the kind of world vision that people in a world of self-reliant communities would create, because our experience is limited to worlds created largely from the top down, i.e., by national governmental and nongovernmental organizations and by international governmental and nongovernmental organizations. Much would be learned by actual experience with local people endeavoring to create self-reliant external relations. Much also would be learned by working with people in creating strategies for change. Since the whole world cannot be reorganized at once, this experience would provide valuable insight on self-reliance strategies that would be a part of visions of desirable worlds. A *transformation process* would be spurred by two factors:

1. *Norms establishing the right to equitable external exchange, and representation in decision-making processes that affect local communities.* Included would be the right of a local community to decide which external organizations could penetrate the community and which collectivities it would join. Eventually this would, of course, mean that the nation-state would lose its paramount position in global organization. Aggregations in which local communities are involved would be a result of self-reliant choices of local communities, subject to change as conditions change. This, of course, does *not* mean that national governments would necessarily be disbanded. Those that are satisfying the needs of citizens as a unit for collective decision-making would continue. It might be expected that smaller countries containing a cohesive nationality group would continue as national units for a long time, as would governments of countries whose boundaries were relevant for certain functional activities. But it might be expected that the ways in which very large nations relate to the world would change. I would expect that regions of a country as large as the United States would relate directly to the world on some issues: e.g., the Western region might have separate relations with people in the Pacific Basin on issues concerning the Pacific Ocean and the Southeastern region might have separate relations with Caribbean countries on issues of particular importance to that region.

2. *Knowledge and competence that make it possible for local communities to evaluate and make decisions about external relationships.* As local communities begin to develop competence in external relations, they would begin playing a more dynamic role in a number of arenas – in province, region, nation and internationally. This would

160

enable them to play an increasingly effective role, for example, on decisions about foreign investments in all of these arenas. This new local competence in external relations would gradually transform the foreign-policy making process of national governments into a democratic process. This would dramatically transform the 'nation-state system', since one of its most significant characteristics has been the assumption that the people are incompetent to make foreign-policy decisions. This has been the norm in all countries – rich and poor, North and South, democratic and authoritarian.

This transformation process would be closely watched as a source of insight in the creation of visions of desirable worlds – i.e., there would be a dialectical process between visions and experience. This process would deepen knowledge about the most pressing problem in global organization· how to enable the people of the world to have equitable relations with those parts of global systems that impact their daily lives.[4]

NOTES

1 This argument is developed more fully in Chadwick F. Alger. ' «Foreign» Policies of United States Publics,' *International Studies Quarterly,* 21 (June 1977), 277–318.
2 This is described more fully in Chadwick F. Alger and David G. Hoovler, 'The Feudal Structure of Systems of International Organizations,' *Proceedings of the 5th IPRA Conference,* 1975, and Johan Galtung, 'Non-Territorial Actors: The Invisible Continent: Towards a Typology of International Organization,' Chair in Conflict and Peace Research, University of Oslo, Paper No. 4.
3 This argument is developed more fully in Chadwick F. Alger, 'Extending Responsible Public Participation in International Affairs,' *Exchange Magazine,* Vol. XIV (Summer 1978), 17–21, based on experience using this approach in Columbus, Ohio. Methods used in gathering information on the international links of a metropolitan area are described in Chadwick F. Alger, 'Your Community in the World: The World in Your Community: Discovering the International Activities and Foreign Policies of People, Groups and Organizations,' Mershon Center Informal Publications, Ohio State University, 1974. This manual includes all questionnaires used in the research. A manual of exercises using this approach in undergraduate teaching is available in Chadwick F. Alger and David G. Hoovler, *You and Your Community in the World* (Columbus, Ohio: Learning Package Series 23, Consortium for International Studies Education of the International Studies Association, 1978).
4 These ideas are developed more fully in Chadwick F. Alger, 'Creating Visions of a World of Self-Reliant People', a working paper for the Project on Goals, Processes and Indicators of Development (GPID), United Nations University, 1979, and in Chadwick F. Alger, 'People in the Future Global Order', *Alternatives,* 4 (October 1978), 233–362, and *Bulletin of Peace Proposals,* No. 2 (1978), 129–143.

Towards a Growing Contradiction between Research and Diplomacy?

RAIMO VÄYRYNEN

Are there any similarities between *diplomacy* and *research* and to what extent does research have an impact on the formation and conduct of diplomacy? The search for similarities may be a somewhat hazardous exercise, because these two modes of activities aim at fundamentally different targets. According to a somewhat idealistic formulation by Harold Nicholson, the chief aim of diplomacy is international stability. [1] In a more pragmatic approach diplomacy is seen to be a means of promoting a certain set of political, military and economic goals, which may have support among the population, but which may equally well be fairly particularist in their nature. Diplomacy is, in other words, a method of articulating domestic goals in the international arena, confronting them with the goals of possibly stronger nations, and finally adjusting them to the level which it is possible to attain.

For this purpose the diplomatic system has to *compile information* in order to be aware of the goals and action strategies of other governments as well as of the overall international setting in which they have to be realized. The information compiled has to be evaluated and analyzed; hence one of the prerequisites of diplomacy is to *process information* in order to design appropriate action strategies compatible with the foreign policy goals. The actual decision-making is conditioned by the amount and quality of information so compiled and processed, though the final decisions may be based on premises other than the available information. In terms of information, research and diplomacy can be distinguished from each other by saying that in diplomacy the analysis is geared to serving certain organizational functions, while in research the analysis aims at broadening the understanding and conceptualization of the world.

Johan Galtung makes a distinction between three *diplomatic styles,* i.e. *elite-oriented* diplomacy based on personal manipulation, *treaty-oriented* diplomacy aiming at explicit agreements, and *structure-oriented* diplomacy based, in turn, on structural manipulation and the analysis of social and economic forces. It is obvious that the kind of information needed varies from one style to another, and hence there are also differences in the preferred skills and educational orientation of the diplomats. Galtung summarizes this correlation in the following manner:

It is rather obvious what kind of training one would expect these people to have: the first type should preferably have a background of solid upper-class training in general, the second type should be a legal expert in order to negotiate and draft ratifiable treaties that are consistent with other legal norms . . . and the third type should be a social scientist of any discipline or persuasion.[2]

In the empirical investigations it has been shown that there has indeed been a change in the hypothetized direction; diplomats originate increasingly in middle-class families compared with upper-class families and are increasingly educated in social sciences instead of the legal profession.[3]

A concomitant of the change from treaty-oriented to structure-oriented diplomacy is the shift from *bilateral* to *multilateral* or conference diplomacy. Here again the need for social science education is emphasized, because the prime motive of multilateral diplomacy is not to draft legal instruments, but to compile and analyze information on such functional matters as international customs policy or the regulation of maritime transports. In the multilateral fora diplomats are normally specialists in certain organizations or in certain functions or fields. In bilateral diplomacy there is a related shift in the type of information needed; instead of political gossips or rumours, a diplomat has to trace information on the social or economic policy pursued by the host country.

The question is not, however, only one of the compilation of economic facts. One factor that Galtung has largely omitted is the growing *involvement of diplomacy in trade promotion*. Nicholson had already a comment on that tendency when he wrote in the early 1950s that

commercial ambitions and interests exercise an ever increasing influence upon foreign policy. It is only comparatively recently that they have produced an alteration in diplomatic method. Even in my own day, it was regarded by the older diplomatists as most improper that the German Government would use its Embassy at Constantinople to obtain concessions to German industrialists. It was not merely that those of the ancient tradition regarded it as undignified that diplomatists should concern themselves with questions of commerce: it was also feared that if commercial competition were to be added to political rivalry, the task of diplomacy would become even more complicated than it was already.[4]

Nowadays the impact of economic interests on diplomacy is more real than ever before. The relationship between commercial ambitions and diplomatic methods has changed, however, from the days of elite-oriented diplomacy, when the contradiction described by Nicholson existed. In fact a characteristic of structure-oriented diplomacy is that the promotion of commercial interests is both politically and organizationally tied to the practice of foreign relations. Ambassadors dine with potential buyers, and at a lower level commercial and industrial attachés promote trade through the diplomatic framework. At home foreign ministries and interest associations in the field of foreign economic relations are closely coordinating their activities. In other words the *corporative features* in foreign trade and diplomacy have intensified.[5]

The linkage between foreign trade and diplomacy also makes new demands on the diplomatic style as well as on the nature of the information needed. In trade promotion it is not sufficient to receive information only from other ambassadors or legal experts; one has to approach the business community, both at home and abroad. This is typical of structure-oriented diplomacy. In fact one could hypothetize that the structure-oriented diplomatic style was very much encouraged, and perhaps even caused, by the intensification of cooperation between the foreign ministries and foreign-trade organizations. This, in turn, has played a more conspicuous part since the early 1930s, when the Great Depression forced economic and diplomatic circles to give up their earlier hesitations and try to conquer or preserve markets by their joint efforts.[6]

From this point of view the alliance between diplomacy and foreign trade in the 1930s marked the beginning of structure-oriented diplomacy. This conclusion also illustrates one characteristic of Galtung's typology of diplomatic styles; although there is an overall transition from elite-oriented, through treaty-oriented, to structure-oriented diplomacy, these stages, besides being ideal types, overlap each other in the time perspective. In a way one may speak of *emerging, dominant* and *receding* diplomatic styles, without postulating any sharp edges between them.

So far we have explored relatively little the *relationship between the research community and the diplomatic community*. This relationshiop can be characterized by several variables, including the *similarity* of their orientation and composition as well as the *intensity* of their interaction. One may hypothetize that the nature of this relationship varies from one diplomatic style to another. In the era of elite-oriented diplomacy the relationship between these two communities appears to have been rather *symbiotic*, because of the similarity in the educational and cultural background of their members. Both institutions were elite-oriented and hierarchical; both professors and ambassadors had a superior status. The work of the research community was less differentiated than nowadays and partly for this reason it was easier to be even a full or at least an associate member of both of these communities. From earlier days there are several examples of diplomats who were also renowned researchers.[7] The flow of people from one community to another was relatively easy, and no doubt more frequent than nowadays. This was partly due to the lack of diplomatic staff in newly independent countries, which had to recruit their diplomats from the universities, for example.

These conclusions can be extended, with some qualifications, also to the period of treaty-oriented diplomacy. During this era the most sought-for skills were possessed by the professors of international law, who almost invariably became involved in the diplomatic work (and some of them still are). It may be, however, that they did not always become ambassadors, but assumed rather the role of a high-level expert. *Expertise* rather than more 'soft' cultural, social and scientific talents became more pronounced. This is probably one reason why treaty-oriented diplomacy never really replaced elite-oriented diplomacy and gave way in a relatively easy fashion to structure-oriented diplomacy. It seems to me that the aftermath of World War II was the peak of treaty-oriented diplomacy, since lawyers were needed in large numbers to solve the political and legal problems left by the war in interstate relations.

Both of these phases were characterized by the existence of a relatively strict *hierarchy* in the academic and diplomatic community. The interaction between them was 'top-heavy' and primarily took place between the top representatives of the two communities. The emergence of structure-oriented diplomacy has coincided with a certain breakdown of the hierarchies. This process has, however, been less rapid in the diplomatic communities than in the academic ones. This decrease in the similarity of the nature of these two communities is obviously one relevant factor in accounting for the present relations between them.

The high degree of hierarchy in the diplomatic system has been described by Galtung, on the basis of his own experiences, in a diplomatic conference:

a delegation is run in a relatively feudal manner: information from periphery to center, orders from center to periphery. The center elaborates the statements in consultation with its home base, not in consultation with the delegation – sometimes in consultation with neither, very rarely with both.

165

Being dissatisfied with this state of affairs, Galtung proposes an alternative to the feudal practice:

> there should be no excuse for not running delegations in a more democratic manner – less like an old-fashioned bilateral tutorial system and more like a modern seminar to express it in the university jargon – drawing on the experience and dedication of all members.

The hierarchic character of the diplomatic delegations and of the entire system, for that matter, results in the situation in which the leading foreign ministry officials express the 'national interest', which may be their own view or simply a compromise between various subnational interests. Those who are advocating ideas incompatible with this 'national interest' are stamped as 'idealistic', while those who have compatible standpoints are 'realistic'.[8]

Here we find a dilemma. On the one hand, the diplomatic service increasingly needs the information and interpretation that scholars can give. The *information explosion* and the *increasing complexity of the international system* lead to a situation in which the foreign ministries – which are seldom organized to meet the needs of structure-oriented diplomacy – find it increasingly difficult to cope with the accumulating information. One solution to this problem has been the establishment of research sections of various calibre to compile and process information. At least in smaller countries, they have usually, however, proved to be relatively inefficient and in fact incapable of carrying out the tasks to be performed.

Even if they have been able to muddle through this terrain, they have been faced with the problem of *interpreting* the information and explaining where a particular development is heading. There are no doubt diplomats who are very good at this task, but despite that I would venture to generalize the conclusion that Galtung has drawn from a multilateral diplomatic conference:

> there is a considerable market at such conferences for high level expertise. The delegates are undernourished, it seems, on three things; facts, a synthesis of where one stands and where the conference is leading, and some guide-lights, some philosophy, some perspective.[9]

In this sort of perspective there is, of course, the danger that the researchers start considering themselves somehow superior to the 'poor' young diplomats, who do not have sufficient training and ability to interpret the world.

These types of dangers notwithstanding, there is a certain *conflict*

166

between the diplomats and the researchers.[10] No doubt there is also nowadays a certain flow of people between the academic and the diplomatic community, but it is probably less frequent and more 'visible' than what it used to be in the era of elite-oriented diplomacy. This does not, of course, mean that there are no contacts between the two communities. On the contrary a number of various kinds of consultative councils have been established – in the field of disarmament, UN affairs and development problems, for instance – to promote collaboration with researchers and to exploit their knowledge and recommendations. This type of cooperation is by no means useless to the scholars involved, because in that way they gain experience of the working style in the foreign ministries or information which may otherwise be difficult to come by.

The conflict remains, however. It is partly anchored in the different world views of researchers and diplomats, but this is indeed only a partial explanation. The conflict is probably more related to the way in which the role of research in the diplomatic community is conceptualized. If the prevalent approach is based on the application of the hierarchic principle, the situation becomes unbearable to a true researcher. In this alternative the top of the foreign ministries defines the role of research as a goal-oriented activity in which the research impulses come from the top that also determines which problems are researchable and which are not. In addition to that a relatively high degree of loyalty is required from those carrying out research to satisfy the needs of a foreign ministry.[11] This approach, however, overlooks the fact that 'loyalty' depends on identification, and identification is to a large extent a function of the volume of meaningful and equalitarian interaction with other people.[12]

In spite of some contrary tendencies, the hierarchical nature of the academic research community is declining and the cooperation patterns are becoming in a long-term perspective more interwoven and egalitarian, even though much still remains to be done in this respect. In the foreign service and in diplomatic delegations the hierarchies, connected with the promotion of some particular interests, are more resistant to change. In this situation the role of research and researchers cannot but be subordinated; in the most clear-cut case they have to produce pragmatic, empirical knowledge, devoid of any theoretical considerations, for the top of the hierarchy on the topics dictated by them. If this type of attitude prevails in the foreign ministries, the contradictions between research and diplomacy will grow, because of the increasing gap in the structural properties of these two systems.

Meaningful cooperation between researchers and diplomats will be possible only if the foreign services become more open and more receptive to innovative ideas, together with their theoretical underpinnings and implications, which the researchers *may* have. This does not, of course, mean that diplomats should be uncritical towards the ideas raised by the scholarly community; on the contrary, they should be critical, because researchers often have a deficient sense of politics and its realities.

The organization of the relationship between the diplomatic and the research community contains considerable problems. One solution is to strengthen the research component of the foreign office as such and introduce this sort of action into its everyday routine. Even in a permissive environment it is, however, difficult to guarantee the freedom and independence of research, because the organizational needs tend to emphasize pragmatic reviews of the present and future shape of international relations. From this perspective it would be more fruitful to develop the cooperation between the foreign office and the independent research community. Despite contradictions, which may even be growing, this is probably a better solution, although there will always be voices saying that the researchers will lose their virginity in this cooperation. This may indeed be the case, but the solution is not the elimination of the cooperative links, but rather the preservation of the capacity for independent and critical judgement by researchers themselves. It is a sign of weakness on the part of the research community if it is not capable of egalitarian, critical and independent cooperation with the diplomatic community.

NOTES

1 Harold Nicholson, *The Evolution of Diplomacy*. New York 1966, p. 122 (the first edition was published in 1954).
2 Johan Galtung & Mari Holmboe Ruge, Patterns of Diplomacy. A Study of Recruitment of Career Patterns in Norwegian Diplomacy. *Journal of Peace Research*, Vol. 3, No. 2 (1965), pp. 101–35 (the quotation is from p. 107).
3 *Ibid*, pp. 113–26, and Matti Alestalo, Muuttuva diplomatia ja diplomaatit. *University of Helsinki, Department of Sociology. Research Reports*, No. 136, 1969, 218 pp.
4 See Nicholson *op.cit.* 1966, p. 109.
5 For the evidence of this development in Finland see, e.g., Lauri Karvonen, Korporativa drag i Finlands utrikeshandelspolitik. *Meddelanden från statsvetenskapliga fakulteten vid Åbo Akademi*, ser. A:131. Abo 1978. This is a new development as such, but the close collaboration between the Finnish Ministry of Foreign Affairs and various foreign organizations started already during the interwar period, see Juhani Paasivirta, *Suomen diplomaatti-edustus ja ulkopolitiikan hoito itsenäistymisestä talvisotaan*. Porvoo 1968, pp. 204–24.
6 This is at least what happened in Finland, see Paasivirta *op.cit.* 1968, pp. 215–18.
7 On the Finnish case see *ibid.*, pp. 233–66.
8 See Johan Galtung, How Can World Interests Be Better Promoted? Some Ideas Based on the Caracas Conference. *Instant Research on Peace and Violence*, Vol. 4, No. 4 (1974), pp. 188–89.

168

9 *Ibid.*, p. 193.
10 Galtung & Holmboe Ruge *op.cit.* 1965, p. 126.
11 This kind of research programme has been launched, for example, by Keijo Korhonen, who has been in leading positions in the Finnish diplomatic service as well as professor of political history at the University of Helsinki, see his Turvallisuuspolitiikasta ja sen tutkimisesta, Mika Hokkinen (ed.), *Turvallisuuspolitiikka ja sen tutkimus*. Department of Political History, University of Turku, Turku 1975, pp. 25–42.
12 Galtung & Holmboe Ruge *op.cit.* 1965, p. 111.

Research on Intelligence*

NILS PETTER GLEDITSCH AND OWEN WILKES

1. Intelligence and research

'Intelligence', according to an authoritative US military publication, is 'the product resulting from collection, evaluation, analysis, integration, and interpretation of all information concerning one or more aspects of foreign countries or areas which is immediately or potentially significant to the development and execution of plans, policies, and operations' (Department of Defense, 1974). This definition of intelligence has great similarities with common definitions of research.[1] We might say that intelligence is a special form of goal-directed research in the military and foreign-policy field, aiming to contribute to 'military planning and operations'. But since the definition also speaks of 'potential relevance', it is clear that intelligence can include basic research, where the goal-direction may be neither particularly strong nor particularly clear.

The practice of intelligence organisations also illuminates some of the similarities with research. Whether the information is collected by technical means, as in SIGINT, or signals intelligence, or by human beings, as in HUMINT, human intelligence, the data collection must be subjected to the same requirements as that of other research. The analysis also has the same character: formulating competing

* Shortened version of PRIO-publication S-16/79, presented to the Eighth General Conference of the International Peace Research Association, at Königstein, German Federal Republic, in September 1979. The work has been supported by a grant from the Norwegian Research Council for Science and the Humanities (12.48.41.078). Thanks are due to Tor Andreas Gitlesen and Ingvar Botnen for research assistance and to the participants of the symposium on intelligence at the IPRA conference for their comments. The very first draft of what became this article was written as a statement for, among others, the police when the authors were questioned for revealing in a previous report (Wilkes and Gleditsch, 1979) details of CIA/NSA technical intelligence activities in Norway. This earlier report has led to a charge against Gleditsch for violation of the 'spy paragraph' of the penal code. We think it is in the tradition of Galtung's own work to introduce new fields to the scrutiny of researchers, even when extremely controversial, and also to use unconventional methodology. We can only regret that we were unable to conform to another established tradition of Galtung's work by coming up with exactly ten researchable problems. In the context of a *Festschrift* it is also proper to record our gratitude to Galtung's unwavering solidarity throughout the development of the case. Needless to say, neither he nor anyone else but ourselves is responsible etc. etc.

hypotheses and choosing between them on an empirical basis. The intelligence analyst may more frequently than the average researcher be in the position where he has to choose between hypotheses on the basis of incomplete data, but a good analyst will formulate his conclusions with proper caution.

In spite of these similarities, there is very little research on intelligence. There is a growing body of biographical and anecdotal literature, including some excellent journalistic history,[2] and an even larger body of fiction. But intelligence has been subjected to very little systematic scrutiny by academics.[3] The main reason for this relates to an important distinction between intelligence and most research: the secrecy of the process as well as the end product.

One consequence of the lack of research on intelligence is the proliferation of myths, positive as well as negative. Signals intelligence is said to have completely changed the course of the Second World War, and today's spy satellites are seen as essential for stable deterrence, the avoidance of nuclear war, and the achievement of arms control. Or, from a different perspective, the dirty tricks practised by intelligence services are seen as the source of all internal unrest in the third world. Such gross simplifications are not only an obstacle to our understanding of history and current affairs, but also prevent proper democratic control over intelligence operations.

This article is a part of a wider effort to elucidate the role of one important, and growing, part of modern intelligence: technical intelligence. This is done by first formulating very briefly eight researchable problems, then discussing the data needs for answering them, and finally reviewing existing studies.

2. Eight researchable problems

The first three problems concern international issues:

2.1. The strategic balance between the superpowers

There is no general agreement as to which superpower is ahead in the strategic arms race. To resolve this disagreement is an important task in order to understand the dynamics of the arms race. Among the inadequacies of existing studies are a failure to evaluate the relative importance of different indicators, and an over-emphasis on easily quantifiable indicators of strategic power like the number of missiles and bombers to the exclusion of more elusive concepts like accuracy or morale. One factor that is left out of most strategic comparisons is the strategic infrastructure, of which command and control and intelligence facilities are important parts. In the area of HUMINT the Soviet

Union can more easily achieve its objectives, in part because of the more open nature of the USA. On the other hand, the US is commonly judged to be well ahead in intelligence-gathering technology. This may have important consequences for military strategy. To what extent, for instance, does the acquisition of a superior strategic reconnaissance and targeting ability facilitate a counterforce strategy.

2.2. Trends towards strategic instability

There is a growing concern that increasing counterforce capabilities are leading toward first-strike counterforce doctrines. Since about 1960 the main obstacle to a successful first strike has been the invulnerability of submarine-based strategic missiles. Recent developments in anti-submarine warfare capabilities are beginning to threaten this invulnerability and thus the presumed stability of the arms race. The main reason for this is not the development of new weapons, but an improved ability to *detect* and *track* operational submarines, i.e. a question of improved intelligence (SIPRI, 1979).

2.3. Verification of arms control and disarmament agreements

Progress towards arms control and disarmament agreements, such as SALT II or a complete test ban treaty, is constantly impeded by the objection that national technical means of verification, especially those of the USA, are not adequate to the task. These objections are controversial, and the argument should not be decided simply on faith, but on the basis of a study of the capabilities of existing verification technology. In fact, this means the technical intelligence of the superpowers (the 'national technical means of verification'), since there is virtually no third-country or international machinery for arms control verification (SIPRI, 1980).

The next five research problems refer to issues for the countries that serve as hosts to the intelligence installations of the superpowers. They were formulated with Norway in mind, but, with the partial exception of the one relating to the base policy, are just as relevant to other superpower allies.

2.4. Are technical intelligence installations offensive or defensive?

All countries profess to be defensive in their overall military policy, and the terms offensive and defensive are charged with considerable emotion. However, they can be defined simply by reference to where warfare takes place: on enemy territory or one's own. It is frequently

172

asserted that military installations close to the enemy's border will be interpreted as offensive. On the other hand, intelligence stations are frequently interpreted as essentially defensive, because they provide reliable warning of enemy attack. Moreover, they are seen as stabilizing because they prevent a rash response on the basis of false interpretations of enemy intentions. Our own view is that no technology is essentially defensive or offensive – the crucial issue is strategy and the planned use of the technology. In addition to the defensive early-warning function it is not difficult to point to possible offensive uses of intelligence, such as the use of electronic interception to prepare a pre-emptive attack on the enemy's radar stations. A forward location of a listening station may be crucial for the accomplishment of an offensive task like this, but may also improve the stations (defensive) early-warning function.

2.5. Do intelligence stations add to or detract from the host nation's security?

A small nation that accommodates military bases, including intelligence installations, for a superpower may thus enhance its security by increased capacity for deterring attack and by assuring armed intervention of the superpower in the case of war. On the other hand, its security may suffer in the sense that the probability of involvement in war is increased. Weighing these considerations against each other is a moral and political task. But empirical research can contribute by mapping the extent and offensive potential of the strategic installations, thereby making it clear that the dilemma is real.

2.6. Intelligence stations and base policies

Since joining NATO in 1949 Denmark and Norway have practised a policy of not permitting peacetime foreign military bases (although Denmark has made an exception for the territory of Greenland). Other countries practise more or less severe restrictions. Few if any countries give their allies complete freedom to establish military bases. On the other hand, even fairly restrictive countries like Denmark and Norway may themselves operate with local personnel 'facilities' requested, designed, and paid for by the US for US military purposes. For example, both countries operate a number of SIGINT stations, probably on behalf of the CIA and NSA. Key elements in maintaining the distinction between 'bases' and 'facilities' are nominal host nation control and host nation manning of the stations. To what extent these elements are present, is an empirical question. Here, research can help to elucidate possible inconsistencies between declared and actual policy.

2.7. *The legality of intelligence*

Intelligence-gathering operations, and communications intelligence in particular, raise a number of legal problems. They may infringe various domestic laws relating to individual privacy, but organizations and even nations also have some, limited, defined privacy rights. In international law both the Diplomatic Convention of 1961 and the International Telecommunications Convention of 1973 place certain constraints on the interception of official communications. The restrictions in the diplomatic sphere are particularly severe with regard to the protection of the diplomatic bag and other written communications, but are also interpreted by one prominent author in international law to cover radio communication (Denza, 1976).

2.8. *The question of secrecy*

It is frequently asserted that there is excessive secrecy with regard to military matters and particularly in the area of intelligence. One way to establish whether or not there is 'too much' secrecy is to make a comparison with other countries. Another is to compare the extent of secrecy with what one can reasonably assume the opponent to know. Since the opponent will rarely reveal exactly what he knows, one must make informed guesses. It seems reasonable to assume that as a minimum the opponent must know what is available in public sources, including visual inspection from public places and using their own national technical means of verification.

3. Data needs and resources

All the eight questions mentioned above are researchable in the sense that they can be subjected to theorizing. But are they researchable in an empirical sense?

The answer to this question, in our view, is an emphatic yes. All intelligence activities are subject to great secrecy, and records may never be made or may be destroyed to protect sources and also to prevent post-hoc analysis. In the area of human intelligence, at least, this makes it extremely difficult to reach any reliable conclusions about such important questions as the degree of agent penetration, the reliability of agent reporting, etc. Technical intelligence is different in the sense that any physical sensor must be exposed to the environment it monitors and is therefore itself potentially detectable by technical intelligence, and frequently by very simple means. Much electronic intelligence, for instance, requires large antenna farms, which can frequently be found in publicly accessible places. Manned installations are also traceable through other means, such as telephone directories, advertisements for personnel, military service rosters and trade union records. The ownership of various installations can frequently be ascertained in municipal records or government property directories. The age of installations, generally a clue in determining their function, can often be determined through municipal records or by examining old editions of telephone directories. Most important, much of the technology is commercially promoted and frequently field observations can be compared with advertisements and illustrated articles in electronics journals. In spite of governmental reluctance to release official information about intelligence activities, a great deal of the information is already in the public domain, and available for research purposes.

4. Existing empirical studies

A few beginnings have been made, most of them by journalists, peace movement activists, and US congressional investigators, rather than by academic researchers. Several of them provide some data relevant to some of the questions we have outlined above.

4.1 US congressional studies of American commitments abroad

The US Indochina wars stimulated a review by the US Congress of foreign military commitments. A first, and not trivial task was simply to map how many and what kind of commitments had been entered into by the US, including tacit or covert commitments in the form of foreign bases. A major study by the Senate Foreign Relations committee, initiated in 1969, led in 1971 to the publication of a transcript of reports and hearings totalling 2442 pages (US Congress, 1971). In these volumes several US SIGINT facilities are located and identified. In 1977 the House Committee on International Relations commissioned a report from the Congressional Research Service (CRS) on US commitments in the Mediterranean. The resulting report (US Congress, 1977) identified a number of SIGINT sites as well as NADGE radar sites. In 1978 the CRS completed another study, this time on anti-submarine warfare. This report listed no fewer than 17 US underwater listening stations, based mostly on newspaper and magazine articles.

4.2. Gensuikyo's study of US bases in Okinawa

As a result of revelations that the US Navy routinely brought nuclear weapons into Japanese ports in violation of agreements banning all nuclear weapons from Japan, the Japanese peace movement Gensuikyo undertook an investigation of all the US facilities in Japan and Okinawa to assess the degree to which they assisted US preparations for nuclear war. This study resulted in a book, heavy on technical data, with plans and photos of antenna arrays, location maps, etc.

4.3. Semi-official information and unofficial revelations about electronic interception in Britain

Great Britain is frequently contrasted with the US for its more restrictive secrecy policies. Nevertheless a textbook on the techniques of radio direction-finding has been published by an electronics expert who has spent most of his professional career with the so-called Government Communications Headquarters, the British signals intelligence organization (Gething, 1978). In addition numerous articles by Gething and others describe the Plessey-built hardware operated by the GCHQ. (There is a similar US textbook on electronic counter-measures, Boyd et al., published in classified form in 1961, declassified in 1973.)

The rather pro-intelligence journalist Chapman Pincher has described the location of half a dozen NSA stations in Britain which are 'rather pointlessly camouflaged as military and naval establishments or radio research stations' (Pincher, 1978, p. 161). Duncan Campbell, a journalist highly critical of intelligence activities, has revealed details of telephone tapping and radio interception in a number of articles (cf. for instance Campbell and Hosenball, 1976; Campbell, 1979, as well as a series of articles in the *New Statesman* in 1980).

4.4. US article on West German eavesdropping on the Warsaw Pact

In 1977 the trade journal *Defence Electronics/Electronic Warfare* published a remarkable article on electronic intelligence in West Germany. The article included a map that provided approximate locations for 18 listening stations and described the technical equipment and US-West German cooperative arrangements in some detail.

4.5. The case of Iran

As a result of the Islamic revolution in Iran in early 1979, the US seems to have lost all its intelligence facilities in that country. In the wake of the revolution a great deal of detail about the facilities in Iran has been

176

published in newspapers. But even before the new regime took over, newspapers were able to report on locations. (Cf. e.g. Boyes and Henderson, 1979. This article, for good measure, was reprinted by the US Defense Department's daily reprint service *Current News.*)

4.6. The case of Denmark

In October 1969 a group of Danish students exposed a military operation in the basement of a university building. The military immediately pulled out of what appears to have been a station to tap telex and cable connections between Denmark and other countries, operated by the intelligence service. In the ensuing debate, five electronic intercept stations also operated by military intelligence were named in the press, although little was said about their equipment or possible role.

4.7. The case of Sweden

In 1973 two Swedish journalists, working closely with a former employee of Swedish intelligence, exposed the existence of a hitherto secret intelligence organization, innocently named the Information Bureau (IB). A number of intelligence and covert action projects of the IB were revealed. The ensuing debate also provided some details of signals intelligence performed in another branch of military intelligence and on US-Swedish cooperation in technical intelligence (Bratt, 1973; Guillou, 1976 a,b).

4.8. The case of Norway

The listening stations in Norway were briefly mentioned, without giving any locations, in a book that appeared in 1969 (Johansen, 1969). Eight years later, together with other material on the intelligence service and the special branch of the police, they became part of an exposé which came to be known as 'the lists case'. A book about this case (Elvik, 1977, p. 10) gave the approximate location of seven such stations. On a later occasion, the same journalist reported the assumed location of a US underwater listening station in Norway (Elvik, 1978). Meanwhile, in 1976 the defense minister had given a general description of the listening stations and their location ('in Northern Norway and along the coast'). It is generally thought that this interview was a pre-emptive move to take the sting out of the revelations which erupted ten months later. In a book published by the present authors and two others in 1978 a brief technical description was given of one of the listening stations, as well as a critical discussion of their relation to the

Norwegian base policy. In early 1979 a very detailed report was published by ourselves, naming a total of 11 stations in 9 locations. We were unable, in that report, to locate the underwater listening station, but rejected the location given by Elvik. This report was based on a variety of open sources and field observations. A few months later a New York Times story described an intelligence site in Norway as important for monitoring Soviet missile tests (Burt, 1979).

5. Research as intelligence?

Although the authorities in all the various countries mentioned have been reluctant to publish any official information on intelligence operations, their reactions to the information which has been published has varied a great deal. One of the authors of one of the US congressional studies told us that the Pentagon was quite pleased with his work: it showed them what was already in the public domain, and it gave them an unclassified publication to refer to when asked for information. At the other extreme, the two Swedish journalists and their main informant were sent to jail for terms from eight months to a year. In between, we find milder judicial reactions in Norway against the main actors in the 'lists case' and against several journalists involved in the revelations of Danish signals intelligence. (However, Danish intelligence relaxed its security as a result of this episode and painted over the line reading 'no photography' on signs outside the intelligence stations.) In Japan there was no prosecution at all, and in England Duncan Campbell and his associate were given only a quite nominal sentence for receiving information from a former soldier in signals intelligence, while more serious charges for systematic collection of information on the intelligence stations were dropped midway through the trial.

As this brief survey shows, studies on technical intelligence which involve the naming of specific installations and their equipment may lead to prosecution, although this is by no means always the case. Frequently, and perhaps most clearly in the case of our own 1979 report, research in the area of intelligence is interpreted as intelligence collection and the perpetrators distinguished from traditional spies mainly by their naivety. Since in the introduction we have explicitly identified intelligence as a form of research, it would be pointless to try to deny that research on intelligence stations is itself a form of intelligence. It differs from a great deal of contemporary research on international relations in that the researcher has to depart from his office desk and his library to seek relevant data in the field – just as there is a limit to what anthropologists can say about foreign cultures without visiting them.

An implicit assumption in a great deal of the criticism of 'research as intelligence' is that it tells the enemy a great deal about what he does not know and what we prefer him not to know. These are interesting issues, but in no way relevant to determining the *research value* of the empirical findings. These considerations may, of course, inspire caution not to collect more data than are needed to illuminate the research problems formulated. In a longer version of this article we have tried to show in more detail why field observations, the most frequently criticized form of data collection, are necessary to shed light on all of the issues outlined in section 2 above. We also believe that studies limited to open sources, including field observations from publicly accessible places, are inherently unlikely to reveal secrets not known to the opponent, as distinct from what is kept secret from the public at large. In the name of caution, and in the absence of solid data, essayists may engage in generalizations which are as vague as they are misleading. As one example, we may quote a recognized expert on Soviet foreign policy, who has written:

> The Norwegians clearly conduct some tactical electronic and other surveillance of Soviet developments . . . But this limited tactical surveillance can be tolerated by the USSR. It is surveillance integrated into hostile strategic offensive systems that could not be tolerated. (Jacobson, 1972, p. 152).

We feel, on the contrary, that our own limited study of technical intelligence in Norway went a long way toward demonstrating that Norwegian surveillance is in fact not 'limited tactical surveillance' but part of a world-wide surveillance network, which is very definitely 'integrated into hostile strategic offensive systems'. This kind of armchair speculation can survive only in an environment where researchers have abandoned their empirical curiosity or their will to assert an independent right to know.

NOTES

1 Research is more frequently used to refer to the *process* than to the product. But although the quoted definition of intelligence refers only to the product, the product is defined in terms of a process, and intelligence is also used to denote the process.
2 Two excellent surveys of the non-fictional literature are Blackstock and Schaf (1978) and Williams (1978). A recent example of good journalistic history is Wyden (1979) on the Bay of Pigs.
3 Some exceptions are the classical work by Ransom (1970) and more recent work by Freedman (1977), Dedijer (1978), and Agrell (1979), but the empirical base on the intelligence side leaves much to be desired.

REFERENCES

Agrell, Wilhelm, 1979. 'Military intelligence and the information explosion', *Discussion paper* No. 129, Lund University, Research policy institute.

Blackstock, Paul W. & Frank L. Schaf, Jr., 1978. *Intelligence, espionage, counterespionage, and covert operations. A guide to information sources.* Vol. 2 in the International relations information guide series. Detroit, Gale.

Boyd, J. A. *et al.*, 1978. *Electronic Countermeasures.* Los Altos Hills, California, Peninsula (Classified edition 1961, declassified 1973, republished 1978.)

Boyes, R. & S. Henderson, 1979. 'US military surveillance of the Soviet Union: Monitoring bases in Iran at risk', *Financial Times*, February 9.

Bratt, Peter, 1973. *IB och hotet mot vår säkerhet* (The information bureau and the threat to our security). Stockholm, Gidlunds.

Dedijer, Stephan, 1978. 'The Jones intelligence doctrine for the underveloped countries', *Science and Public Policy*, Vol. 5, No. 5, October, pp. 333–45.

Denza, Eileen, 1976. *Diplomatic law. Commentary on the Vienna convention on diplomatic relations.* Dobbs Ferry, NY/London, Oceana/British institute of international and comparative law.

(Department of Defense), 1974. *Department of Defense Dictionary of Military and Associated Terms.* JCS-publ. No. 1. Washington, D. C., Joint Chiefs of Staff.

Elvik, Halvor, 1977. *Politi, presse, overvåking. Hvitbok om listesaka* (Police, press, and surveillance. White book on the lists case). Oslo, Pax.

– , 1978. 'Grensekrenkelsene i nord: Soviet til aksjon mot lyttesystem i Finnmark' (The border violations in the North. The Soviet Union acts against listening system in Finnmark), *Dagbladet* July 25.

Freedman, Lawrence, 1977. *US Intelligence and the Soviet Strategic Threat.* London, Macmillan.

Gething, P. J. D., 1978. *Radio Direction-Finding and the Resolution of Multicomponent Wave Fields.* Stevenage, Peter Peregrinus.

Jacobsen, C. J. 1972, *Soviet Strategy – Soviet Foreign Policy. Military Considerations Affecting Soviet Foreign Policy.* Glasgow, Glasgow University Press.

Johansen, Jahn Otto, 1969. *Hva vil Sovjet?* (What does the Soviet Union want?) Oslo, Cappelen.

Pincher, Chapman, 1978. *Inside Story.* London, Sidgwick and Jackson.

Ransom, Harry Howe, 1970. *The Intelligence Establishment.* Cambridge, Harvard University Press.

(Stockholm International Peace Research Institute), 1979. 'Strategic anti-submarine warfare and its implications for a counterforce first strike', chapter 9 in *World Armaments and Disarmament. SIPRI Yearbook 1979.* London, Taylor and Francis.

(–) 1980. 'Verification of the SALT II Treaty' Chapter 7 in *World Armaments and Disarmament. SIPRI Yearbook 1980.* London, Taylor and Francis.

(US Congress, 1971) *United States security agreements and commitments abroad.* Hearings before the subcommittee on United States security agreements and commitments abroad, Committee on foreign relations, US Senate. Washington, D.C. US government printing office.

(–), 1977. United States military installations and objectives in the Mediterranean. Report prepared for the subcommittee on Europe and the Middle East, Committee on international relations, House of Representatives. Washington, D.C., US government printing office.

(–), 1978. *Evaluation of fiscal year 1979 arms control impact statements: Toward more informed congressional participation in national security policy-making.* Report prepared for the Subcommittee on international security scientific affairs of the Committee on international relations, House of Representatives. Washington, D.C., US government printing office.

Wilkes, Owen & Nils Petter Gleditsch, 1979. 'Intelligence installations in Norway: Their number, location, function, and legality'. Oslo, International Peace Research Institute. (PRIO-publication S-4/79).

Williams, George, 1978. 'Intelligence and book learning. A comprehensive survey of public sources on secret activities', *Choice,* Vol. 6, No. 9, November, pp. 1125–38.

Wyden, Peter, 1979. *The Bay of Pigs. The Untold Story.* NY, Simon and Schuster.

Whole Philosophies as Data and as Constructs

ARNE NAESS

1. Systems: Large scope combined with low epistemic pretensions

In the heroic stage of development within logical empiricism the term 'wissenschaftliche Weltanschauung' ('scientific world view') was a-voided, but not 'wissenschaftliche Weltauffassung' ('scientific conception of the world'). Gradually the enthusiasm for the latter diminished, mainly for two reasons: science might not yet be ripe for saying something about everything, and, secondly, the problems involved might be mere pseudo-problems or puzzles due to 'Leergang der Sprache'. Personally I accepted world conceptions as long as they were taken as working hypotheses in a spirit of Scientific Attitude. This term I· proposed as a central slogan, not 'physicalism' or any definite working hypothesis.[1] Generalizations from areas well covered by research to those less well or not covered should be considered implicit research *programs*.[2] Their formulation as assertions served only purposes of promotion and encouragement.

As I see it now, the step from a less to a more inclusive hypothesis does not require a drop in scientific attitude, whatever the wideness of the initial hypothesis. This holds at least if the decisive characteristic of that attitude is (as I thought in the thirties) to leave every question open in principle. That is, never to close any investigation except for practical purposes. Action requires decision, whatever the state of evidence.

It seems, however, that the conception of scientific attitude in terms of openness is historically untenable. Historically, science is not colored by 'zetecism', the non-academic, seeking scepticism of Sextus Empiricus. Dogmatism and zetecism alternate. Anyhow, a historically adequate concept of scientific attitude must include reference to the marked preference of scientists for problems which seem at the present to have some chance of being investigated by established methods and kinds of technology. Such an inclusion, however, makes it likely that successive widening of the scope of a hypothesis eventually makes its use incompatible with a scientific attitude. There are good reasons for scientists to avoid seeking a grand synthesis. But why not combine competence in scientific methodology with serious work of a non-scientific nature?

Today there is in analytically oriented philosophy less interest in the question whether an investigation is carried out scientifically or not. What is asked is rather whether the norms of *pro et contra dicere* and of unbiasedness *(Sachlichkeit)* are adhered to. (A covering of witty rhetorical artistry, like that of Paul Feyerabend, is not generally frowned upon, however.) We may therefore inquire in a new spirit what place is to be offered to world views, or even more inclusive constructions: total views or systems. A total view says something about everything, not everything about everything, or even everything about anything. Brushing away the question of the possibility of a *scientific* total view (in spite of Gödel's theorem), we immediately face a more serious problem: is there not an inherent dogmatism in every system pretending totality? Need the pretension of scope be combined with high epistemic pretensions?

2. The methodology of total views does not favor dogmatism

A total view containing its own logic, ontology and methodology can scarcely be disconfirmed empirically. But it can be found inconsistent and in other ways logically defective. If the view is articulated as a philosophical system, there is no a priori reason that it should be held more dogmatically than a partial view – a view of history, psychology, or politics. There seems to be no limit to the dogmatism concerning particular theories. They may also be formed in a way making it impregnable empirically. Example: The conditional reflex theory as formulated in the thirties and forties.

Philosophers like Descartes, Spinoza, Hegel seemed to be utterly convinced that they were right in their most general and abstract views, but the same attitude is found also among philosophers who are against systems. We find utterly convinced people among ordinary language philosophers and various branches of analytically oriented philosophers.

Considering the step by step widening of a combined empirical and logical/methodological system, there is no stage before the practically and perhaps theoretically unobtainable totality at which testability in a wide sense reaches zero. Talking about systems in general, there is not even good reason to believe in any necessary reduction of testability with increased scope. On the contrary, the vulnerability normally increases with intended field of validity.

Some would hold that the value statements preclude testability. But valuations refer to life-situations, and more generally, to the environment. Hypotheses about the universe thus enter any normative system. Excepting isolated, ultimate norms, valuations are held for certain reasons and are changed because of happenings of various kinds. This guarantees sources of vulnerability and testability.

Discussing testability, the most important difference between to-day's research habits and those of previous centuries is in the using of models. The incompleteness and crudeness of models are clearly and explicitly recognized. Their usefulness is dependent (among other factors) upon a degree of simplicity that implies incompleteness and crudeness. System-building in philosophy must, in my view, acknowledge that in so far as its verbalizations are moderately precise and testable, what is worked out is a succession of models, modified step by step through experience and logical analysis.

3. The implicit systems of fighters against systems

But, it may be objected, is not building models of systems a kind of luxury, and also dependent upon more than average knowledge about the world and oneself?

Suppose a man just going to be married is asked whether he has any opinion at all about astrology, and suppose he answers 'Absolutely none!' From the point of view of philosophical systems he may nevertheless have hundreds. One may ask whether he believes as-trological insight may prove that he is completely wrong in marrying on that day, and he may reject the suggestion. It may turn out that after all he entertains opinions making it reasonable not to study astrology. Every decision to act does, in a sense, presuppose a survey of factors considered relevant in the choice situation. *Innumerable factors are by implication dismissed as irrelevant.* A general view is presupposed, even if never articulated.[3]

The effort to *articulate* a general view may for most people in most situations be a luxury, but it seems that rather general, more or less consistent, views and orientations are causally active in individuals and groups. There is no good reason to avoid making explicit what is operating anyhow, with or without scrutiny.

4. Political and general social importance of systems

The above reflections about total views are offered for consideration because of my belief that policies in the industrialized countries, and I am now thinking particularly about Scandinavia, today rather than 20 years ago, touch and increasingly must touch, general and fundamental views about what is the good life and how is it to be realized under the present global conditions. Let me use economics as an example.

The development of the non-marxist science of economics points towards the inevitability of system-thinking.[4] Standard of living was until the success of welfare economics measured in terms of the distribution of single goods (telephones, iceboxes, radio, television). Welfare economics introduced concepts of profiles of goods and services. 'Would you prefer the fairly moderate amounts of goods so-and-so combined with a fairly high standard of housing to fairly rich amounts of goods so-and-so combined with a moderate standard of housing?' Ultimately this tendency from particulars to whole sets of goods and services leads to presenting life style alternatives. The question of meeting marked *demands* of particulars led to questions of how to satisfy *needs,* and this again to question how to secure preferred life styles. Needs in an industrial society vary considerably with life style preferences. At this stage the development statistics of prices on the market could not any longer be a chief source of relevant economic data. Extensive and deep interviews, as in 'life quality' research, were needed. But life style preferences cannot be separated from philosophical questions of value priority.

Thus, the development of economics as a science concerned with how to provide and distribute scarce goods and services has arrived at the gates of philosophy: extensive systems implicitly held by people are basic materials for consideration, not fragments, like preferences exhibited on markets. The systems include value-priorities, which can be explicated by systems of norms of different degrees of fundamentality or generality. They also include important sets of general opinions about society, about what is going to happen in the future, and about many other topics of philosophical import. The value-preferences or norms are scarcely understandable without reference to such hypotheses. In short, economics in the customary narrow sense has become a speciality dealing with fragments of larger wholes involving not only social sciences of diverse kinds, but philosophy. Economic policies of a society, local or national, will have to compare life philosophies in relation to resources, technologies, and other basic factors of general political development.

Those philosophies which diminish or destroy potentialities of self-realization among adherents of others cannot be offered maximum support. Thus, the policy makers need to understand what is going on in the populace as regard life style preferences. Furthermore, study is needed to better understand which technologies and modifiable life conditions are favorable to the growth of life styles and value preferences which destroy the potentialities of others. An example: Life styles with stress on vast and increasing consumption of scarce ('high cost') goods and services require development destructive of environmental characteristics which are vital to representatives of other life styles.

5. An illustration: A Fragment of Ecosophy T

Let me for the sake of illustration present a fragment of a general philosophical system in the form of a simple model. It is a version of the 'Ecosophy T'-model published and defended in various writings.[5] Here I shall not concentrate on a defense of the model, but rather offer some critical comments based on a hypothetical claim that it is adequate as a paradigm.

The lines suggest derivations. Norms are given imperative form.

Some semantical remarks: The sentences are formed more or less as slogans. The one-word sentence 'Self-realization!' may be interpreted in the directions of 'Complete Self-realization!', 'Maximum Self-realization!' or 'More Self-realization'. The term 'self' is to be interpreted in the direction of 'Self' (*ātman*) in certain philosophies of the East in which it is contrasted with 'ego' and 'self'. It is a direction which makes the concept of 'Self' compatible with some versions of Buddhist *anāt-mavada*. There are (of course) also Western conceptions in line with the broad and deep concept of Self, but they are today less known. – These remarks about 'Self-realization' are made in order to avoid the thought that it is a kind of 'ego-trip', or that it is identical with Maslow's somewhat egocentric concept.

A remark on the function of the sentence 'The higher the self-realization by anybody the more its increase depends upon the increase of the self-realization of others': The sentence is meant to suggest hypotheses about the social requirements of high degrees of self-realization. The individual is dependent upon society and, when insight and praxis develop, upon all societies. Thus the individual eventually gets into the situation in which further increase of the level of self-realization depends upon that of all others, and not only upon humans.

Critical remarks:

1. The pyramidal form of the fragment has been criticized as too Aristotelian, and lacking the insight of 'feed back'. The diagram only pictures derivations (in a broad logical sense), not influences.

Experience may (of course) result in modification from the bottom upwards. Either by modification of the interpretation of one or more of the (vague, ambiguous) sentences, or by substitution of some sentences for others.

2. The formulation of norms (imperatives) rather than lines of recommendation or standards of valuation, suggests an absolutist or dogmatic approach to decision. (A point made by Nils Kristian Sundby).

186

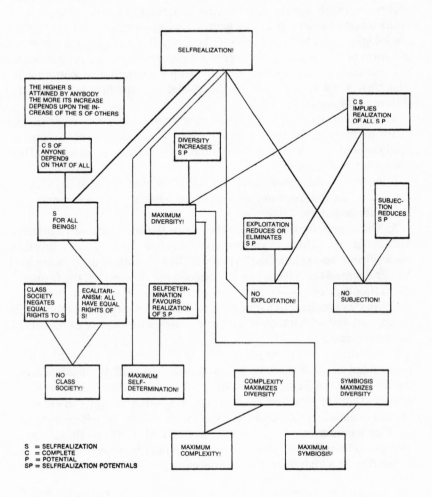

The diagram is only of use to picture the logical relationships between such lines. Making the sentences more precise, their dichotomic, absolutist form should be moderated.

3. Starting with imperatives suggests a 'voluntarist', 'idealist' system. The imperatives also make it difficult to stress the importance of the moment (Øieblikket, Kierkegaard), the dwelling (Heidegger), rather being 'busy'. And how is Eastern non-action accommodated?

Comments of this kind can always be made. They remind us of the limitation of every version of a model relying on slogans. Without clarification of the terms used, vague and superficial impressions will color the interpretations. There are, however, strong methodological

187

reasons for starting an exposition with vague and ambiguous sentences rather than with sentences belonging to a definite scientific approach. (Information theory, theory of games, model logic, general ecology or sociology, . . .) The ambiguities make it possible to formulate a general platform representative of different subgroups within the deep ecological movement.[6] By careful step by step elimination of certain ambiguities, a set of versions of the model are constructed which fit different subgroups.

4. Why start with only one fundamental norm? It favors word-magic to try to cover every principle by means of only one norm. Empirical study of which norms are taken as basic suggests that they are rather numerous and diverse.

It must, on the other hand, be admitted that if we start with 10 fundamentals the question of mutual consistency and independence arises immediately.

5. The simplicity of the model is due to the tolerance of vagueness and ambiguity. Efforts towards 'maximal self-determination', 'no class society' and 'no exploitation' will normally be conflicting. As soon as a higher degree of preciseness is introduced into the model, the formidable difficulties of consistency and elimination of norm-conflicts will necessitate complicated formulations. The simplicity of the model will disappear, and with it one of the basic motives for the use of models in system construction.

Concluding, the comments point to obvious weaknesses which may be avoided in other models. I look forward to studying models comparable to that of Ecosophy T which are clearly different in their point of departure. In Scandinavia there are Christian activists in environmental questions who would not start with a norm of self-realization. Neither would groups deeply influenced by Marxism or Buddhism, I assume. The different starting points do not, however, exclude the possibility of a high degree of overlapping further down the stream of derivations.

NOTES

1 Wie fórdert man heute [1937] die empirische Bewegung?, Filosofiske Problemer No.19, Oslo 1956.
2 'Die Funktion der Verallgemeinerung', *Erkenntnis* 7, 1937/38, pp. 198–210.
3 More about this in my 'Reflections about Total Views', *Philosophy and Phenomenological Research*, 25, 1964, No. 1.
4 Details in Sections 24 and 25 in the Chapter on Economics in my *Økologi, samfunn og livsstil*, 5th, ed., Oslo 1976.
5 Cp. 'Notes on the Methodology of Normative Systems', *Methodology and Science*, 10, 1977, pp. 64–79. More details: *Økologi, samfunn og livsstil*, 5th ed., Universitetsforlaget, Oslo 1976.
6 Cp. 'The Deep and the Shallow Ecological Movement', *Inquiry* 16, 1973, pp. 95–100.

Trying to Reconcile Galtung and Durkheim

ERIK ALLARDT

Many of us who have worked with social indicators on problems of social development are in great debt to Johan Galtung. His, at the same time fearless and theoretically elegant, formulations not only in the work towards a system of world indicators but also in the realm of methodology have liberated us from many unproductive constraints. It has been assuring to realize that a social scientist can try to be unashamedly value-oriented, that there might be potential and better worlds than the present one, and that the aim can be to break invariances rather than to seek them.[1]

Johan Galtung's proposals for creating programmes and defining concrete indicators have had a considerable impact as well. Yet, my intention is not to describe in detail how and to what extent I have borrowed ideas from Johan Galtung[2] but rather to indicate concerns which are different from his. It is not a question of contradictions or antagonisms but rather of a difference in emphasis. Three points in particular appear important to me.

Personal Growth as a Problem

In their work towards a World Indicators Programme Johan Galtung and his co-workers posited a list of ten value dimensions chosen as basic social concerns.[3] *Personal Growth* is at the top of the list as the most basic value. For at least two reasons I find it very difficult to make personal growth the overriding value or social concern to which other values should be subordinated. To postulate one value as more basic than others in a list of social concerns is not only an ethical but also a causal question. The value given the highest priority ought to have a considerable impact on other goods or other forms of goodness: in other words, it should have a high degree of convertibility or transferability. There seems to be nothing warranting such an assumption regarding personal growth. Except for the fact that man's survival as a biological being is a precondition for all other concerns, it seems unfounded to give any single social concern a priority over other concerns. In the so-called Comparative Scandinavian Welfare Study, conducted by the Research Group for Comparative Sociology at the University of Helsinki,[4] it was striking that the correlations between different components of well-being were fairly weak, and that the strength of convertibility was rather modest. It is not only dubious but also dangerous to posit one value as basic. On the other hand it is of importance to indicate and formulate the values defining the good life openly. However, all of these values are worth special and independent attention: they can not be substitutes for each other.

It has to be admitted that I also have a personal difficulty regarding the assumption of personal growth as the basic value. Personal growth, sometimes also described as the need for self-actualization and self-realization, easily becomes a very egotistical goal. This is so if personal growth becomes something individuals can claim for themselves. However, personal growth as a value is also problematic if it is something that is handed down from one individual to another. To work for the personal growth of others has in the situation of the present welfare-states been a privilege of the few. In fact, this pattern can be considered as one of the problematic features of the welfare-state. The gist of the matter is to make it possible for everyone to contribute to the well-being and personal growth of others. But the latter objective also means that solidarity has become more important than, or at least equally as important as, personal growth. The positing of personal growth as the basic value is an expression of a quest for liberation. This quest is quite typical of Johan Galtung, whereas the emphasis on solidarity, at least in sociology, is Durkheimian. I am aware of the danger of too much solidarity. Many cruelties have been committed in the name of solidarity. However, the same verdict may be issued as regards personal growth, at least as soon as it is advanced as a demand. Without any serious pretentions to be analytic I should like to suggest that the values of personal growth and of solidarity are both needed in order to counterbalance each other. Personally I probably have an inclination to side with Durkheim in an emphasis on solidarity in society, but I can also see a danger in such an orientation. I don't know of any other sociologist who to such an extent has constituted a healthy counterbalance to my Durkheimian inclinations as Johan Galtung. Yet, the tensions between the values of personal growth and solidarity, and between Galtung and Durkheim, will probably haunt me through all my sociological life.

Solidarity as a Problem

In their programme for a world indicators system Johan Galtung and his associates have listed solidarity as one of their ten values. In my own study comparing the well-being in Denmark, Finland, Norway, and Sweden, the basic values were labelled *Having, Loving,* and *Being.*

Having was an overriding concept for the components of the material level of living, whereas Loving represented indicators measuring solidarity and togetherness, and Being stood for different aspects of personal growth. It seems obvious that the different aspects of solidarity were given a greater weight in the Comparative Scandinavian Welfare Study than in the world indicators programme by Johan Galtung and his colleagues. There is also a clear difference in the content of the word solidarity in the two indicator programmes. In Galtung's system the opposite of solidarity is fragmentation, and in addition it is assumed that the value of solidarity is fairly close to an absence of marginalization. In my own indicator system fragmentation and marginalization are but minor aspects of the absence of solidarity. I have assumed that people generally have a strong need to feel togetherness in groups, which clearly is something much more than just the absence of fragmentation and marginalization.

There is one particular aspect of the relations of solidarity and of human relations generally which ought to be more closely observed in attempts to build indicators of well-being and quality of life. Relations of togetherness, of solidarity, and of companionship are strongly tied to the language we use. Actually the relations of togetherness can be seen as occurrences in the language. Feelings of togetherness usually require a long and shared linguistic development. Thus, in addition to the linguistic component in relations of togetherness there is also a historical aspect involved. Relations of solidarity have as a rule a background in a shared history and in a shared sameness of experiences. This is also why it is important for most people to have and to search for their roots.

To me relations of solidarity and the existence of roots are phenomena which are important to consider both in social science and in daily life. Again, I am very much aware of and also disturbed by what too much solidarity and an excessive emphasis on roots can cause in forms of cruelty and misery. Therefore, it is important to search for safeguards and balancing factors. The first and most important device is that it is always of the utmost importance to consider other values too as soon as solidarity comes into the focus of attention. Solidarity is an important value but it should never be exercised, suggested or conceived of without a simultaneous consideration of other values, such as the material resources for biological survival, ecological balance, equality, and personal growth. The second device for avoiding the negative consequences of solidarity is to observe that 'small is beautiful'. This is also the reason why I in our Comparative Scandinavian Welfare Study constructed indicators aiming at measuring community cohesiveness, family attachment, friendship patterns, and the absence of isolation, and, on the other hand, avoided measures of, for instance, national solidarity.

191

At any rate, my personal store of motives both in social science and in daily life is full of ambivalence and contradictions. Again, I find it helpful and even rewarding to describe it as a tension between Galtung and Durkheim.

Ethnicity as a Problem

Considering my interest in solidarity and roots it is not astonishing that I consider ethnicity and ethnic boundaries as important and interesting research problems. In fact, my most recent research is devoted to the study of linguistic minorities.[5] It can be mentioned that as part of its Social Indicator Programme, OECD has listed 'the maintenance and development of cultural heritage relative to its positive contribution to the well-being of the members of various social groups' as one of its social concerns. I accept this social concern as a positive value, and my recent studies of linguistic minorities are in fact a kind of outgrowth of my previous research on welfare and well-being. Ethnic factors such as language, culture, and race create important structural divisions, and I am inclined to agree with those who maintain that ethnicity was the forgotten factor of sociology and political science in the 1950's and 1960's.

It goes without saying that a focus on ethnicity and in particular on the cultural heritage as a positive value creates the same kinds of grave problems as an emphasis on solidarity in general does. The problems are probably even graver, since ethnicity and national feelings are directly related to world peace. It may be that I, as a member of a linguistic minority, the Swedish-speaking Finns, and as a citizen of Finland, a country with a very long joint border with one of the super-powers, am inclined to overstress the ethnic factor. On the other hand, my predicament is not at all an unusual one. At any rate, in this respect my inclinations are clearly different from those of Johan Galtung, who not only is one of the founders of modern peace research but who is in most of his doings a true cosmopolitan. In my defence it might be said that I am clearly aware of the dangers in a one-sided emphasis on ethnicity. The remedies and safeguards are by and large the same as regards a one-sided emphasis on solidarity in general, but there are additional points. As before, it is always important to emphasize also other values than the maintenance of the cultural heritage and the awareness of roots. As before, it is worthwhile to stress that 'small is beautiful'. The right to maintain their cultural heritage is also and perhaps particularly important for small, poor, and peripheral groups. In the last-mentioned respect, in the study of conditions under which peripheries may survive, Johan Galtung[6] as well as other Norwegian scholars[7] have made seminal contributions. One additional safeguard

192

against the evils of too much nationalism is to emphasize both cultural and structural pluralism, or in other words diversity in both culture and structure. Such a value has been strongly stressed in Johan Galtung's world indicators programme, and I cannot but heartily agree with this emphasis.[8]

At any rate, also in the approach to ethnicity I am full of the same kind of ambivalence as in my attempts to study solidarity, its assets and liabilities. I am glad to say that my acquaintance with the work of Johan Galtung has helped me not to become apathetic under the cross-pressures.

The Importance of Social Structure

I cannot deny that I have very much welcomed this opportunity to openly declare some of my inner tensions as a social scientist. To contrast Johan Galtung and Emile Durkheim is not a contrivance fashioned for this particular occasion; I feel that it describes my sentiments as a scientist and my point of departure in the field of sociology.

The subject matter in this note has led me to emphasize points on which I both have difficulties in fully following Johan Galtung and have gained much by reading him. In some theoretical questions I am much more in agreement with him. In particular I have always whole-heartedly enjoyed his ability to analyze social structure and its effects on different social forms, ranging from problems of peace to the development of science.

NOTES

1 Johan Galtung, *Methodology and Ideology. Theory and Methods of Social Research.* Vol. I (Copenhagen: Christian Ejlers, 1977).
2 See for example Erik Allardt, *Att ha, att älska, att vara. Om välfärd i Norden.* (Lund: Argos, 1975) p. 33.
3 J. Galtung, A. Guha, A. Wirak, S. Sjlie, M. Cifuentes and H. Goldstein, 'Measuring World Development II', *Alternatives* I (1975) pp. 523–524.
4 Erik Allardt, 'Dimensions of Welfare in a Comparative Scandinavian Study', *Acta Sociologica* 19 (1976) pp. 236–238.
5 Erik Allardt, *Implications of the Ethnic Revival in Modern, Industrialized Society. A Comparative Study of the Linguistic Minorities in Western Europe.* (Helsinki–Helsingfors: Commentationes Scientiarum Socialium, 1979).
6 Johan Galtung, 'A Structural Theory of Imperialism', *Journal of Peace Research*, No. 1, 1971, pp. 81–117.
7 Stein Rokkan, 'The Survival of Distinctiveness', Mimeo to be published in S. Rokkan and Derek Urwin (eds.), *Economy, Territory, Identity* (University of Bergen, 1979).
8 Johan Galtung et al., *op.cit.* pp. 324–325.

On Chance, Watersheds, Dialectical Succession, and J. Galtung's Recent Idealism

ULF HIMMELSTRAND

After Franklin D. Roosevelt's election as President of the USA in 1932 but before his inauguration, he once visited Miami, Florida. Sitting in an open car with the Mayor of Chicago at his side he participated in a cavalcade through the city. In the crowd lining up along the streets an assassin aimed at the President-Elect. Just as he was about to fire, a bystander nudged the assassin sideways so that the shot hit the Mayor of Chicago. He was killed, and Roosevelt survived to embark upon his new Deal policy to tackle the Great Depression.

If Roosevelt had been killed on this occassion he would automatically have been replaced by the Vice-President-Elect, John Nance Garner, a very conservative Texas Democrat who had no sympathy whatsoever for the New Deal. Quite possibly this could have given US political and economic history a rather different direction from what it actually took under Roosevelt's presidency.

This is not the place for writing counter-factual history. I have rendered this brief account of what happened around Christmas time in Miami 1932 only to illustrate the crucial role that chance and coincidence can play in history. The inevitable question that arises is how we as social scientists can best handle chance and coincidence in historical processes. When mass-events are involved it is possible to use random net models, or the so-called Monte Carlo method for projecting the time paths of a model combining 'deterministic' and stochastic assumptions. This is one approach to handling chance and coincidence in social processes. But even if the USA has experienced several presidential assassinations, they certainly do not constitute a mass phenomenon in any reasonable statistical sense. Stochastic models are thus simply not applicable. Counter-factual history is still possible as a second approach in cases like these. However, in this paper I would rather focus attention on a third approach, which asks not what might have happened with a slightly different chance outcome, but rather why and when small variations in the outcome of chance factors, or small variations in conscious human deliberation, will have large consequences for social and historical processes. Or in more concrete terms relating to the case of Roosevelt and Garner: Why did Roosevelt and

Garner have such very different political profiles, thus allowing chance to play such a decisive role in historical processes? An answer to this kind of question can be found both in terms of the structural universals of electoral competition in Western multi-party political systems, and in terms of the historical specificities of the US party-political system. To maximize electoral support for a political party and its leadership in a broadly aggregating rather than articulating party system such as the one found in the USA, the presidential and vice-presidential candidates are usually picked from rather different segments of the political spectrum within the party. Obviously such structural characteristics of electoral competition and aggregative political parties provide more leeway for distinctly different outcomes as a result of stochastic events, such as the death of a presidential candidate or incumbent, either through the stochastic processes of fatal illness, or ballistics.

Therefore, in explaining historical events that are a result of mixtures of stochastic and deterministic processes, a main explanatory factor is the extent to which a given structure provides branching points with a wide scope for stochastic events. By explaining the origin and change of such structural features, a historical analysis can be pursued in greater depth.

But the attempted assassination of Roosevelt, and its structural context, is only a very limited example of the structural features on which social scientists should focus attention in coming to grips with the role of chance and coincidence in historical processes. There is a whole family of structural features which are crucial in this kind of historical explanation. In this paper I will primarily make some observations on the function of 'watershed structures' and 'dialectical succession' in social processes of a historical nature. Unlike counter-factual history and the most common stochastic models, so-called watershed models and models of dialectical change have profound practical significance. Relatively small variations in factors of chance or human deliberation could have distinctively different effects in such structural contexts.

On Watersheds

The mathematical properties of a watershed model can be illuminated by Herbert A. Simon's so-called Berlitz model of language learning (see Paul F. Lazarsfeld, ed., *Mathematical Thinking in the Social Sciences*, Glencoe: The Free Press 1954, pp. 402–05). According to the Berlitz model, success in solving a given task such as learning a language (or, as Herbert Simon himself suggests, in struggling for social or political reform or revolution) depends on the Difficulty of the task (D), and on the rate or effort at which the Activity (A) to accomplish the task is performed (see Fig. 1). If the task is very difficult for the given actor, and the activity invested is rather limited, for instance in terms of the number of hours spent on it (A_0, D_0), then failure is inevitable. If the task is less difficult, and considerable activity is invested into accomplishing it from the very onset (A_0^1, D_0^1), then success is easily attainable.

Figure 1. Simon's Berlitz Model

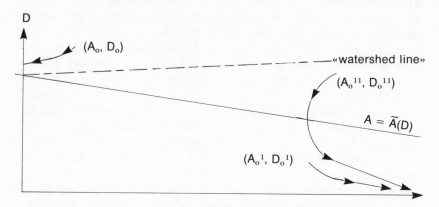

In Fig. 1 the time paths (lines with arrows) for these two cases have been indicated from starting points (A_0, D_0) and (A_0^1, D_0^1). However, the model also takes into account the motivational effects, or the pleasantness of the activity, given variations in values of A and D. If the activity is unpleasant, because of the high level of difficulty, the rate of activity will decrease to a point where it ceases completely, or to a point where a sufficient mastery of the task has been achieved to make it increasingly pleasant. The line $A = \bar{A}(D)$ represents all the points at which the pleasant aspects of the actitivy at any given level of difficulty become predominant. I will call this the line of intrinsic motivational replenishment – intrinsic in the sense that motivation is replenished from within the activity system itself through increasing mastery and thus decreasing difficulty of the task.

Taking this line of intrinsic motivational replenishment into account, we can specify a third time path starting from (A_0^{11}, D_0^{11}). This time path is characterized by decreasing efforts to begin with, up to the line $A = \bar{A}(D)$, and thereafter by an increase in the rate of activity until the task has been accomplished $(D \rightarrow O)$.

The most interesting aspect of the Berlitz model in the context of this paper, however, is the 'watershed' that divides successful and unsuccessful time paths, and which has been indicated in the figure by a broken line. Any time path taking off above the divide of the watershed

196

line ends in failure; any time path starting below that line ends in success, and proceeds towards that end by way of a more or less curved trajectory, depending on whether it takes off above or below the line of intrinsic motivational replenishment.

Leaving aside the question how to estimate the quantitative parameter defining the watershed line, and how to introduce stochastic events in the model as applied to mass-learning, I will here concentrate on some aspects of the practical application of this kind of model. Obviously a rational actor committed to the accomplishment of learning a language, or struggling for reform or revolution, and conscious of the structure of the model and the existence of a watershed line, will take every precaution to take off from a point below the watershed line. This can be done by choosing a task of reasonable difficulty, or by dividing the entire task into sub-parts that can be more easily accomplished, and by investing sufficient effort and activity from the very start. But what is 'reasonable difficulty' and 'sufficient effort'? At least in the struggle for social reform or revolution this is a matter of conjecture rather than of applied science, because of the problems of measuring the relevant variables and estimating the parameters in such historical and macrosociogical settings.

But if we agree that social science at present has little if anything to offer on this point (except by creating a more general awareness of the notion and existence of watershed lines, wherever they are located), then the question remains how we as social scientists can improve our ability to give advice on the structure, location, and dynamics of social and political watersheds. To this question I will return after having added a few points about the structures and processes of 'dialectical succession' – another context where relatively small variations of chance events or human deliberation may have far-reachingly different outcomes.

Dialectical Succession

Gudmund Hernes, in a mathematically argued paper on 'Structural Change in Social Processes' *(American Journal of Sociology,* November 1976), has pointed out that there is a logical isomorphism between theories of 'ecological succession' and 'dialectical transformation'. Both refer to 'systems which while they destroy themselves are pregnant with new ones'. For instance, trees of a species that is victorious in the competition with other species within a given habitat may, over time, by their very victory and increasing density impoverish the very basis of their existence – the soil that provides nourishment – and at the same time promote the spread of their successors – other species growing up from seeds in the shade of the dominant species, and with less stringent demands on the quality of soil.

Similarly, under capitalism according to Marxian theory, 'the bourgeoisie, by advancing industry, precipitates entire sections of the ruling classes into the proletariat, and simultaneously produces increasing riches, increasing poverty and an increasing proletariat. By concentration of industry the workers are also concentrated, become conscious of their own exploitation and potential, and organize as a class'.

I will not here quarrel with Hernes about his condensation of Marx, but rather point out a weakness in some versions of Marxism – more precisely so-called 'scientific socialism' – which looks at the dialectical succession of socialist proletarian rule after the self-destruction of capitalism as inevitable and automatic. Dialectical, unlike ecological, succession requires the intervention of human consciousness to grasp the problems involved, and to find solutions to them. But consciousness can easily be blocked. The seeds of a new socialist rule growing in the shadow of concentrated capital require the emergence of a new consciousness fit not only for wage-struggle within capitalism, but also capable of transcending capitalism by envisaging and struggling for a new system of socialist production relations. However, we know that the form that socialism has taken in the Soviet Union has created doubts in the working-classes of capitalist countries about the virtues of socialism. The resulting confusion is further magnified by the emergence of other brands of socialism in Yugoslavia and China, and by the fact that even other roads to a democratic socialism are conceivable in countries which today are capitalist. Unless a new and less ambiguous socialist consciousness develops in this context of uncertainty and confusion about the resolution of the contradictions of mature capitalism, it is quite possible that stagnant capitalism will survive for a considerable period of time, perhaps propped up with fascistic political designs. To borrow once more from the language of ecological theories, we may get 'desertification' rather than 'succession'.

In a sense this kind of situation is also a 'watershed'. But if this is the problem, what is the solution? Unfortunately a widespread awareness of the problem is not always promptly followed by a more general acceptance of relevant and effective problem solutions.

On this point let us return to the question raised earlier: How can social scientists improve their ability to give advice on the structure, location, and dynamics of social and political watersheds?

The Science of Social and Political Watersheds

In my view a major task of social scientists today is to analytically and, wherever possible, empirically illuminate (1), the structural contradictions to be resolved in mature capitalism as well as in 'actually existing socialism', (2) the nature of the 'watersheds' dividing successful and unsuccessful efforts to resolve those contradictions, (3) the strength of forces – both 'deterministic', stochastic, and consciously deliberating – operating at the 'watershed', and (4) the relevance and probable future effectiveness of proposals made to resolve those structural contradictions.

I doubt very much whether this task can be accomplished with a high degree of precision in estimating the relevant parameters. The exact location of social and political watersheds cannot be determined. The relative strength of forces operating at these watersheds cannot be precisely determined because of the incommensurability of some of the component forces involved. Only the scratch test of history can determine what forces eventually turn out to be stronger. But at least it would seem possible to scientifically assess the attributes of contradictions, watersheds, and solutions, and whether forces are gaining or losing strength. Such an assessment I have attempted in a forthcoming book (U. Himmelstrand, G. Ahrne, L. Lundberg and L. Lundberg, *Beyond Welfare Capitalism, Issues, Actors and Forces in Societal Change*, London: Heinemann, Autumn 1980).

But in most contexts high precision in parameter estimation would seem less important for political action than the creation of a widespread awareness and conscious recognition of the nature of our problems, and of the relevance of various proposals for the solution of the problems at hand. Creating such an awareness is also part of our task as social scientists, I believe. Too often solutions proposed do not fit the given problem simply because the nature of the problem is insufficiently understood.

The Relevance of Johan Galtung's Recent Idealism

Over the years my thinking about several of the matters raised in this paper has been influenced a great deal by attending or participating in discussions in which Johan Galtung has played a major intellectual role, and I am thinking particularly of his well-known notion of 'structural violence', and his insistence on the role of the social scientist in breaking, and not only seeking invariant relationships.

But Johan himself has moved away from his earlier preoccupation with structural features of society towards an approach which Marxists would call idealistic. He and his collaborators are now primarily concerned with value systems and cosmologies – particularly those of the *alpha* and *beta* types, which are sufficiently well-known to Galtung's many readers not to require any further elaboration here. To me it seems that the Galtung-group has increasingly lost sight of the structural constraints and options which limit or open up areas of application and implementation for ideologies, value systems, and cosmologies.

There is no doubt in my mind that most Marxists have paid too little attention to the content and meaning of value systems, cosmologies, and similar 'superstructural' phenomena, and that many if not all of them have tended to view the relationship between base and superstructure in too simplistic terms, such as superstructural mirroring or instrumentalism. Ideological and state 'apparatuses' are seen simply as tools for maintaining and reproducing given social relations of production in the interest of the dominant social class. Gramsci's notion of 'bourgeois hegemony' has helped to loosen the tight grip of instrumentalism, but still within the same general framework. Here the Weberian tradition, which the Galtung group would seem to be pursuing, has made more important contributions.

But why lose sight of the overall structural features of society in the study of the 'superstructure'? A main task for social scientists at present would seem to be a theoretical analysis of relations of compatibility and contradiction between cosmologies and value systems, on the one hand, and the structural options and constraints of mature capitalism, on the other. Similar questions of compatibility could be raised with regard to potential future social systems with which present-day capitalism may be pregnant, according to theories of dialectical succession.

Obviously the *beta*-cosmologies and value patterns idealistically favoured by the Galtung group are incompatible with Scandinavian welfare capitalism, and even more incompatible with the 'raw capitalism' to which Monsieur Barre, Mrs Thatcher, and others are trying to make us return. The question then is whether the Galtung group is able to envisage some alternative future, determined not on the basis of wishful idealistic philosophies but in terms of the material forces unfolding in the present, which would be more compatible with *beta*-cosmologies and value patterns. Judging from comments received from the Galtung group on some recent papers of mine regarding societal change in Sweden, Galtung and his collaborators seem to have a serious hang-up with regard to any proposals or attempts by the labour movement and socialist parties to move beyond capitalism. Even when such proposals contain *beta* elements, undernourished as they often seem, they remain unnoticed by the Galtung group. For them the labour movement, whether bolshevik or reformist and social-democratic, seems irrevocably sold on the *alpha* type of cosmologies and value patterns.

Yet, in a mature capitalist society, the only hope for change, apart from a long period of continued capitalist dominance, with or without fascism and global wars, stems from the potential of the labour movement where it is strong and well-organized enough, as in the Nordic countries. If the labour movement in these and other countries cannot help us to push in a direction beyond capitalism towards a society where *beta* elements can be rooted and grow more freely, then there is no other force sufficiently strong to move us in that direction. No Galtung group of idealistic intellectuals can accomplish that feat on its own. The future is bleak without a labour movement conscious of its historical mission.

But is there at all a labour movement at present exhibiting any signs of being pregnant with new and fruitful ideas on structural transformation, while still pursuing its regular wage-struggle and struggle for state welfare policies within the existing structure of contradictory capitalism? This is an empirical question more urgent, in my view, than the building of beautiful and complex but structurally disconnected typologies of cosmological thinking. I happen to think that more recent ideological trends among European labour movements, even when they represent minority factions only, and more recent writings of Marxist theoreticians like André Gorz and Rudolf Bahro and others, deserve more respect and attention from scholars like Johan Galtung and his collaborators. These labour movements represent the only cutting edges we have for opening up new roads towards the future. If these edges are blunt and often handled rather inconsistently as a result of contradictory forces, social scientists should not turn their faces away in perfectionistic disgust but help to sharpen these edges where they can be found in material reality rather than in the dreamworld of theoretical constructs. Furthermore, social scientists should point out and help to resolve the contradictions which cause the edges to cut so inconsistently.

As regards ideological trends in reformist labour movements, I will here briefly describe only the historical self-image of Swedish Social Democracy.

Three Historical Stages of Labour Reformism

The first task that the reformist labour movement set for itself at the beginning of this century was not to introduce socialism but to *remove poverty*. This could be done not only through wage- struggle but also by political means. This was seen as requiring the introduction of *political democracy*. The struggle for universal suffrage, undertaken in close collaboration with liberal politicians, and the struggle against poverty, thus characterized this first stage of labour reformism.

Once political democracy was achieved and the struggle against poverty had been launched, and workable labour majorities had been attained in the early thirties, the second stage of Swedish labour history began. The strategy of the Swedish labour movement during this stage was to promote *stable economic growth within the framework of the capitalist order* in order to provide a larger 'national cake' to be shared more equitably both through *unionized wage-struggle* and *welfare-state redistribution*. Again, this was not a socialist policy in a strict sense, but a consistent social-liberal policy of capitalist economic growth and market-conforming state interventions to make the economy less sensitive to business cycles, plus welfare redistributions of wealth. The social democrats could pursue this social-liberal policy much more consistently than the Liberal Party ever could have done owing to their liberal hang-ups with regard to the state, and their non-existing relationships with the trade union movement.

Today Swedish social democrats agree that the second stage of the reformist labour movement has come to an end, now that the post-war period of sustained economic growth has ground to a halt. It is no longer sufficient to struggle to remove remaining poverty by promoting the creation and redistribution of wealth within the framework of a private capitalist economy. Now the main task is rather to *control the use of wealth,* which has become highly concentrated and centralized, and which tends to behave in a manner that threatens needed productive and social investment, employment levels, and the quality of working life as well as the quality of leisure-time use.

Proposals for wage-earners funds, regional and national development funds, and similar proposals from the labour movement are aimed primarily at controlling wealth by transferring an increasing portion of ownership and power over capital investments to new categories of owners, namely to locally and regionally organized labour and social ownership. This is conceived as the third stage of labour history, the stage of *economic democracy*.

The debate about the shape of 'economic democracy' through wage-earners' funds or similar arrangements is still going on in Sweden, concurrently with a debate on how to influence the direction of technological change so as to humanize industrial labour, and to change the content of production in response to human and societal needs. To summarize that debate in this paper is impossible. Let me only emphasize that there is a significant current in this debate calling for a more decentralized system of workers' self-management and alternative technologies that would satisfy several of the *beta*-values vindicated by the Galtung group. In this debate our 'eurocommunist' party, VPK, is also involved. The *alpha*-element in socialist thought – central state interventions and planning – is not absent from the debate but is seen mainly as a counter-cyclical corrective, and as a device to prevent a basically decentralized economy of workers' self-management from producing too much social inequality and from neglecting production of socially needed goods and services over-sensitive to swings in market forces.

There are certainly also some leading social democrats who seem to think of 'economic democracy' mainly as an attractive catchword for what will remain a marginal refinement of private capitalism. They shun ideas of radical decentralized redistribution of power, and find no attraction in the *beta*-ideology of 'small is beautiful'. They view wage-earners' funds and similar arrangements mainly as a way of replenishing existing enterprises with risk-assuming capital in the interest of continued economic growth.

At the present watershed of Swedish political and economic history our Social Democratic Party faces a crisis of identities straddling the watershed. It is not an easy matter for an established political party to change and go beyond an earlier approach in moving forward from one stage to another in its historical development. The past history of a party has shaped its image and established its identity. To give up or rather to transcend that identity, and to switch to a new approach is probably as difficult as to shift unsynchronized gears in an old motor-car negotiating a steep upward gradient – particularly if you lack the necessary skills in double-declutching. In such a situation you are likely to maintain the car in second gear as long as possible, until the vehicle is at a near standstill, before you try to shift into first gear. And then, if you fail, you may come to a complete stop, or even roll backwards a bit until you finally make it.

Metaphorically speaking this is what seems to have happened to the Social Democratic Party in its transition from the stage of welfare-capitalism to the stage of economic democracy. The party has been identified as a party of successful but piecemeal social reform within welfare-capitalism. Those who were satisfied with that approach, and fail to understand the objective need for another approach at the present juncture, are likely to be confused about the identity of the Social Democratic Party in this transitional phase; and others who certainly would favour structural reform towards some kind of economic democracy may fail to understand or to believe that the party is really about to transcend its previous identity as a party of social reform within welfare capitalism.

Understandably the party leadership is uncertain about the proper way to handle this transitional situation so as to maximize electoral support and once again obtain a workable and durable parliamentary majority. Still, opinion surveys conducted by my collaborators and myself (and reported in our forthcoming book) would seem to indicate that a majority of the electorate are aware of the need to move beyond welfare-capitalism. But, as every party strategist knows, the translation of public opinion into electoral support for a new approach is a complicated affair. It requires an educational effort from the party to prove that the party is indeed choosing a new track at the present cross-roads, and that current proposals for economic democracy really address themselves to the problems of welfare-capitalism of which a majority of the electorate is aware. This educational task is further complicated by the fact that the bourgeois parties at present in government positions can and do cynically exploit the equally widespread fears of Eastern-European socialism in their attacks on wage-earners' funds, in spite of the fact that these proposals have nothing in common with 'actually existing socialism' in Eastern-European settings.

These anti-socialist bourgeois slogans do not imply that all the bourgeois are entirely free from identity problems similar to those found in the Social Democratic Party. The Liberal and Center parties contain significant minorities of members and cadres who are responsive to demands for more decentralized forms of economic democracy and for alternative technologies, and who furthermore favour a closer collaboration with the social democrats rather than with the conservatives within the bourgeois block.

I have not delivered this brief lecture on Swedish labour history mainly because I think that the Galtung group and other idealistic sociologists need such a lecture, which they probably do. I simply want to set the stage for my concluding remarks, which concern the role of social scientists today at an assumed social and political watershed, or if you prefer another metaphor, at the cutting edges of the labour movement facing the challenge of dialectical succession.

Concluding Remarks

As I have indicated earlier, an actor who is *aware* of the fact that he is close to the kind of watershed represented in Simon's watershed model, is likely to increase his efforts in order to be sure that he is placed on that side of the watershed which ordinarily leads to a successful accomplishment of the task at hand. An alternative strategy is to divide the complete task into smaller and less difficult sub-tasks. However, there is a danger in such a strategy of segmentalization unless the actor can be reasonably certain that one sub-task leads to another without diverting him from the trajectory by which the goal can be attained. The actor must be *aware* of this danger and define his sub-tasks in such a manner that he can avoid it.

If we take our point of departure in models of dialectical succession, with the amendments I have suggested with regard to the possible blocking of emerging consciousness about the dialectics of the situation, we again find that an *awareness* of the precise nature of the situation may alert potential successors to the need to make an extra effort to bring about the succession.

A key word in the above paragraphs is 'awareness'. To provide a scientific basis for such awareness is an important aspect of the work of social scientists. In a sense this is a task which at present requires the building or at least a recognition of relevant and scientifically based social cosmologies compatible with the structural features of dialectical succession at social and political watersheds. These theoretical, empirical and educational tasks, my dear Johan, are the frontiers at which your intellectual efforts are most needed at present. If you feel less at home with the establishment of the labour movement than with progressive managers and with liberals and populists of the ecological type, then there are important intellectual tasks of conscientization at those frontiers as well, as I have indicated in my remarks on the crises of identity found not only among socialists and labour parties.

And what about chance? Chance is partly, if not entirely, a product of the ignorance of scientists, and in social science also a result of the ignorance of the actors who are part of our field of study – and perhaps also a result of our ignorance about the degree and areas of ignorance of actors.

Even if our ignorance is reduced, ignorance will always remain – and therefore also those 'chance events' which are a product of ignorance. But to the extent that we succeed in reducing ignorance, the question remains: the ignorance of whom? The ignorance of the scientist alone, who will thus be able provide a more reliable and valid basis for the manipulation of human beings considered only as objects? Or can we also help to reduce the ignorance of our 'objects', thus transforming them into reasonably enlightened subjects, that is to actors in the proper sense? This requires a new relationship between social scientists and their 'objects' of study. Action research of the type undertaken by Orlando Fals Borda and Alain Touraine are cases in point. But also more conventional research can serve this purpose if supplemented by a more active role of social scientists in opinion formation and educational endeavours.

Johan Galtung is one of the most gifted educators there is among contemporary social scientists. In this paper I have challenged him not only as a leading social scientist today but also as an educator facing urgent and neglected educational tasks. A *Festschrift* will certainly not be the end of Johan Galtung.

Why Mathematics in Social Sciences?

SOLOMON MARCUS

Mathematics can be invoked:

1. as a kind of snobbery:
2. because (like some drugs) it does not do any damage;
3. because it is useful;
4. because you cannot avoid it.

Like any other field, the social sciences have experienced each of the above types of union with mathematics. The first and the second type differ psychologically rather than logically. They both are, in most cases, examples of a misunderstanding of what mathematics really are and what a real use of mathematics means.

It would be desirable to avoid the first type, which falsifies both the nature of mathematics and the nature of (social) sciences, and which is prejudicial to research. Let us take, for instance, those papers in which many algebraic symbols are introduced without motivation, because no syllogistic reasoning is made, obliging the author to refer often to them, and yet they are submitted to no calculation. Instead of gaining in concision, clarity and precision, the author succeeds in this way in obscuring the ideas, because the capacity of the natural language to direct the intuitive understanding of things is in this way considerably reduced, and the reader's attention is orientated in a wrong direction, giving him the impression that he has to achieve a formalization of the problem and of its solution.

Another aspect of the first two types is the introduction of a scientific jargon that is not really used. Let us take, for instance, the words *entropy* and *redundancy*. Sometimes, they occur without a real use of the corresponding informational theoretic concepts. Entropy has become a beautiful metaphor; we can admit that scientific terms, like any other word in the language, may acquire a figurative use (there is a book of poetry called *Entropy*). But the reader has to be warned that *entropy* is not synonymous with *disorder* or *indetermination* as common words in English. With respect to *redundancy,* the mistakes are more frequent. Many authors believe that *redundancy* is synonymous with *uselessness, superfluity, or waste.* But there is only a vague relation between the informational theoretic concept of *redundancy* and the common concept of *waste* or *uselessness;* the former gives a global characterization of a message and expresses the relation between the elements of information and the elements that control the information, whereas the latter are concerned with individual objects that are considered parasitic in some situations.

In order to avoid types 1 and 2 and to stimulate types 3 and 4, it is necessary to learn how can we distinguish between them. Which are the symptoms of the presence of mathematics?

There is a type of mathematical thinking that uses no mathematical formulas or mathematical jargon. James R. Newman *(The World of Mathematics,* Vol. 2, Simon and Schuster, New York, 1956, pp. 1167–1172), in his commentary on Sir Francis Galton (born in 1822) observes that Galton was not a mathematician, but he was mathematically minded. Karl Pearson, in his biography of Galton *(The Life Letters and Labours of Francis Galton,* Cambridge, 1914–1930, Vol. 2, p. 424) calls him the master builder of the modern theory of statistics. If Galton was 'almost obsessed by the need to count and to measure' (see, for instance, his *Classification of Men According to Their Natural Gifts),* today mathematical thinking is characterized by means of other features, related more to structural, qualitative mathematics than to the quantitative type: the capacity to discover analogies between apparently completely different phenomena; the ability to cope with combinatorial aspects; the possibility of retaining some aspects of things by ignoring the other aspects; the taste of order and relations and, above all, the capacity to proceed step by step, from simple to complex, by using at each stage the results obtained at the preceding ones. Jacob T. Schwartz ('Mathematics as a Tool for Economic Understanding', in Lynn Arthur Steen editor, *Mathematics Today,* Springer Verlag, New York–Heidelberg–Berlin, pp. 269–295) observes that 'mathematical arguments remain sound even if they are long and complex'. Jacob Schwartz contrasts this fact with the situation of common sense arguments, which can generally be trusted only if they remain short; even moderately long non-mathematical arguments rapidly become far-fetched and dubious. How does mathematics succeed in presenting long arguments, whereas the common sense intuitive arguments fail in this respect? The common sense arguments are developed almost exclusively by means of expressions in natural languages, which are suitable for expressing empirical, spontaneous, emotional and intuitive thinking, but which are not equipped to face the requirements of rigorous logical thinking. Mathematics keeps, as an important component, the natural language (because we are always thinking in such a language, our mother tongue), but it adds to it an artificial, symbolic component,

207

which enables us to shorten the assertions as much as necessary and to convert great parts of our judgments into various types of calculus. But in fact even the natural component of the mathematical language is not so empirical as the usual natural language, because it is considered in its written aspect and in a very standard form, and is thus able, to a great extent, to face ambiguities and excessive redundancy. So, used with great care, the written natural language sometimes allows, even in the absence of an artificial symbolism (or at least with a very poor one), the presentation of relatively long arguments. So, we get an intermediate situation with respect to the dichotomy considered by Jacob Schwartz. Long arguments can sometimes be presented in a rigorous way, with no use of mathematical formalism. In this respect we could ask whether the rigorous thinking is identical to the mathematical one; the answer seems to be affirmative only if we admit that the mathematical thinking may sometimes avoid an artificial component.

Examples of contemporary scholars who are mathematically minded, but not mathematically trained, are many. This is especially true for researchers using computers in Humanities and Social Sciences; they often have a great capacity for algorithmic thinking, but almost no (or very poor) technical mathematical knowledge.

A significant example of a very deep mathematical thinking that often requires no mathematical technics is given by Johan Galtung's papers and lectures. Galtung organizes his ideas around a few basic points, giving a global, holistic view of his thinking. He has a remarkable gift of being able to confront, to order, to systematize, and to synthesize very heterogeneous opinions. He brings the matters to the point where it is almost obvious what mathematical tools are required in order to go further and deeper into the subject. This point is one where mathematics are invoked as an obligation or at least as a favourable way of finding out the consequences of the premises (types 3 and 4). Two such examples come to mind: Galtung's analogy between chemical structures and social structures (see his paper in the second volume of *Mathematical Approaches to International Relations,* published in 1977 by the Romanian Academy of Social and Political Sciences), where the reader is strongly invited (in an implicit way), to imagine a common mathematical frame for the chemical and the social analogous structures (type 3), and his paper *On Alpha and Beta and their Many Combinations* (published in E. Masini, editor, *Visions of Desirable Societies,* Pergamon Press, 1979), whose natural continuation cannot avoid the use of rooted trees (as an ideal model of alpha structures) and of complete graphs (as an ideal model of beta structures) (type 4).

What guarantees the usefulness of a mathematical tool? Usually we have to compare the input and the output of our reasoning. If there is a non-trivial difference between them and if the output has some relevance with respect to the problem we are investigating, then we fall into one of the types 3 and 4 of union. Such a non-trivial path from the input to the output can avoid the mathematical symbolism and formulas only if you master the natural logic very rigorously.

The divorce between mathematical thinking and mathematical formulas may happen in the opposite sense too. Unfortunately, there are many papers rich in mathematical symbolism and terminology, but very poor in mathematical ideas. More exactly, and excepting the unions of type 1 or 2, things happen as follows. Let us try to build a mathematical model B of a social phenomenon A. For instance, if A is a hierarchical social structure, B could be a rooted tree. If we remain here, we can say that B is adequate to A, but it is not yet relevant. What we need is to find out some theorems about B which have some interesting, significant interpretation with respect to A. Adequacy without relevance is the most frequent disease of mathematical models in Social Sciences; it corresponds to a situation somewhere between type 2 and type 3, because its adequacy potentially promises a power of relevance.

At this point, may I introduce myself. I was for a long time a pure mathematician, working on the pathology of real sets and functions. I was attracted by scientific facts that contradict our intuitive knowledge. Like art, science is for me a beautiful frustrated expectation. Such frustrations are frequent in Mathematical Analysis, in view of its systematic use of processes with infinitely many steps. More than 20 years ago I was fascinated by the infinity of human language, another source of interesting frustrations. So, I began to be interested in Mathematical Linguistics. I was curious to see how mathematical models are born in a human context. Ten years ago I began to discover that mathematical models of language have a universal power, because language is the basic human activity; it is a term of reference for any other human activity. The models I previously developed in Linguistics (*Algebraic Linguistics,* Academic Press, New York, 1967; *Introduction mathématique à la linguistique structurale,* Dunod, Paris, 1967) were applied in Praxiology by Maria Nowakowska (*Language of Motivation and Language of Action,* Mouton, Paris, 1973), in Musicology by Bogdan Cazimir ('Sémiologie musicale et linguistique mathématique', *Semiotica,* Vol. 15, 1976, No. 1, pp. 48–57). I provided mathematical-linguistic models for poetry (*Mathematische Poetik,* Athenäum Verlag, Frankfurt am Main, 1973), for folklore (*Sémiotique formelle du folklore* – in collaboration, Klincksieck, Paris, 1978), for the theatre ('Semiotics of Theatre; A Mathematical-Linguistic Approach', *Revue roumaine de linguistique,* Vol. 25, 1980, No. 3, pp. 161–189). I began to be interested in a generative approach to both individual and social action during my work concerning the fairy-tales. I was attracted by Chowsky's dichotomy competence-performance, and I tried to project it in the study of learning processes, under the influence of Mircea Malitza's work (see now J. Botkin, M. Elmandjra, M. Malitza, *No Limits to Learning. Bridging the Human Gap,* Pergamon Press, Oxford, 1979). Human and social action have a surface and a deep structure; the former takes the form of an infinite language over a finite vocabulary whose elements are elementary actions, whereas the latter is expressed by a generative grammar, i.e. a creative device that produces both the real and the potential actions. This is the kernel of a new attitude toward social action (see our papers 'Applications de la théorie des langages formels en économie et organisation', *Revue roumaine de linguistique,* Vol. 13, 1976, No. 2, pp. 583–594 and 'Learning as a generative process', *Revue roumaine de linguistique,* Vol. 24, 1979 – *Cahiers de linguistique théorique et appliquée,* Vol. 16, 1979, No. 2). The main work on the generative approach to Economics is due to Gheorghe Păun (see, for instance, his 'Generative Grammars for Some Economical Activities', *Foundations of Control Engineering,* Vol. 2, 1977, No. 1, pp. 15–25). A formal linguistic approach to international relations was developed by S. Marcus ('Languages, Grammars and Negotiations', in *Mathematical Approaches to International Relations'* Vol. 2, editors M. Bunge, J. Galtung, M. Malitza, Romanian Academy of Social and Political Sciences, Bucharest, 1977, pp. 378–388), whereas the generative approach to this subject is developed by Hayward R. Alker, Jr., and William Greenberg ('On Simulating Collective Security Regime Alternatives', in G. M. Bonham and M. J. Shapiro eds., *Thought and Action in Foreign Policy,* Birkhäuser, Basel, 1977) and by Dwain Mefford *(The Language of Crisis and its Evolving Grammar,* preprint, The Center for International Studies, Massachusetts Institute of Technology, 1979). The main interest of this generative approach lies in the contradiction between the finite character of the generative device and the infinite nature of the language generated by this device. So, International Relations are not only a real confrontation, but also a world of infinite possibilities whose plausibility lies in the structure of the corresponding generative grammar. A generative typology of economic processes (see Păun's papers) is far from being that suggested by the common feeling.

A new impulse for our interest in modelling social phenomena began in 1977, with our participation in the project *Goals, processes and indicators of development,* initiated by the United Nations University (Tokyo). The soul and the brain of this project is its coordinator, Johan Galtung. I felt myself to be on the same wavelength with him when he told us that, with respect to the possible dichotomies quantitative-qualitative and deterministic-probabilistic in building models for social

210

sciences, he prefers the qualitative and the deterministic models. Galtung thought especially that the graph-theoretic facts related to balance, to stability, to connectedness, and other such phenomena, following the lines of the well-known Harary–Norman–Cartwright book. Our team tries to go further in this direction, for instance by studying Mario Bunge's definition of a social indicator, his model of cohesiveness of a social group, but our main orientation is different. Following a line coming from Condorcet's example showing that majority rule leads to the famous voting paradox, we try to understand Arrow's impossibility theorem, with its strange dictator, when dealing with social decision. In this respect, a whole class of problems concerning various types of restrictions in building global models appear in a very natural way. Paradoxes and antinomies were first discovered in Logic, in Mathematics, then in Linguistics, in Semiotics, and in Social Sciences. Democracy seems to be not only a question of political will, but also something requiring a very difficult learning process, because the possible democracy is not that accessible to the common understanding. Self-reference is crucial in any social forecasting, but self-reference leads to paradoxes. *Kamilla Lányi* ('A Paradox in Forecasting', *Mat, Közgazdusági Folyoirat,* Vol. 10, 1977, Nos. 1–2, pp. 49–50) discusses situation in which the econometrician is asked to give predictions for events, the realization of which depends heavily on the decision maker, while the decision itself depends on the forecast given by the econometrician; the conclusions drawn have a bearing on a number of concrete decision problems. Howard C. Petith ('A Vintage Capital Paradox', *International Economic Review,* Vol. 19, 1978, No. 2, pp. 533–535) considers the problem of choosing the capital to labour ratio which leads to a steady state that, out of all steady states with the same savings ratio, has the highest level of consumption; he shows that for the vintage model this optimal capital to labour ratio is not, in general, the one that satisfies the competitive profit-maximizing conditions. As J. A. Rickard observes, the immediate impression given by the above result is that welfare could be increased by the choice of a non-competitive capital to labour ratio. However, C. J. Bliss has shown that competition is necessary for intertemporal utility maximization and consequently the above impression must be false. Then there is the problem of a Gallup poll: How people can modify their opinion tomorrow if they learn today what was their opinion yesterday?

A new type of impossibility theorem is due to Gh. Păun (GPID paper, in print) and concerns the aggregation of some social indicators $i_1, \ldots,$ i_n into a synthetic indicator i. He proves that there exists no such aggregation that is at the same time monotonous (when $i_1, \ldots, i_n$ increase, i does not decrease), anticatastrophic (to small modifications of $i_1, \ldots, i_n$ corresponds a small modification of i), and non-compensatory (if i_j decreases, i cannot remain the same because i_k increases). In contrast with the Arrow theorem, where very plausible requirements concerning a social decision are proved to be contradictory, here only the first requirement is intuitively satisfied. But they seem to be independent, whereas Pǎun's theorem asserts just their incompatibility.

Then, there is the fascinating world of Nonstandard Models initiated by Abraham Robinson. H. Jerome Keisler (University of Wisconsin) constructed a nonstandard conceptualization of time, making logically defensible the intuitive reasoning by which each moment is followed by a next moment, yet two successive moments are infinitely close together; so, it is possible to represent a physical or social process as taking place one step at a time, each step infinitely close to the next. The antinomy between discrete and continuous time is thus synthesized in a plausible manner. By means of this model of time, Keisler obtains a model of an exchange economy in which prices would be determined by the aggregate effect of a large number of traders acting in a succession of infinitesimally spaced moments. Keisler was able to set forth explicit upper and lower bounds on the momentary price fluctuations to make market stability possible. If prices change too slowly, they will not converge to equilibrium in a finite amount of time, while if they change too rapidly, they will never have a chance to become stabilized (see Lynn Arthur Steen, 'The Mathematical World of Model Theory', *Science News,* Vol. 107, 1975, pp. 108–111).

René Thom's Catastrophe Theory and Smale's economic models in terms of Differential Topology are other attractive fields for the social scientist. They are well enough known to need no inclusion here.

So, why are we, as mathematicians, engaged in Social Sciences at all? Because Mathematics is a basic tool with which to go beyond common sense, the intuitive social truth, and to understand the hidden part of social phenomena. We discover a lot of restrictions and paradoxes that fascinate our imagination. We investigate problems that could be neither formulated nor solved without Mathematics. The unavoidable union between Mathematics and Social Sciences becomes a marriage of reciprocal love.

Problems of Social Forecasting

BY I. BESTUCHEV-LADA

Until recently the notion of 'forecasting' has been primarily associated with spontaneous ('self-induced') phenomena and processes of a natural, biological or technical character, unconnected directly with the vital activity of the human community and with people's plans and decisions: forecasting of weather, earthquakes, mineral deposits, crop yields, hydrological conditions of water reservoirs, course of illness (based on medical diagnosing), machine performance, etc. In the area of social phenomena in economics, demography, politics, etc. the term 'forecast' usually signified nothing but an attempt at anticipating the state of a particular phenomeon in the future and was not, as a rule, directly connected with plans and decisions of a social-economic or social-political character.

On the other hand, the great importance of scientific foresight for raising the degree of objectivity and justification of plans, programmes, projects and decisions was established quite a long time ago, relatively speaking.

The Soviet Union and other countries set up hundreds of special sectors, departments, and whole research establishments to undertake this particular line of research. The latter has come to be known as 'forecasting' or 'forecast-making', although it is clear that this essentially differs from, say, weather forecasting, and is not limited to attempts at anticipating the future state of any particular phenomena. The object of this research is not just to foretell what will happen at any particular time in the future and when it will happen – although this is a matter of no mean importance by itself – but, above all, to raise the level of objectivity and, consequently, the efficiency of planning and administration of social affairs.

This rapidly developing branch of modern science – an entirely new trend of scientific research, in point of fact – called for a theoretical explanation and produced a science of prognostics, that is, a science of the laws of forecasting.

Scientific prediction has a long history behind it. It was pioneered by K. Marx, F. Engels, and V. I. Lenin, who laid down certain principles that have subsequently been developed by Marxist-Leninist theory and

213

confirmed by the practice of socialist and communist construction for over half a century. It is quite obvious, besides, that forecasting by itself cannot constitute a particular 'science of the future', for this is an inalienable function of each science. All this generated a series of theoretical problems now more topical than ever: what is the true relation between foreseeing and forecasting, between forecasting and planning, between forecasting and prognostics? What are the most effective methods of forecasting social processes and the ways of enhancing their efficiency? What are the problems involved in social forecasting and which of them emerge into the foreground at present?

The development of social forecasting at first gave rise to the following question: why apply a new term which seemed, at first glance, to duplicate the long-established notion of foresight, on the one hand, and that of planning, on the other? A closer examination, however, revealed a confusion of different ideas due to an almost total absence of appropriate philosophic categories well worked out. Foresight and control are common generic terms in the strict sense of this term, covering as they do, respectively, all the methods and processes whereby to obtain and reduce information about the future. These abstract categories manifest themselves in a variety of specific forms in actual practice. The forms of specifying foresight are of a purely descriptive and predictive character: these are prediction, foretelling, anticipation, forecasting, etc.; on the other hand, the forms of specifying control are connected with certain solutions to long-range problems, bearing an instructive and decision-imposing character: these are planning, programming, designing, and managerial decision-making. Forecasting, as one of the forms of specified foresight, holds a place apart in this series: it is not, by itself, connected with the solution of long-range problems, but the assessments of the future it offers are strictly conditional and totally subordinated to the idea of optimizing plans and decisions.

To identify the specific category of forecasting in full measure, one has to consider it in the historically established context of other approaches to the problems of the future: religious and eschatological, utopian, philosophic and historical, to mention just a few. This involves some practically unstudied problems of relation between hypothesis and forecast, forecast and law, diagnosing and forecasting, problems of reverse connection between the prognostic and constructive approaches (the so-called 'self-organizing' and 'self-destructive' forecasts), problems of type characterization of forecasts, etc.

One more question: What is the area of social forecasting? This question, too, gave rise to rather long-lasting controversy. There was a suggestion that forecasting had to be subdivided in terms of time; some sought to prove that forecasting must do no more than precede a plan, while others said it must cover only an area inaccessible to planning. Actual practice showed, however, that forecasting can and must cover not only both areas, but the very progress of plan fulfilment as well. In other words, forecasting has to be done without interruption and parallel to planning of any range, depending on the particular problems of research. No doubt was expressed that forecasting was bound to be comprehensive and to embrace as wide a range of social phenomena as possible. But some insisted in this context that scientific forecasting had to comprise economic and social forecasting in addition to scientific and technological, while others objected by saying that the forecasting of social developments, according to its character, could be only economic in practice, that is, instrumental in the attainment of national economic objectives, while scientific, technical and demographic forecasting was limited to auxiliary functions.

This course of argument also revealed some confusion of terms brought about by the extreme dearth of appropriately elaborated notions. Indeed, the forecasting of social developments represents a very involved, though integrated, complex (one cannot forecast any social phenomenon, such as, for instance, the prospects of town-building, in the absence of information on other, all the other if possible, related developments, for example, on the prospects of science, technology, economics, population growth, social relations). As stated earlier on, this is not a particular 'science of the future', but an agglomeration of the forecasting functions of the existing sciences – technical, economic, philosophic, etc. – brought together by the science of prognostics specializing in the investigation of these particular functions. From this point of view, all the forecasts of social phenomena – scientific-technological (prospects of the development of science and technology as social phenomena) and medical-biological, geocosmic, social-economic and military-political – are entitled to exist in their own right. But in actual practice what arises in each particular case – depending on the particular task in hand – is a definite target-oriented group of forecasts, with one playing the dominant role and others (all the others, if possible) in auxiliary roles. For instance, the target-oriented group dealing with economic forecasting of national importance is dominated by economic forecasts, with scientific-technological, demographic, and other forecasts fulfilling the subsidiary function. In principle, however, any forecast can form a target-oriented group of its own.

A tendency to oppose scientific forecasting to social forecasting arises from a confusion of the notions of social and sociological forecasts, which are seen as identical more often than not.

However, there must be a notion to cover the forecasts of all social phenomena. It is properly denoted by the term 'social forecasting', which covers scientific-technological (in the above-mentioned sense), medical-biological, geocosmic, economic, political, sociological and other forecasts. The latter group of forecasts (it is these that are described as social quite often) refers to the prospects of development of social relations, properly speaking: social requirements and structure, social organization and administration.

There are some almost totally unstudied questions of relationship between the forecasting functions of various sciences, a relationship between prognostics, on the one hand, and mathematics, cybernetics, economics and sociology, on the other.

So, what all this suggests is the need for a special effort to work out the philosophic issues involved in social forecasting, which have received inadequate attention until now.

There has been a controversy of no lesser duration over the particular methods of working out social forecasts. Everybody agreed that extrapolation, perfectly justified in forecasting spontaneous processes, offered but relatively limited opportunities for dealing with social phenomena noted for frequent qualitative change, with some particular decision (including one based on a forecast) being capable of fundamentally changing the very course of a forecast process. It was also found to be beyond dispute that a poll of experts would not by itself guarantee the dependability of a forecast: experts are humans, and it is only human to err. Finally, it was felt doubtful that mathematical modelling, which had perfectly justified itself in applied economics and sociology, would do any good in predicting any particular future developments. Why, then, have the existing methods of forecasting proved highly effective in predicting developments involving thousands of millions of dollars for some countries?

First, because, as stated earlier on, forecasting is designed not so much to foretell what will happen in the future, as to optimize plans, programmes, and decisions. Second, because highly effective methods of forecasting were not confined to extrapolation, poll-taking, and modelling, but represented a combination of all three approaches. Besides, the logical sequence of the major stages of forecasting investigation has been generally identified: elaboration of the starting model of a forecast object, construction of dynamic and statistical rows in relation to the particular parameters of this model with their conditional extrapolation towards the forecast date, construction of preliminary forecasting models of a prospective and standard-fixing character, their approval through a poll of experts (and sometimes individual population groups), and a correlation of the ultimate prospective and standard-fixing models with a view to working out recommendations for planning and administration.

One area that has been developed on a large scale in the Soviet Union is that of methods of scientific and technological forecasting based on licence analysis. This country as well as some others have done much in the investigation of all three of the above-mentioned approaches to making social forecasts. This most valuable experience requires to be theoretically generalized so as to serve as a basis for producing yet more effective methods of forecast-making.

Inasmuch as social forecasting is not limited to a mere attempt at anticipation, but aims to optimize planning and administration, the entire complex of problems involved in social forecasting must be geared to meeting this particular objective. It must, above all, be introduced in the modern context – one of confrontation of the two world social systems, the general crisis of capitalism, socialist and communist construction in the countries of victorious socialism, the scientific and technological revolution and its social implications. The next task to tackle is not so much to forecast the individual outlines of our future world (interesting and important though it is), as to analyse the trends and – on this basis – the prospects for any particular social phenomena, the principal objective being to identify the 'critical points' in the subsequent development of appropriate processes which will call for inevitable qualitative change. Finally, having identified these points and direction of change (both probable and desirable), one can pass on to the 'superobjective' of forecasting – that of working out recommendations for planning and administration as an effective way to overcoming an impending 'critical situation' by bringing the most probable and the most desirable versions of development into as close a relationship as possible.

It is necessary to point out that the coming of such 'critical situations' was identified in respect of nearly all forecast objects in the very early stages of social forecasting. There is no prospect for the world's present fuel- and energy- as well as raw material-producing capacities, automation of production and agriculture, transport and communications, town-building and colonization of the earth's surface, research and information systems, public education and health services to continue to develop in their traditional ways beyond a few decades hence. They all face clearly discernible limits, which, once attained, will require a substantial repatterning of the respective aspects of the vital activities of the human community. To work out the forecasts of the probable and desirable social implications of the scientific and technological revolution for each of these aspects means providing important assistance for the continued improvement of long-range planning and control of social processes.

a Johan Galtung

DANILO DOLCI

non è un ramo la città terrestre
cui fiorisce cristallo da cristallo,
ramaglia stalattitica;
né un ramo di rami assorbenti
per capillari vene –
        o arcipelago
di mandorle chiuse a isterilirsi:
fluire e rifluire
        in linfe e voli –
e il centro
        è nella terra

arrivano i riflessi del trascorso –
nella sua eco, altro è ormai il fuoco
altra è la luce, quando torna

bambini adulti rompono mondi
per scoprire come sono dentro

(cosmico polline fluttua
tra buio e buio –
        coagula cercando
la forma nel fluttuare dei riverberi

più vasto a chi più vede –
stupore di incontrare in altro cielo
ogni pelle una riva
continua)

non saper concepire differenti cosmi –
non saper maturare domande

l'occhio
quando non vince l'orizzonte
tenta scoprire oltre
scrutandosi

il vedere matura l'occhio –
il veduto matura
dentro

come il vedere interroga
matura
soluzioni –
se arriva a connubio
invisibili confluendo linfe
si illuminano
dentro

arduo maturare senza
sole di sguardo

tutta occhio la pelle –
oltre la nausea di costruire esiguo
paradiso nello sgretolio del mondo
oltre ogni pelle tenti seminarti:
semini nuovo
vedere

in altro si nasconde ogni variare:
la creatura non elude –
tenta
risolvere la storia

bruciarsi l'occhio rischia
esplodere

(canta il canto se nuovo –
una è la notte?)

se opaco punto schiarische illumina
altro buio –
ognuno proteo ognuno
in aggrovigliato buio brancola

infiniti occhi non vedono
se non comunicano

tra esuberanti bulbi di galassie
trasparenti e invisibili
aria nel guscio lo scorgere di un occhio –
un occhio solo

ogni confine strazia –
rompe
venule trafigge
l'occhio

The Editors

HANS-HENRIK HOLM, Institute of Political Science, University of Aarhus, Århus, Denmark, is the author of *Johan Galtung: 'Missionary' or 'Superstar'?*, Århus 1975; 'Danish Third World Policy: The Feed-back Problem', *Cooperation and Conflict*, Vol. 14 (1979), and articles on the New International Order.

ERIK RUDENG, Ministry of Education, Oslo, Norway, is the author of Ch. XII, *The New Cambridge Modern History*, Comparison Volume, Cambridge University Press, Cambridge 1979 (with Johan Galtung and Tore Heiestad); 'On the decline and fall of empires', HSDP-GPID Series, United Nations University, Tokyo 1979 (with Johan Galtung and Tore Heiestad; *Norway in the 1980's* (in Norwegian), Gyldendal, Oslo 1980 (with Johan Galtung and Dag Poleszynski).

The Contributors

HERB ADDO, Institute of International Relations, University of the West Indies, St. Augustine, Trinidad, is the author of 'Contemporary Adaption Dialectic of the World Economic System: An Introductory Probing', *Caribbean Yearbook of International Relations* (1976); 'The New International Economic Order and Imperialism: A Context for Evaluation', *IPRA Studies in Peace Research* (1979); 'Caribbean Plight', United Nations University, *Red Series* (1980).

CHADWICK ALGER, Mershon Center, The Ohio State University, is the author of 'Foreign Policies of United States Publics', *International Studies Quarterly* (1977); 'The Researcher in the United Nations: Evolution of a Research Strategy' in James N. Rosenau (ed.): *In Search of Global Patterns*, The Free Press, New York 1976. He is the co-author of *You and Your Community in the World*, Columbus, Ohio: Consortium for International Studies Association (1978).

ERIK ALLARDT, Research Group for Comparative Sociology, University of Helsinki, is the author of *Att ha, att älska, att vara. Om välfärd i Norden*, Arges, Lund 1975 (in Japanese: Mochi aishi kodosuru, Tokyo 1978); *Implications of the Ethnic Revival in Modern Industrialized Society. A Comparative Study of the Linguistic Minorities in Western Europe*, Societas Scientiarum Fennica, Helsinki 1979. With W. Wesolowski he has edited *Social Structure and Change. Finland and Poland. Comparative Perspective*, Polish Scientific Publishers, Warszawa 1978.

SAMIR AMIN, UNITAR, Dakar, Senegal, is the author of *Accumulation on a World Scale*, 2 vols. (1974); *Imperialism and Unequal Development* (1977); *Class and Nation in Historical Perspective and the Present Crisis* (1980), all three Monthly Review Press, New York.

ANNA ANFOSSI, Instituto di Scienze umane, University of Turin, Torino, is the author of *Socialità e organizzazione in Sardegna: Studio sulla Zona di Oristano – Bosa – Macomer*, Franco Angeli, Milano 1968; *Prospettive sociologiche sull'organizzazione aziendale:* 'Scientific Management' – 'Relazioni umane' – Sistemi, Franco Angeli, Milano 1971; 'Le interazioni tra organizzazioni' in *Studi organizzativi* (1979).

IGOR BESTUZHEV-LADA, Institute of Social Research, USSR Academy of Sciences, Moscow, is the author of *Future Concepts in the West*, 1979 (in Russian); *The Soviet Society Way of Life: Social Indicators*, 1980 (in Russian); and has recently contributed to i.a. F. Andrews (ed.), *Comparative Studies on the Quality of Life*, Ann Arbor 1980.

ADAM CURLE, Bradford University, is the author of *Making Peace*, Tavistock, London 1971; *Mystics and Militants*, Tavistock, London 1972; *Education for Liberation*, Tavistock, London 1973.

DANILO DOLCI, Centro Studi e Iniziative, Palermo, Nobel Peace Prize Laureate, is the author of *Creatura di creature*, Feltrinelli (1979); *A New World in the Making*, Monthly Review Press, New York 1965; *The Man Who Plays Alone*, Pantheon Books 1969 and Doubleday 1970, New York.

RICHARD A. FALK, Princeton University, is the author of *A Global Approach to National Policy*, Harvard University Press, Cambridge, Mass. 1975. With Sam S. Kim he has edited *The War System: An Interdisciplinary Approach*, Westview Press 1980. He has edited *The Vietnam War and International Law*, Princeton University Press 1976.

NILS PETTER GLEDITSCH, International Peace Research Institute, Oslo, has edited with Ottar Hellevik *Kampen om EF* (The Norwegian Common Market struggle), Pax, Oslo 1977; with Owen Wilkes, Sverre Lodgaard, and Ingvar Botnen *Norge i atomstrategien* (Norway in the nuclear strategy), Pax, Oslo 1978.

PATRICK HEALEY, sociologist, was previously director of Extension Studies at the University of Papua New Guinea, Port Moresby, and is now with the Department of Adult Education, Ontario Institute for Studies in Education, Toronto, Canada.

PETER HEINTZ, Soziologisches Institut der Universität Zürich, Switzerland, is the author of *Ein soziologiszhes Paradigma der Entwicklung mit besonderer Berücksichtigung Lateinamerikas*, Enke, Stuttgart 1969 (Spanish version: Un paradigma sociológico del desarrollo con especial rererencia a América Latina, Buenos Aires 1970). He had edited *A Macrosociological Theory of Societal Systems with Special Reference to the International System*, Vol I and II, Huber, Bern 1972. With Suzanne Heintz he has edited *The Future of Development*, Huber, Bern 1973 (German edition (enlarged): Die Zukunft der Entwicklung, Huber, Bern 1974).

ULF HIMMELSTRAND, Department of Sociology, University of Uppsala, Sweden, is the author of *Social Pressures, Attitudes and Democratic Processes*, Uppsala 1960; *Scientific-technological Revolution: Social Aspects*, London 1977 (with Ralf Dahrendorf et al.); *Beyond Welfare Capitalism. Issues, Actors and Forces in Societal Change*, London 1980 (with Göran Ahrne et al.).

ALAIN JOXE, Ecole des Hautes Etudes en Sciences Sociales, Paris, is the author of *Socialisme et crice nucléaire*, l'Herne, Paris 1973; *Le Chili sous Allende*, ed. Gallimard, Paris 1974; *Le rempart social, essai sur l'impérial-militarisme*, Galilée, Paris 1979.

OTTO KLINEBERG, Ecole des Hautes Etudes en Sciences Sociales, and International Center for Intergroup Relations, Paris, is the author of pioneering, classical works in social psychology: *Race Differences*, Harper and Row, New York 1935; *Social Psychology*, Holt, Rinehart & Winston, New York 1940 and 1954; *The Human Dimen-*

sion in International Relations, Holt, Rinehart and Winston, New York 1964; *Students, Values and Politics*, The Free Press, New York 1979 (with M. Zavalloni *et al.*).

SOLOMON MARCUS, Faculty of Mathematics, University of Bucharest, Romania, is the author of *Algebraic Linguistics; Analytical Models*, Academic Press, New York and London 1967; *Mathematische Poetik*, Editura Academiei, Bucuresti, Athenäum Verlag, Frankfurt am Main 1973. He is the co-author of *La Sémiotique Formelle du Folklore*, Klincksieck, Paris 1978.

MIHAILO MARKOVIC, Serbian Academy of Sciences and Arts, Belgrade, is the author of *From Afference to Praxis*, University of Michigan Press, Ann Arbor 1974; *The Contemporary Marx*, Spokesman Books, Nottingham 1974; *Praxis, Yugoslav Essays on Philosophy of Social Sciences*, Reidel, Dordrecht 1979.

ELEONORA MASINI, World Future Studies Federation, Rome, is the author of *Social and Human Forecasting*, Rome, 1973; *Space for Man*, Rome 1974.

ARNE NAESS, Institute of Philosophy, University of Oslo, is the author of *Interpretation and Preciseness*, Oslo University Press, Oslo 1953; *Gandhi and the Nuclear Age*, Oslo 1965; *Scepticism*, London and Oslo 1968, New York 1969.

ROY PREISWERK, Institute of Development Studies, Geneva, Switzerland, has edited with Dominique Perrot, *Ethocentrism and History: Africa, Asia and Indian America in Western Textbooks*, NOK Publishers, New York and Lagos 1978; with Johan Galtung and Peter O'Brien *Self-Reliance: A Strategy for Development*, Bogle-l'Ouverture, London 1980. He has edited *The Slant of the Pen: Racism in Children's Books*, World Council of Churches, Geneva 1980.

BERT V. A. RÖLING, Polemological Institute of the University of Groningen, The Netherlands, is the author of *International Law in an Expanded World*, De Brug, Amsterdam 1960; *Polemologie. Inleiding tot de wetenschap van oorlog en vrede* (Polemology, Introduction to the Science of War and Peace), van Gorcum, Assen 1973; *The Law of War and Dubious Weapons* (with Olga Suković), SIPRI, Almquist and Wiksell, Stockholm 1976.

HIROHARU SEKI, Institute of Oriental Culture, University of Tokyo, is the author of 'Introduction to the Behavioral Sciences', *Kodokagaku Nyumon*, Kodansha 1970; 'The Metastasis of the Nuclear Deterrence', *Peace Research in Japan* (1974); 'Forecasting in Cross-National Perspective – Japan', *Forecasting in International Relations*, edited with Youshikazu Sakamoto and N. Choucri, MIT Press 1978.

DIETER SENGHAAS, Department of Social Science, University of Bremen, is the author of *Abschreckung und Frieden*, Frankfurt 1980; *Aggressivität und kollektive Gewalt*, Stuttgart 1972; *Weltwirtschaftsordnung und Entwicklungspolitik*, Frankfurt 1978.

ANDRZEJ SICINSKI, Institute of Philosophy and Sociology, Polish Academy of Sciences, has edited in Polish *Studies in the Theory and Methodology of Social Forecasting*, Warszawa 1976; he has co-edited in English *Images of the World in the Year 2000*, Mouton, The Hague and Paris 1976; he is the author of 'The Concepts of «Need» and «Value» in the Light of the Systems Approach', *Social Science Information* (1978).

RAIMO VÁYRYNEN, Department of Political Science, University of Helsinki, is the author of *Militarization, Conflict Behavior and Interaction: Three Ways of Analyzing the Cold War* (1973); *Transfer of Technology, Transnational Corporations and Technological Dominance* (1977); *Industrialization, Economic Development and the World Military Order* (1979).

HÅKAN WIBERG, Department of Peace Research, University of Lund, is the author of *Konfliktteori och fredsforskning* (Conflict Theory and Peace Research), Scandinavian University Books, Stockholm 1976; *Visions of the Future – A Cross-national Study*, Lund 1977. With H. Ornauer, A. Sicinski, and J. Galtung he has edited *Images of the World in the Year 2000*, Mouton, Paris and The Hague 1976.

OWEN WILKES, Stockholm International Peace Research Institute, is the author of chapters on space warfare (1977), on the command and control of ballistic-missile submarines (1979), on anti-submarine warfare (1979), and the verification of arms control agreements (1980) in the SIPRI yearbooks.